Constitutional Law

2016 Supplement

Constitutional Law

Seventh Edition

Geoffrey R. Stone
Harry Kalven, Jr., Distinguished Service Professor of Law
University of Chicago Law School

Louis Michael Seidman
Carmack Waterhouse Professor of Constitutional Law
Georgetown University Law Center

Cass R. Sunstein
Felix Frankfurter Professor of Law
Harvard Law School

Mark V. Tushnet
William Nelson Cromwell Professor of Law
Harvard Law School

Pamela S. Karlan
Kenneth & Harle Montgomery Professor of Public Interest Law
Stanford Law School

Published by Wolters Kluwer in New York.

Wolters Kluwer Legal & Regulatory US serves customers worldwide with CCH, Aspen Publishers, and Kluwer Law International products. (www.WKLegaledu.com)

To contact Customer Service, e-mail customer.service@wolterskluwer.com, call 1-800-234-1660, fax 1-800-901-9075, or mail correspondence to:

    Wolters Kluwer
    Attn: Order Department
    PO Box 990
    Frederick, MD 21705

Printed in the United States of America.

1 2 3 4 5 6 7 8 9 0

ISBN 978-1-4548-7559-8

SUSTAINABLE FORESTRY INITIATIVE   Certified Sourcing   www.sfiprogram.org   SFI-01028

About Wolters Kluwer Legal & Regulatory US

Wolters Kluwer Legal & Regulatory US delivers expert content and solutions in the areas of law, corporate compliance, health compliance, reimbursement, and legal education. Its practical solutions help customers successfully navigate the demands of a changing environment to drive their daily activities, enhance decision quality and inspire confident outcomes.

Serving customers worldwide, its legal and regulatory portfolio includes products under the Aspen Publishers, CCH Incorporated, Kluwer Law International, ftwilliam.com and MediRegs names. They are regarded as exceptional and trusted resources for general legal and practice-specific knowledge, compliance and risk management, dynamic workflow solutions, and expert commentary.

Contents

Table of Cases

Table of Authorities

Constitutional Law

BIOGRAPHICAL NOTES ON SELECTED U.S. SUPREME COURT JUSTICES

Page lxx.   Justice Scalia died in 2016.

THE SUPREME COURT SINCE 1789

Page lxxxviii. Justices Sotomayor and Kagan are listed in the wrong column of the chart. Justice Sotomayor was appointed to replace Justice Souter. Justice Kagan was appointed to replace Justice Stevens.

I
THE CONSTITUTION AND THE SUPREME COURT

C. The Basic Framework

Page 38. At the end of the Note, add the following:

For a detailed and revealing historical account of the relationship between civil liberties and judicial review during the first part of the twentieth century, see Weinrib, Civil Liberties outside the Courts, 2014 Sup. Ct. Rev. 297.

D. The Sources of Judicial Decisions

Page 52. After section 4 of the Note, add the following:

5. *Stun guns.* In Caetano v. Massachusetts, 136 S. Ct. 1027 (2016), the Court disapproved of three reasons given by a lower court to justify the state's categorical ban on stun guns.

> The [Massachusetts] court offered three explanations to support its holding that the Second Amendment does not extend to stun guns. First, the court explained that stun guns are not protected because they "were not in common use at the time of the Second Amendment's enactment." This is inconsistent with *Heller*'s clear statement that the Second Amendment "extends . . . to . . . arms . . . that were not in existence at the time of the founding." *District of Columbia v. Heller*, 554 U.S. 570, 582 (2008).
>
> The court next asked whether stun guns are "dangerous per se at common law and unusual," in an attempt to apply one "important limitation on the right to keep and carry arms," *Heller*, 554 U.S. at 627; *see id.* (referring

to "the historical tradition of prohibiting the carrying of 'dangerous and unusual weapons'"). In so doing, the court concluded that stun guns are "unusual" because they are "a thoroughly modern invention." . . . By equating "unusual" with "in common use at the time of the Second Amendment's enactment," the court's second explanation is the same as the first; it is inconsistent with *Heller* for the same reason.

Finally, the court used "a contemporary lens" and found "nothing in the record to suggest that [stun guns] are readily adaptable to use in the military." . . . But *Heller* rejected the proposition "that only those weapons useful in warfare are protected." 554 U.S. at 624-25

For these three reasons, the explanation the Massachusetts court offered for upholding the law contradicts this Court's precedent. . . .

With a more elaborate opinion, Justice Alito (joined by Justice Thomas) concurred in the judgment. The reasoning of the Massachusetts Supreme Judicial Court, he wrote, "defies our decision in *Heller*, which rejected as 'bordering on the frivolous' the argument 'that only those arms in existence in the 18th century are protected by the Second Amendment.' 554 U.S. at 582. . . . [T]he pertinent Second Amendment inquiry is whether stun guns are commonly possessed by law-abiding citizens for lawful purposes *today*. . . . While less popular than handguns, stun guns are widely owned and accepted as a legitimate means of self-defense across the country. Massachusetts' categorical ban of such weapons therefore violates the Second Amendment."

Justice Alito further emphasized that the Second Amendment "vindicates the 'basic right' of 'individual self-defense,'" and noted that the defendant had acquired the stun gun in order to defend herself against a violent ex-boyfriend. He concluded that "[t]he decision below [does] a grave disservice to vulnerable individuals like Caetano who must defend themselves because the State will not. . . . The Supreme Judicial Court suggested that Caetano could have simply gotten a firearm to defend herself. . . . But the right to bear other weapons is 'no answer' to a ban on the possession of protected arms. *Heller*, 554 U.S. at 629. Moreover, a weapon is an effective means of self-defense only if one is prepared to use it, and it is presumptuous to tell Caetano she should have been ready to shoot the father of her two young children if she wanted to protect herself. Courts should not be in the business of demanding that citizens use *more* force for self-defense than they are comfortable wielding."

Page 44.   After section 4 of the Note, add the following:

5. *Federal supremacy reaffirmed.* In James v. City of Boise, 136 S. Ct. 685 (2016), the Supreme Court reaffirmed that its interpretations of federal law are

supreme and binding on state courts. In *Hughes v. Rowe,* 449 U.S. 5 (1980) (*per curiam*), the Supreme Court had interpreted 42 U.S.C. § 1988 to permit a prevailing defendant in a civil rights suit to recover fees only if "the plaintiff's action was frivolous, unreasonable, or without foundation." The Idaho Supreme Court concluded that it was not bound by the Court's interpretation, reasoning that "[although] the Supreme Court may have the authority to limit the discretion of lower federal courts, it does not have the authority to limit the discretion of state courts where such limitation is not contained in the statute." The Idaho Supreme Court proceeded to award attorney's fees under section 1988 without first determining whether the plaintiff's action was frivolous, unreasonable, or without foundation. In reversing, the Supreme Court stated:

> "It is this Court's responsibility to say what a [federal] statute means, and once the Court has spoken, it is the duty of other courts to respect that understanding of the governing rule of law.' (citations omitted)"   As Justice Story explained 200 years ago, if state courts were permitted to disregard this Court's rulings on federal law, "the laws, the treaties, and the constitution of the United States would be different in different states, and might, perhaps, never have precisely the same construction, obligation, or efficacy, in any two states. The public mischiefs that would attend such a state of things would be truly deplorable." *Martin v. Hunter's Lessee*, 14 U.S. (1 Wheat) 304, 348 (1816).

F.   *"Case or Controversy" Requirements and the Passive Virtues*

Page 106.   Before the Note, add the following:

CLAPPER v. AMNESTY INTERNATIONAL USA

133 S. Ct. 1138 (2013)

JUSTICE ALITO delivered the opinion of the Court.

Section 702 of the Foreign Intelligence Surveillance Act of 1978, 50 U.S.C. § 1881a (2006 ed., Supp. V), allows the Attorney General and the Director of National Intelligence to acquire foreign intelligence information by jointly authorizing the surveillance of individuals who are not "United States persons" and are reasonably believed to be located outside the United States. Before doing so, the Attorney General and the Director of National Intelligence normally must obtain the Foreign Intelligence Surveillance Court's approval. Respondents are United

States persons whose work, they allege, requires them to engage in sensitive international communications with individuals who they believe are likely targets of surveillance under § 1881a. Respondents seek a declaration that § 1881a is unconstitutional, as well as an injunction against § 1881a-authorized surveillance. The question before us is whether respondents have Article III standing to seek this prospective relief.

Respondents assert that they can establish injury in fact because there is an objectively reasonable likelihood that their communications will be acquired under § 1881a at some point in the future. But respondents' theory of *future* injury is too speculative to satisfy the well-established requirement that threatened injury must be "certainly impending." And even if respondents could demonstrate that the threatened injury is certainly impending, they still would not be able to establish that this injury is fairly traceable to § 1881a. As an alternative argument, respondents contend that they are suffering *present* injury because the risk of § 1881a-authorized surveillance already has forced them to take costly and burdensome measures to protect the confidentiality of their international communications. But respondents cannot manufacture standing by choosing to make expenditures based on hypothetical future harm that is not certainly impending. We therefore hold that respondents lack Article III standing.

I

A ...

The present case involves a constitutional challenge to § 1881a. Surveillance under § 1881a is subject to statutory conditions, judicial authorization, congressional supervision, and compliance with the Fourth Amendment. Section 1881a provides that, upon the issuance of an order from the Foreign Intelligence Surveillance Court [FISC], "the Attorney General and the Director of National Intelligence may authorize jointly, for a period of up to 1 year . . . , the targeting of persons reasonably believed to be located outside the United States to acquire foreign intelligence information." Surveillance under § 1881a may not be intentionally targeted at any person known to be in the United States or any U.S. person reasonably believed to be located abroad. Additionally, acquisitions under § 1881a must comport with the Fourth Amendment. Moreover, surveillance under § 1881a is subject to congressional oversight and several types of Executive Branch review.

Section 1881a mandates that the Government obtain the Foreign Intelligence Surveillance Court's approval of "targeting" procedures, "minimization" procedures, and a governmental certification regarding proposed surveillance. Among other things, the Government's certification must attest that (1) procedures are in place "that have been approved, have been submitted for approval, or will be submitted with the certification for approval by the [FISC] that are reasonably designed" to ensure that an acquisition is "limited to targeting persons reasonably believed to be located outside" the United States; (2) minimization procedures adequately restrict the acquisition, retention, and dissemination of nonpublic information about unconsenting U.S. persons, as appropriate; (3) guidelines have been adopted to ensure compliance with targeting limits and the Fourth Amendment; and (4) the procedures and guidelines referred to above comport with the Fourth Amendment.

The Foreign Intelligence Surveillance Court's role includes determining whether the Government's certification contains the required elements. . . .

B

Respondents are attorneys and human rights, labor, legal, and media organizations whose work allegedly requires them to engage in sensitive and sometimes privileged telephone and e-mail communications with colleagues, clients, sources, and other individuals located abroad. [Respondents] claim that they communicate by telephone and e-mail with people the Government "believes or believed to be associated with terrorist organizations," "people located in geographic areas that are a special focus" of the Government's counterterrorism or diplomatic efforts, and activists who oppose governments that are supported by the United States Government.

Respondents claim that § 1881a compromises their ability to locate witnesses, cultivate sources, obtain information, and communicate confidential information to their clients. Respondents also assert that they "have ceased engaging" in certain telephone and e-mail conversations. According to respondents, the threat of surveillance will compel them to travel abroad in order to have in-person conversations. In addition, respondents declare that they have undertaken "costly and burdensome measures" to protect the confidentiality of sensitive communications. . . .

III

A

Respondents assert that they can establish injury in fact that is fairly traceable to § 1881a because there is an objectively reasonable likelihood that their communications with their foreign contacts will be intercepted under § 1881a at some point in the future. This argument fails. . . .

[Respondents'] argument rests on their highly speculative fear that: (1) the Government will decide to target the communications of non-U.S. persons with whom they communicate; (2) in doing so, the Government will choose to invoke its authority under § 1881a rather than utilizing another method of surveillance; (3) the Article III judges who serve on the Foreign Intelligence Surveillance Court will conclude that the Government's proposed surveillance procedures satisfy § 1881a's many safeguards and are consistent with the Fourth Amendment; (4) the Government will succeed in intercepting the communications of respondents' contacts; and (5) respondents will be parties to the particular communications that the Government intercepts. . . .

[Respondents'] theory of standing, which relies on a highly attenuated chain of possibilities, does not satisfy the requirement that threatened injury must be certainly impending. Moreover, even if respondents could demonstrate injury in fact, the second link in the above-described chain of contingencies—which amounts to mere speculation about whether surveillance would be under § 1881a or some other authority—shows that respondents cannot satisfy the requirement that any injury in fact must be fairly traceable to § 1881a.

First, it is speculative whether the Government will imminently target communications to which respondents are parties. Section 1881a expressly provides that respondents, who are U.S. persons, cannot be targeted for surveillance under § 1881a. . . .

Accordingly, respondents' theory necessarily rests on their assertion that the Government will target *other individuals*—namely, their foreign contacts.

Yet respondents have no actual knowledge of the Government's § 1881a targeting practices. Instead, respondents merely speculate and make assumptions about whether their communications with their foreign contacts will be acquired under § 1881a. For example, journalist Christopher Hedges states: "I have no choice but to *assume* that any of my international communications *may* be subject to government surveillance, and I have to make decisions . . . in light of that *assumption*." Similarly, attorney Scott McKay asserts that, "[b]ecause of the [FISA Amendments Act], we now have to *assume* that every one of our international communications *may* be monitored by the government." . . .

[Because] § 1881a at most *authorizes*—but does not *mandate* or *direct*—the surveillance that respondents fear, respondents' allegations are necessarily conjectural. Simply put, respondents can only speculate as to how the Attorney General and the Director of National Intelligence will exercise their discretion in determining which communications to target.

Second, even if respondents could demonstrate that the targeting of their foreign contacts is imminent, respondents can only speculate as to whether the Government will seek to use § 1881 authorized surveillance (rather than other methods) to do so. The Government has numerous other methods of conducting surveillance, none of which is challenged here. Even after the enactment of the FISA Amendments Act, for example, the Government may still conduct electronic surveillance of persons abroad under the older provisions of FISA so long as it satisfies the applicable requirements, including a demonstration of probable cause to believe that the person is a foreign power or agent of a foreign power. The Government may also obtain information from the intelligence services of foreign nations. . . . Even if respondents could demonstrate that their foreign contacts will imminently be targeted—indeed, even if they could show that interception of their own communications will imminently occur—they would still need to show that their injury is fairly traceable to § 1881a. But, because respondents can only speculate as to whether any (asserted) interception would be under § 1881a or some other authority, they cannot satisfy the "fairly traceable" requirement.

Third, even if respondents could show that the Government will seek the Foreign Intelligence Surveillance Court's authorization to acquire the communications of respondents' foreign contacts under § 1881a, respondents can only speculate as to whether that court will authorize such surveillance. . . .

We decline to abandon our usual reluctance to endorse standing theories that rest on speculation about the decisions of independent actors. In sum, respondents' speculative chain of possibilities does not establish that injury based on potential future surveillance is certainly impending or is fairly traceable to § 1881a.

B

Respondents' alternative argument—namely, that they can establish standing based on the measures that they have undertaken to avoid § 1881a-authorized surveillance—fares no better. Respondents assert that they are suffering ongoing injuries that are fairly traceable to § 1881a because the risk of surveillance under § 1881a requires them to take costly and burdensome measures to protect the confidentiality of their communications. Respondents claim, for instance, that the threat of surveillance sometimes compels them to avoid certain e-mail and phone conversations, to "tal[k] in generalities rather than specifics," or to travel so that they can have in-person conversations. . . .

Respondents' contention that they have standing because they incurred certain costs as a reasonable reaction to a risk of harm is unavailing—because the harm respondents seek to avoid is not certainly impending. In other words, respondents cannot manufacture standing merely by inflicting harm on themselves based on their fears of hypothetical future harm that is not certainly impending. Any ongoing injuries that respondents are suffering are not fairly traceable to § 1881a.

If the law were otherwise, an enterprising plaintiff would be able to secure a lower standard for Article III standing simply by making an expenditure based on a nonparanoid fear. . . .

Thus, allowing respondents to bring this action based on costs they incurred in response to a speculative threat would be tantamount to accepting a repackaged version of respondents' first failed theory of standing.

Another reason that respondents' present injuries are not fairly traceable to § 1881a is that even before § 1881a was enacted, they had a similar incentive to engage in many of the countermeasures that they are now taking. . . .

IV

A

Respondents incorrectly maintain that "[t]he kinds of injuries incurred here—injuries incurred because of [respondents'] reasonable efforts to avoid

greater injuries that are otherwise likely to flow from the conduct they challenge—are the same kinds of injuries that this Court held to support standing in
cases such as" *Laidlaw* [and] Meese v. Keene, 481 U.S. 465 (1987). . . .

[Each] of these cases was very different from the present case.

In *Laidlaw*, plaintiffs' standing was based on "the proposition that a company's continuous and pervasive illegal discharges of pollutants into a river would
cause nearby residents to curtail their recreational use of that waterway and would
subject them to other economic and aesthetic harms." Because the unlawful discharges of pollutants were "concededly ongoing," the only issue was whether
"nearby residents"—who were members of the organizational plaintiffs—acted
reasonably in refraining from using the polluted area. *Laidlaw* is therefore quite
unlike the present case, in which it is not "concede[d]" that respondents would
be subject to unlawful surveillance but for their decision to take preventive measures. *Laidlaw* would resemble this case only if (1) it were undisputed that the
Government was using § 1881a-authorized surveillance to acquire respondents'
communications and (2) the sole dispute concerned the reasonableness of respondents' preventive measures.

In *Keene*, the plaintiff challenged the constitutionality of the Government's
decision to label three films as "political propaganda." The Court held that the
plaintiff, who was an attorney and a state legislator, had standing because he demonstrated, through "detailed affidavits," that he "could not exhibit the films without incurring a risk of injury to his reputation and of an impairment of his political
career." Unlike the present case, *Keene* involved "more than a 'subjective chill'"
based on speculation about potential governmental action; the plaintiff in that
case was unquestionably regulated by the relevant statute, and the films that he
wished to exhibit had already been labeled as "political propaganda." . . .

B

Respondents also suggest that they should be held to have standing because
otherwise the constitutionality of § 1881a could not be challenged. It would be
wrong, they maintain, to "insulate the government's surveillance activities from
meaningful judicial review." Respondents' suggestion is both legally and factually incorrect. First, " '[t]he assumption that if respondents have no standing to
sue, no one would have standing, is not a reason to find standing.' "

Second, our holding today by no means insulates § 1881a from judicial review.
As described above, Congress created a comprehensive scheme in which the
Foreign Intelligence Surveillance Court evaluates the Government's certifica-
tions, targeting procedures, and minimization procedures—including assess-
ing whether the targeting and minimization procedures comport with the Fourth
Amendment. Any dissatisfaction that respondents may have about the Foreign
Intelligence Surveillance Court's rulings—or the congressional delineation of
that court's role—is irrelevant to our standing analysis.

Additionally, if the Government intends to use or disclose information obtained or derived from a § 1881a acquisition in judicial or administrative proceedings, it must provide advance notice of its intent, and the affected person may challenge the lawfulness of the acquisition. . . .

Finally, any electronic communications service provider that the Government directs to assist in § 1881a surveillance may challenge the lawfulness of that directive before the FISC. Indeed, at the behest of a service provider, the Foreign Intelligence Surveillance Court of Review previously analyzed the constitutionality of electronic surveillance directives issued pursuant to a now-expired set of FISA amendments.

* * *

We hold that respondents lack Article III standing because they cannot demonstrate that the future injury they purportedly fear is certainly impending and because they cannot manufacture standing by incurring costs in anticipation of non-imminent harm. We therefore reverse the judgment of the Second Circuit and remand the case for further proceedings consistent with this opinion.

It is so ordered.

JUSTICE BREYER, with whom JUSTICE GINSBURG, JUSTICE SOTOMAYOR, and JUSTICE KAGAN join, dissenting.

I . . .

No one here denies that the Government's interception of a private telephone or e-mail conversation amounts to an injury that is "concrete and particularized." Moreover, the plaintiffs, respondents here, seek as relief a judgment declaring unconstitutional (and enjoining enforcement of) a statutory provision authorizing those interceptions; and, such a judgment would redress the injury by preventing it. Thus, the basic question is whether the injury, *i.e.,* the interception, is "actual or imminent."

II

A . . .

The addition of § 1881a in 2008 changed [prior] law in three important ways. First, it eliminated the requirement that the Government describe to the court each specific target and identify each facility at which its surveillance would be directed, thus permitting surveillance on a programmatic, not necessarily individualized, basis. Second, it eliminated the requirement that a target be a "foreign power or an agent of a foreign power." Third, it diminished the court's authority to insist upon, and eliminated its authority to supervise, instance-specific

13

privacy-intrusion minimization procedures (though the Government still must use court-approved general minimization procedures). Thus, using the authority of § 1881a, the Government can obtain court approval for its surveillance of electronic communications between places within the United States and targets in foreign territories by showing the court (1) that "a significant purpose of the acquisition is to obtain foreign intelligence information," and (2) that it will use general targeting and privacy-intrusion minimization procedures of a kind that the court had previously approved.

B . . .

Plaintiff Scott McKay [says] in an affidavit (1) that he is a lawyer; (2) that he represented "Mr. Sami Omar Al-Hussayen, who was acquitted in June 2004 on terrorism charges"; (3) that he continues to represent "Mr. Al-Hussayen, who, in addition to facing criminal charges after September 11, was named as a defendant in several civil cases"; (4) that he represents Khalid Sheik Mohammed, a detainee, "before the Military Commissions at Guantanamo Bay, Cuba"; (5) that in representing these clients he "communicate[s] by telephone and email with people outside the United States, including Mr. Al-Hussayen himself," "experts, investigators, attorneys, family members . . . and others who are located abroad"; and (6) that prior to 2008 "the U.S. government had intercepted some 10,000 telephone calls and 20,000 email communications involving [his client] Al-Hussayen." . . .

[Another] plaintiff, Joanne Mariner, says in her affidavit (1) that she is a human rights researcher, (2) that "some of the work [she] do[es] involves trying to track down people who were rendered by the CIA to countries in which they were tortured"; (3) that many of those people "the CIA has said are (or were) associated with terrorist organizations"; and (4) that, to do this research, she "communicate[s] by telephone and e-mail with . . . former detainees, lawyers for detainees, relatives of detainees, political activists, journalists, and fixers" "all over the world, including in Jordan, Egypt, Pakistan, Afghanistan, [and] the Gaza Strip." . . .

III

Several considerations, based upon the record along with commonsense inferences, convince me that there is a very high likelihood that Government, *acting under the authority of* § 1881a, will intercept at least some of the communications just described. First, the plaintiffs have engaged, and continue to engage, in electronic communications of a kind that the 2008 amendment, but not the prior Act, authorizes the Government to intercept. These communications include discussions with family members of those detained at Guantanamo, friends and acquaintances of those persons, and investigators, experts and others with knowledge of circumstances related to terrorist activities. These persons are foreigners located outside the United States. They are not "foreign power[s]" or "agent[s] of . . .

foreign power[s]." And the plaintiffs state that they exchange with these persons "foreign intelligence information," defined to include information that "relates to" "international terrorism" and "the national defense or the security of the United States."

Second, the plaintiffs have a strong *motive* to engage in, and the Government has a strong *motive* to listen to, conversations of the kind described. A lawyer representing a client normally seeks to learn the circumstances surrounding the crime (or the civil wrong) of which the client is accused. A fair reading of the affidavit of Scott McKay, for example, taken together with elementary considerations of a lawyer's obligation to his client, indicates that McKay will engage in conversations that concern what suspected foreign terrorists, such as his client, have done; in conversations that concern his clients' families, colleagues, and contacts; in conversations that concern what those persons (or those connected to them) have said and done, at least in relation to terrorist activities; in conversations that concern the political, social, and commercial environments in which the suspected terrorists have lived and worked; and so forth. Journalists and human rights workers have strong similar motives to conduct conversations of this kind.

At the same time, the Government has a strong motive to conduct surveillance of conversations that contain material of this kind. The Government, after all, seeks to learn as much as it can reasonably learn about suspected terrorists (such as those detained at Guantanamo), as well as about their contacts and activities, along with those of friends and family members. And the Government is motivated to do so, not simply by the desire to help convict those whom the Government believes guilty, but also by the critical, overriding need to protect America from terrorism.

Third, the Government's *past behavior* shows that it has sought, and hence will in all likelihood continue to seek, information about alleged terrorists and detainees through means that include surveillance of electronic communications. As just pointed out, plaintiff Scott McKay states that the Government (under the authority of the pre-2008 law) "intercepted some 10,000 telephone calls and 20,000 email communications involving [his client] Mr. Al-Hussayen."

Fourth, the Government has the *capacity* to conduct electronic surveillance of the kind at issue. To some degree this capacity rests upon technology available to the Government. [This] capacity also includes the Government's authority to obtain the kind of information here at issue from private carriers such as AT&T and Verizon. We are further told by *amici* that the Government is expanding that capacity.

Of course, to exercise this capacity the Government must have intelligence court authorization. But the Government rarely files requests that fail to meet the statutory criteria. As the intelligence court itself has stated, its review under § 1881a is "narrowly circumscribed." There is no reason to believe that the communications described would all fail to meet the conditions necessary for approval.

15

Moreover, compared with prior law, § 1881a simplifies and thus expedites the approval process, making it more likely that the Government will use § 1881a to obtain the necessary approval.

The upshot is that (1) similarity of content, (2) strong motives, (3) prior behavior, and (4) capacity all point to a very strong likelihood that the Government will intercept at least some of the plaintiffs' communications, including some that the 2008 amendment, § 1881a, but not the pre-2008 Act, authorizes the Government to intercept. . . .

Consequently, we need only assume that the Government is doing its job (to find out about, and combat, terrorism) in order to conclude that there is a high probability that the Government will intercept at least some electronic communication to which at least some of the plaintiffs are parties. The majority is wrong when it describes the harm threatened plaintiffs as "speculative."

IV

A

The majority more plausibly says that the plaintiffs have failed to show that the threatened harm is *"certainly impending."* But [*certainty*] is not, and never has been, the touchstone of standing. The future is inherently uncertain. Yet federal courts frequently entertain actions for injunctions and for declaratory relief aimed at preventing future activities that are reasonably likely or highly likely, but not absolutely certain, to take place. And that degree of certainty is all that is needed to support standing here.

The Court's use of the term "certainly impending" is not to the contrary. . . .

Taken together the case law uses the word "certainly" as if it emphasizes, rather than literally defines, the immediately following term "impending."

B

1

More important, the Court's holdings in standing cases show that standing exists here. The Court has often *found* standing where the occurrence of the relevant injury was far *less* certain than here. Consider a few, fairly typical, cases. Consider *Pennell*. A city ordinance forbade landlords to raise the rent charged to a tenant by more than 8 percent where doing so would work an unreasonably severe hardship on that tenant. A group of landlords sought a judgment declaring the ordinance unconstitutional. The Court held that, to have standing, the landlords had to demonstrate a " '*realistic danger of sustaining a direct injury* as a result of the statute's operation.' " It found that the landlords had done so by showing a likelihood of enforcement and a "probability," that the ordinance would make the landlords charge lower rents—even though the landlords had not shown (1) that they intended to raise the relevant rents to the point of causing unreasonably severe hardship; (2) that the tenants would challenge those increases; or (3) that the city's hearing examiners and arbitrators would find against the landlords. Here, even more so than in *Pennell*, there is a *"realistic danger"* that the relevant harm will occur. . . .

How could the law be otherwise? Suppose that a federal court faced a claim by homeowners that (allegedly) unlawful dam-building practices created a high risk that their homes would be flooded. Would the court deny them standing on the ground that the risk of flood was only 60, rather than 90, percent?

Would federal courts deny standing to a plaintiff in a diversity action who claims an anticipatory breach of contract where the future breach depends on probabilities? The defendant, say, has threatened to load wheat onto a ship bound for India despite a promise to send the wheat to the United States. No one can know for certain that this will happen. Perhaps the defendant will change his mind; perhaps the ship will turn and head for the United States. Yet, despite the uncertainty, the Constitution does not prohibit a federal court from hearing such a claim. . . .

Neither do ordinary declaratory judgment actions always involve the degree of certainty upon which the Court insists here. See, *e.g.*, . . . Aetna Life Ins. Co. v. Haworth, 300 U.S. 227, 239-244 (1937).

2

In some standing cases, the Court has found that a reasonable probability of *future* injury comes accompanied with *present* injury that takes the form of reasonable efforts to mitigate the threatened effects of the future injury or to prevent it from occurring. . . .

Virtually identical circumstances are present here. Plaintiff McKay, for example, points out that, when he communicates abroad about, or in the interests of, a client (*e.g.*, a client accused of terrorism), he must "make an assessment" whether his "client's interests would be compromised" should the Government "acquire the communications." If so, he must either forgo the communication or travel abroad. . . .

4

In sum [the] word "certainly" in the phrase "certainly impending" does not refer to absolute certainty. As our case law demonstrates, what the Constitution requires is something more akin to "reasonable probability" or "high probability." The use of some such standard is all that is necessary here to ensure the actual concrete injury that the Constitution demands. The considerations set forth in Parts II and III, *supra*, make clear that the standard is readily met in this case.

* * *

While I express no view on the merits of the plaintiffs' constitutional claims, I do believe that at least some of the plaintiffs have standing to make those claims. I dissent, with respect, from the majority's contrary conclusion.

17

SUSAN B. ANTHONY LIST v. DRIEHAUS

134 S. Ct. 2334 (2014)

JUSTICE THOMAS delivered the opinion of the Court.

Petitioners in this case seek to challenge an Ohio statute that prohibits certain "false statements" during the course of a political campaign. The question in this case is whether their preenforcement challenge to that law is justiciable—and in particular, whether they have alleged a sufficiently imminent injury for the purposes of Article III. We conclude that they have.

I

The Ohio statute at issue prohibits certain "false statement[s]" "during the course of any campaign for nomination or election to public office or office of a political party." As relevant here, the statute makes it a crime for any person to "[m]ake a false statement concerning the voting record of a candidate or public official," or to "[p]ost, publish, circulate, distribute, or otherwise disseminate a false statement concerning a candidate, either knowing the same to be false or with reckless disregard of whether it was false or not." "[A]ny person" acting on personal knowledge may file a complaint with the Ohio Elections Commission (or Commission) alleging a violation of the false statement statute. If filed within 60 days of a primary election or 90 days of a general election, the complaint is referred to a panel of at least three Commission members. The panel must then hold an expedited hearing, generally within two business days, to determine whether there is probable cause to believe the alleged violation occurred. Upon a finding of probable cause, the full Commission must, within 10 days, hold a hearing on the complaint. . . .

II

Petitioner Susan B. Anthony List (SBA) is a "pro-life advocacy organization." During the 2010 election cycle, SBA publicly criticized various Members of Congress who voted for the Patient Protection and Affordable Care Act (ACA). In particular, it issued a press release announcing its plan to "educat[e] voters that their representative voted for a health care bill that includes taxpayer-funded abortion." The press release listed then-Congressman Steve Driehaus, a respondent here, who voted for the ACA. SBA also sought to display a billboard in Driehaus' district condemning that vote. The planned billboard would have read: "Shame on Steve Driehaus! Driehaus voted FOR taxpayer-funded abortion." The advertising company that owned the billboard space refused to display that message, however, after Driehaus' counsel threatened legal action.

On October 4, 2010, Driehaus filed a complaint with the Ohio Elections Commission alleging, as relevant here, that SBA had violated [the statute] by falsely stating that he had voted for "taxpayer-funded abortion." Because Driehaus filed his complaint 29 days before the general election, a Commission panel held an expedited hearing. On October 14, 2010, the panel voted 2-to-1 to find probable cause that a violation had been committed. The full Commission set a hearing date for 10 business days later, and the parties commenced discovery. Driehaus noticed depositions of three SBA employees as well as individuals affiliated with similar advocacy groups. He also issued discovery requests for all evidence that SBA would rely on at the Commission hearing, as well as SBA's communications with allied organizations, political party committees, and Members of Congress and their staffs.

On October 18, 2010—after the panel's probable-cause determination, but before the scheduled Commission hearing—SBA filed suit in Federal District Court, seeking declaratory and injunctive relief on the ground that [the statute] violate[s] the First and Fourteenth Amendments of the United States Constitution. The District Court stayed the action under Younger v. Harris, 401 U.S. 37 (1971), pending completion of the Commission proceedings. The Sixth Circuit denied SBA's motion for an injunction pending appeal. Driehaus and SBA eventually agreed to postpone the full Commission hearing until after the election.

When Driehaus lost the election in November 2010, he moved to withdraw his complaint against SBA. The Commission granted the motion with SBA's consent. Once the Commission proceedings were terminated, the District Court lifted the stay and SBA amended its complaint. As relevant here, the amended complaint alleged that [the statute is] unconstitutional both facially and as applied. Specifically, the complaint alleged that SBA's speech about Driehaus had been chilled; that SBA "intends to engage in substantially similar activity in the future"; and that it "face[d] the prospect of its speech and associational rights again being chilled and burdened," because "[a]ny complainant can hale [it] before the [Commission], forcing it to expend time and resources defending itself."

The District Court consolidated SBA's suit with a separate suit brought by petitioner Coalition Opposed to Additional Spending and Taxes (COAST), an advocacy organization that also alleged that the same Ohio false statement provisions are unconstitutional both facially and as applied. According to its amended complaint, COAST intended to disseminate a mass e-mail and other materials criticizing Driehaus' vote for the ACA as a vote "to fund abortions with tax dollars," but refrained from doing so because of the Commission proceedings against SBA. COAST further alleged that it "desires to make the same or similar statements about other federal candidates who voted for" the ACA, but that fear "of finding itself subject to the same fate" as SBA has deterred it from doing so. . . .

III

A

[This] case concerns the injury-in-fact requirement, which helps to ensure that the plaintiff has a "personal stake in the outcome of the controversy." Warth v. Seldin, 422 U.S. 490, 498 (1975) (internal quotation marks omitted). An injury sufficient to satisfy Article III must be "concrete and particularized" and "actual or imminent, not 'conjectural' or 'hypothetical.' " [*Lujan.*] An allegation of future injury may suffice if the threatened injury is "certainly impending," or there is a " 'substantial risk' that the harm will occur." [*Clapper.*]

B

One recurring issue in our cases is determining when the threatened enforcement of a law creates an Article III injury. When an individual is subject to such a threat, an actual arrest, prosecution, or other enforcement action is not a prerequisite to challenging the law. . . .

IV

Here, SBA and COAST contend that the threat of enforcement of the false statement statute amounts to an Article III injury in fact. We agree: Petitioners have alleged a credible threat of enforcement.

A

First, petitioners have alleged "an intention to engage in a course of conduct arguably affected with a constitutional interest." Both petitioners have pleaded specific statements they intend to make in future election cycles. SBA has already stated that representatives who voted for the ACA supported "taxpayer-funded abortion," and it has alleged an "inten[t] to engage in substantially similar activity in the future." COAST has alleged that it previously intended to disseminate materials criticizing a vote for the ACA as a vote "to fund abortions with tax dollars," and that it "desires to make the same or similar statements about other federal candidates who voted for [the ACA]." Because petitioners' intended future conduct concerns political speech, it is certainly "affected with a constitutional interest."

B

Next, petitioners' intended future conduct is "arguably . . . proscribed by [the] statute" they wish to challenge. The Ohio false statement law sweeps broadly, and covers the subject matter of petitioners' intended speech. Both SBA and COAST have alleged an intent to "[m]ake" statements "concerning the voting record of a candidate or public official," and to "disseminate" statements "concerning a candidate . . . to promote the election, nomination, or defeat of the candidate[.]"

20

And, a Commission panel here already found probable cause to believe that SBA violated the statute when it stated that Driehaus had supported "taxpayer-funded abortion"—the same sort of statement petitioners plan to disseminate in the future. Under these circumstances, we have no difficulty concluding that petitioners' intended speech is "arguably proscribed" by the law.

Respondents incorrectly rely on Golden v. Zwickler, 394 U.S. 103 (1969). In that case, the plaintiff had previously distributed anonymous leaflets criticizing a particular Congressman who had since left office. The Court dismissed the plaintiff's challenge to the electoral leafletting ban as nonjusticiable because his "*sole concern* was literature relating to the Congressman and his record," and "it was most unlikely that the Congressman would again be a candidate." (emphasis added). Under those circumstances, any threat of future prosecution was "wholly conjectural."

Here, by contrast, petitioners' speech focuses on the broader issue of support for the ACA, not on the voting record of a single candidate. Because petitioners' alleged future speech is not directed exclusively at Driehaus, it does not matter whether he "may run for office again." As long as petitioners continue to engage in comparable electoral speech regarding support for the ACA, that speech will remain arguably proscribed by Ohio's false statement statute.

Respondents, echoing the Sixth Circuit, contend that SBA's fears of enforcement are misplaced because SBA has not said it " 'plans to lie or recklessly disregard the veracity of its speech.' " The Sixth Circuit reasoned that because SBA "can only be liable for making a statement 'knowing' it is false," SBA's insistence that its speech is factually true "makes the possibility of prosecution for uttering such statements exceedingly slim."

The Sixth Circuit misses the point. SBA's insistence that the allegations in its press release were true did not prevent the Commission panel from finding probable cause to believe that SBA had violated the law the first time around. And, there is every reason to think that similar speech in the future will result in similar proceedings, notwithstanding SBA's belief in the truth of its allegations. Nothing in this Court's decisions requires a plaintiff who wishes to challenge the constitutionality of a law to confess that he will in fact violate that law.

C

Finally, the threat of future enforcement of the false statement statute is substantial. Most obviously, there is a history of past enforcement here. . . .

[Commission] proceedings are not a rare occurrence. Petitioners inform us that the Commission " 'handles about 20 to 80 false statement complaints per year,' " and respondents do not deny that the Commission frequently fields complaints alleging violations of the false statement statute. Moreover, respondents have not disavowed enforcement if petitioners make similar statements in the future. In fact, the specter of enforcement is so substantial that the owner of the billboard refused to display SBA's message after receiving a letter threatening Commission proceedings. On these facts, the prospect of future enforcement is far from "imaginary or speculative."

We take the threatened Commission proceedings into account because administrative action, like arrest or prosecution, may give rise to harm sufficient to justify pre-enforcement review. The burdens that Commission proceedings can impose on electoral speech are of particular concern here. As the Ohio Attorney General himself notes, the "practical effect" of the Ohio false statement scheme is "to permit a private complainant . . . to gain a campaign advantage without ever having to prove the falsity of a statement." [Moreover], the target of a false statement complaint may be forced to divert significant time and resources to hire legal counsel and respond to discovery requests in the crucial days leading up to an election. And where, as here, a Commission panel issues a preelection probable-cause finding, "such a determination itself may be viewed [by the electorate] as a sanction by the State."

Although the threat of Commission proceedings is a substantial one, we need not decide whether that threat standing alone gives rise to an Article III injury. The burdensome Commission proceedings here are backed by the additional threat of criminal prosecution. We conclude that the combination of those two threats suffices to create an Article III injury under the circumstances of this case.

That conclusion holds true as to both SBA and COAST. Respondents, relying on Younger v. Harris, 401 U.S. 37 (1971), appear to suggest that COAST lacks standing because it refrained from actually disseminating its planned speech in order to avoid Commission proceedings of its own. In *Younger*, the plaintiff had been indicted for distributing leaflets in violation of the California Criminal Syndicalism Act. When he challenged the constitutionality of the law in federal court, several other plaintiffs intervened, arguing that their own speech was inhibited by Harris' prosecution. The Court concluded that only the plaintiff had standing because the intervenors "d[id] not claim that they ha[d] ever been threatened with prosecution, that a prosecution [wa]s likely, or even that a prosecution [was] remotely possible."

That is not this case. Unlike the intervenors in *Younger*, COAST has alleged an intent to engage in the same speech that was the subject of a prior enforcement proceeding. Also unlike the intervenors in *Younger*, who had never been threatened with prosecution, COAST has been the subject of Commission proceedings in the past. . . .

Page 107.   Before section 3 of the Note, add the following:

The Court offered a new account of the foundations of the zone-of-interests test in Lexmark International v. Static Control Components, 134 S. Ct. 1377 (2014).

Static Control Components contended that Lexmark had violated the Lanham Act by engaging in certain false and misleading conduct. In particular, Static Control Components claimed that Lexmark falsely advised companies that it was illegal to use Static Control's products to refurbish cartridges used for printing. Lexmark responded that courts should use "prudential standing" doctrines, and especially the zone-of-interests test, to deny standing to Static Control Components.

The Court unanimously disagreed. In an opinion by Justice Scalia, the Court said that the zone-of-interests test should be understood as posing an issue of statutory construction:

> Whether a plaintiff comes within "the 'zone of interests'" is an issue that requires us to determine, using traditional tools of statutory interpretation, whether a legislatively conferred cause of action encompasses a particular plaintiff's claim. As Judge Silberman of the D.C. Circuit recently observed, "'prudential standing' is a misnomer" as applied to the zone-of-interests analysis, which asks whether "this particular class of persons ha[s] a right to sue under this substantive statute." [In] sum, the question this case presents is whether Static Control falls within the class of plaintiffs whom Congress has authorized to sue under [the Lanham Act]. In other words, we ask whether Static Control has a cause of action under the statute. That question requires us to determine the meaning of the congressionally enacted provision creating a cause of action. In doing so, we apply traditional principles of statutory interpretation.

In a potentially important footnote, the Court added:

> The zone-of-interests test is not the only concept that we have previously classified as an aspect of "prudential standing" but for which, upon closer inspection, we have found that label inapt. Take, for example, our reluctance to entertain generalized grievances —i.e., suits "claiming only harm to [the plaintiff's] and every citizen's interest in proper application of the Constitution and laws, and seeking relief that no more directly and tangibly benefits him than it does the public at large." Lujan v. Defenders of Wildlife, 504 U.S. 555, 573-574 (1992). While we have at times grounded our reluctance to entertain such suits in the "counsels of prudence" (albeit counsels "close[ly] relat[ed] to the policies reflected in" Article III), Valley Forge Christian College v. Americans United for Separation of Church and State, Inc., 454 U.S. 464, 475 (1982), we have since held that such suits do not present constitutional "cases" or "controversies." They are barred for constitutional reasons, not "prudential" ones.

(The problem of widely diffused harms is considered at page 110 of the main volume.)

On the merits, the Court concluded that Static Control did indeed have a right to sue, because the zone-of-interests test is "an appropriate tool for determining who may invoke the cause of action," because that test is not meant to be especially demanding, and because that "lenient approach is an appropriate means of preserving the flexibility of the APA's omnibus judicial-review provision, which permits suit for violations of numerous statutes of varying character that do not themselves include causes of action for judicial review." Under the Lanham Act, a plaintiff must allege an injury to a commercial interest in reputation or sales. Under that test, standing was available here:

> To begin, Static Control's alleged injuries — lost sales and damage to its business reputation — are injuries to precisely the sorts of commercial interests the Act protects. . . . There is no doubt that it is within the zone of interests protected by the statute.
>
> Static Control also sufficiently alleged that its injuries were proximately caused by Lexmark's misrepresentations. . . . [A]lthough diversion of sales to a direct competitor may be the paradigmatic direct injury from false advertising, it is not the only type of injury cognizable under [the Lanham Act].
>
> First, Static Control alleged that Lexmark disparaged its business and products by asserting that Static Control's business was illegal. When a defendant harms a plaintiff's reputation by casting aspersions on its business, the plaintiff's injury flows directly from the audience's belief in the disparaging statements. As we have observed, a defendant who " 'seeks to promote his own interests by telling a known falsehood to or about the plaintiff or his product' " may be said to have proximately caused the plaintiff's harm.
>
> In addition, Static Control adequately alleged proximate causation by alleging that it designed, manufactured, and sold microchips that both (1) were necessary for, and (2) had no other use than, refurbishing Lexmark toner cartridges. . . . To invoke the Lanham Act's cause of action for false advertising, a plaintiff must plead (and ultimately prove) an injury to a commercial interest in sales or business reputation proximately caused by the defendant's misrepresentations. Static Control has adequately pleaded both elements.

Query: How, exactly, does the Court's formulation of the zone-of-interests test change preexisting law?

Page 110.   Before subsection c of the Note, add the following:

To what extent can procedural violations count as injury in fact to establish constitutional standing? Consider Spokeo, Inc. v. Robins, 136 S. Ct. 1540 (2016).

The Fair Credit Reporting Act of 1970 requires consumer reporting agencies to "follow reasonable procedures to assure maximum possible accuracy of" consumer reports, and imposes liability on "[a]ny person who willfully fails to comply with any requirement [of the Act] with respect to any" individual. 15 U.S.C. §§ 1681e(b), 1681n(a). Robins brought a class action alleging that Spokeo's online "people search engine" generated a profile of him that contained inaccurate information and thus violated the FCRA's requirements. The District Court dismissed, finding that Robins had not satisfied Article III's injury-in-fact test. The Court of Appeals for the Ninth Circuit reversed, concluding that Robins had established injury in fact because "Spokeo violated *his* statutory rights" and because his "personal interests in the handling of his credit information [were] *individualized.*" The Supreme Court granted *certiorari.*

Writing for the Court, Justice Alito began by explaining the purpose of Article III's standing requirements:

> Although the Constitution does not fully explain what is meant by "[t]he judicial Power of the United States," Art. III, § 1, it does specify that this power extends only to "Cases" and "Controversies," Art. III, § 2. And "'[n]o principle is more fundamental to the judiciary's proper role in our system of government than the constitutional limitation of federal-court jurisdiction to actual cases or controversies.'" *Raines v. Byrd,* 521 U.S. 811, 818 (1997).
>
> Standing to sue is a doctrine rooted in the traditional understanding of a case or controversy. The doctrine developed in our case law to ensure that federal courts do not exceed their authority as it has been traditionally understood. . . . The doctrine limits the category of litigants empowered to maintain a lawsuit in federal court to seek redress for a legal wrong. . . . In this way, "[t]he law of Article III standing [serves] to prevent the judicial process from being used to usurp the powers of the political branches," [and] confines the federal courts to a properly judicial role . . . .
>
> Our cases have established that the "irreducible constitutional minimum" of standing consists of three elements. *Lujan v. Defenders of Wildlife,* 504 U.S. 555, 560 (1992). The plaintiff must have (1) suffered an injury in fact, (2) that is fairly traceable to the challenged conduct of the defendant, and (3) that is likely to be redressed by a favorable judicial decision. . . . The plaintiff, as the party invoking federal jurisdiction, bears the burden of establishing these elements. . . . Where, as here, a case is at the pleading

stage, the plaintiff must "clearly . . . allege facts demonstrating" each element. . . .

The Court then elaborated on the meaning of the injury-in-fact test's particularization and concreteness requirements, finding that the Ninth Circuit's standing analysis was "incomplete" because it failed to address the question "whether the particular procedural violations alleged in th[e] case entail[ed] a degree of risk sufficient to meet the concreteness requirement."

For an injury to be "particularized," it "must affect the plaintiff in a personal and individual way." . . . Particularization is necessary to establish injury in fact, but it is not sufficient. An injury in fact must also be "concrete." Under the Ninth Circuit's analysis, however, that independent requirement was elided. . . . [T]he Ninth Circuit concluded that Robins' complaint alleges "concrete, *de facto* " injuries for essentially two reasons. . . . First, the court noted that Robins "alleges that Spokeo violated *his* statutory rights, not just the statutory rights of other people." . . . Second, the court wrote that "Robins's personal interests in the handling of his credit information are *individualized rather than collective.*" . . . Both of these observations concern particularization, not concreteness. We have made it clear time and time again that an injury in fact must be both concrete *and* particularized. . . .

A "concrete" injury must be "*de facto* "; that is, it must actually exist. . . . When we have used the adjective "concrete," we have meant to convey the usual meaning of the term—"real," and not "abstract." . . . Concreteness, therefore, is quite different from particularization. . . . "Concrete" is not, however, necessarily synonymous with "tangible." Although tangible injuries are perhaps easier to recognize, we have confirmed in many of our previous cases that intangible injuries can nevertheless be concrete. . . .

In determining whether an intangible harm constitutes injury in fact, both history and the judgment of Congress play important roles. Because the doctrine of standing derives from the case-or-controversy requirement, and because that requirement in turn is grounded in historical practice, it is instructive to consider whether an alleged intangible harm has a close relationship to a harm that has traditionally been regarded as providing a basis for a lawsuit in English or American courts. *See Vermont Agency of Natural Resources v. United States* ex rel. *Stevens*, 529 U.S. 765, 775–777 (2000). In addition, because Congress is well positioned to identify intangible harms that meet minimum Article III requirements, its judgment is also instructive and important. Thus, we said in *Lujan* that Congress may "elevat[e] to the status of legally cognizable injuries concrete, *de facto* injuries that were previously inadequate in law." . . . Similarly, Justice Kennedy's concurrence in that case explained that "Congress has the power to define injuries and articulate chains of causation that will give rise to a case or controversy where none existed before." . . .

Congress' role in identifying and elevating intangible harms does not mean that a plaintiff automatically satisfies the injury-in-fact requirement whenever a statute grants a person a statutory right and purports to authorize that person to sue to vindicate that right. Article III standing requires a concrete injury even in the context of a statutory violation. For that reason, Robins could not, for example, allege a bare procedural violation, divorced from any concrete harm, and satisfy the injury-in-fact requirement of Article III. *See* Summers v. Earth Island Institute, 555 U.S. 488, 496 (2009) ("[D]eprivation of a procedural right without some concrete interest that is affected by the deprivation . . . is insufficient to create Article III standing"); *see also Lujan, supra,* at 572.

This does not mean, however, that the risk of real harm cannot satisfy the requirement of concreteness. *See, e.g.,* Clapper v. Amnesty Int'l USA, 568 U.S. ——(2013). For example, the law has long permitted recovery by certain tort victims even if their harms may be difficult to prove or measure. . . . Just as the common law permitted suit in such instances, the violation of a procedural right granted by statute can be sufficient in some circumstances to constitute injury in fact. In other words, a plaintiff in such a case need not allege any *additional* harm beyond the one Congress has identified. *See* Federal Election Comm'n v. Akins, 524 U.S. 11, 20–25 (1998) (confirming that a group of voters' "inability to obtain information" that Congress had decided to make public is a sufficient injury in fact to satisfy Article III); Public Citizen v. Department of Justice, 491 U.S. 440, 449 (1989) (holding that two advocacy organizations' failure to obtain information subject to disclosure under the Federal Advisory Committee Act "constitutes a sufficiently distinct injury to provide standing to sue").

The Court concluded that although "Congress plainly sought to curb the dissemination of false information by adopting procedures designed to decrease that risk," Robins "[could not] satisfy the demands of Article III by alleging a bare procedural violation." It reasoned:

A violation of one of the FCRA's procedural requirements may result in no harm. For example, even if a consumer reporting agency fails to provide the required notice to a user of the agency's consumer information, that information regardless may be entirely accurate. In addition, not all inaccuracies cause harm or present any material risk of harm. An example that comes readily to mind is an incorrect zip code. It is difficult to imagine how the dissemination of an incorrect zip code, without more, could work any concrete harm.

Justice Thomas concurred in the judgment and wrote a separate opinion "to explain how, in [his] view, the injury-in-fact requirement applies to different types of rights." He stated:

> The judicial power of common-law courts was historically limited depending on the nature of the plaintiff's suit. Common-law courts more readily entertained suits from private plaintiffs who alleged a violation of their own rights, in contrast to private plaintiffs who asserted claims vindicating public rights. . . . Historically, common-law courts possessed broad power to adjudicate suits involving the alleged violation of private rights, even when plaintiffs alleged only the violation of those rights and nothing more. . . . Generally, only the government had the authority to vindicate a harm borne by the public at large, such as the violation of the criminal laws, and [e]ven in limited cases where private plaintiffs could bring a claim for the violation of public rights, they had to allege that the violation caused them "some extraordinary damage, beyond the rest of the [community]. . . .

Noting that this distinction underlies modern standing doctrine, Justice Thomas explained:

> Congress can create new private rights and authorize private plaintiffs to sue based simply on the violation of those private rights. . . . A plaintiff seeking to vindicate a statutorily created private right need not allege actual harm beyond the invasion of that private right. . . . A plaintiff seeking to vindicate a public right embodied in a federal statute, however, must demonstrate that the violation of that public right has caused him a concrete, individual harm distinct from the general population. . . . Thus, Congress cannot authorize private plaintiffs to enforce *public* rights in their own names, absent some showing that the plaintiff has suffered a concrete harm particular to him.

Justice Thomas concluded:

> The Fair Credit Reporting Act creates a series of regulatory duties. Robins has no standing to sue Spokeo, in his own name, for violations of the duties that Spokeo owes to the public collectively, absent some showing that he has suffered concrete and particular harm. . . . But a remand is required because one claim in Robins' complaint rests on a statutory provision that

28

could arguably establish a private cause of action to vindicate the violation of a privately held right. Section 1681e(b) requires Spokeo to "follow reasonable procedures to assure maximum possible accuracy of the information *concerning the individual about whom the report relates.*" § 1681e(b) (emphasis added). If Congress has created a private duty owed personally to Robins to protect *his* information, then the violation of the legal duty suffices for Article III injury in fact. If that provision, however, vests any and all consumers with the power to police the "reasonable procedures" of Spokeo, without more, then Robins has no standing to sue for its violation absent an allegation that he has suffered individualized harm. On remand, the Court of Appeals can consider the nature of this claim.

Justice Ginsburg wrote a dissenting opinion (joined by Justice Sotomayor) in which she argued that Robins' injury was sufficiently "concrete." She wrote:

Robins would not qualify, the Court observes, if he alleged a "bare" procedural violation . . . one that results in no harm, for example, "an incorrect zip code." Far from an incorrect zip code, Robins complains of misinformation about his education, family situation, and economic status, inaccurate representations that could affect his fortune in the job market. The FCRA's procedural requirements aimed to prevent such harm. . . . I therefore see no utility in returning this case to the Ninth Circuit to underscore what Robins' complaint already conveys concretely: Spokeo's misinformation "cause[s] actual harm to [his] employment prospects."

Page 118.   At the end of the Note, add the following:

The Court distinguished *Raines* and relied on *Coleman* to uphold the standing of the Arizona Legislature in Arizona State Legislature v. Arizona Independent Redistricting Comm., 135 S. Ct. 2652 (2015). At issue was a proposition adopted by Arizona voters through the initiative process that vested redistricting decisions in an independent redistricting commission. The Arizona legislature brought suit, alleging that the proposition violated Article I, § 4, cl. 1 of the Constitution which provides that "[the] Times, Places and Manner of holding Elections for Senators and Representatives, shall be prescribed in each state by the Legislature [thereof]." The Arizona legislature maintained that by depriving it of the power to engage in redistricting, the proposition violated its rights. In an opinion by Justice Ginsburg, the Court held that the Legislature had standing to raise this claim. The Court noted that in *Raines* it was significant that the plaintiffs had not been authorized to represent their respective houses of Congress. In contrast, "the Arizona legislature was an institutional plaintiff, asserting an institutional injury, and it commenced this action after authorizing votes in both chambers." Because the proposition would nullify votes by the Legislature on redistricting plans, the Legislature had standing to raise the claim. Justice Scalia, joined by Justice Thomas, dissented on the standing question.

6. Perry *and* Windsor. The Court divided five-to-four on standing questions in two important cases involving same-sex marriage. The facts of United States v. Windsor, 133 S. Ct. 2675 (2013), were as follows. New York recognized the marriage of Edith Windsor and Thea Spyer, who wed in Ontario, Canada in 2007. Spyer died in 2009, leaving her estate to Windsor, who sought to claim the federal estate tax exemption for surviving spouses. She was barred from doing so by section 3 of the federal Defense of Marriage Act (DOMA), which defines "marriage" and "spouse" as excluding same-sex partners. Windsor paid $363,053 in estate taxes and sought a refund, which the Internal Revenue Service denied. Windsor brought suit, objecting that DOMA is inconsistent with the Fifth Amendment.

While the case was pending, the Attorney General notified the Speaker of the House of Representatives that the Department of Justice would no longer defend the constitutionality of section 3. In response, the Bipartisan Legal Advisory Group (BLAG) of the House of Representatives sought to intervene in the litigation to defend the constitutionality of section 3. The district court allowed intervention and ruled in Windsor's favor, ordering the Treasury to refund her tax with interest. The court of appeals affirmed. Although the United States agreed with the court's conclusion, it did not comply with the judgment, but instead sought certiorari in the Supreme Court.

In an opinion by Justice Kennedy (joined by Justices Breyer, Ginsburg, Sotomayor, and Kagan), the Court held that there was no standing problem:

> In this case the United States retains a stake sufficient to support Article III jurisdiction on appeal and in proceedings before this Court. The judgment in question orders the United States to pay Windsor the refund she seeks. An order directing the Treasury to pay money is "a real and immediate economic injury," indeed as real and immediate as an order directing an individual to pay a tax. That the Executive may welcome this order to pay the refund if it is accompanied by the constitutional ruling it wants does not eliminate the injury to the national Treasury if payment is made, or to the taxpayer if it is not. The judgment orders the United States to pay money that it would not disburse but for the court's order. The Government of the United States has a valid legal argument that it is injured even if the Executive disagrees with § 3 of DOMA, which results in Windsor's liability for the tax. Windsor's ongoing claim for funds that the United States refuses to pay thus establishes a controversy sufficient for Article III jurisdiction. It

would be a different case if the Executive had taken the further step of pay-ing Windsor the refund to which she was entitled under the District Court's ruling.

The Court acknowledged that "[a] party who receives all that he has sought generally is not aggrieved by the judgment affording the relief and cannot appeal from it." But it said that this rule "does not have its source in the jurisdictional limitations of Art. III. In an appropriate case, appeal may be permitted [at] the behest of the party who has prevailed on the merits, so long as that party retains a stake in the appeal satisfying the requirements of Art. III."

The Court also noted that there was a risk that the case lacked "concrete adver-sariness," because the executive branch was in agreement with Windsor. It con-cluded, however, that this problem involved not Article III but prudential consid-erations, and that those considerations were not sufficient to justify a refusal to rule on the merits:

> In the case now before the Court the attorneys for BLAG present a sub-stantial argument for the constitutionality of § 3 of DOMA. BLAG's sharp adversarial presentation of the issues satisfies the prudential concerns that otherwise might counsel against hearing an appeal from a decision with which the principal parties agree. Were this Court to hold that prudential rules require it to dismiss the case, and, in consequence, that the Court of Appeals erred in failing to dismiss it as well, extensive litigation would ensue. The district courts in 94 districts throughout the Nation would be without precedential guidance not only in tax refund suits but also in cases involving the whole of DOMA's sweep involving over 1,000 federal stat-utes and a myriad of federal regulations. For instance, the opinion of the Court of Appeals for the First Circuit, addressing the validity of DOMA in a case involving regulations of the Department of Health and Human Ser-vices, likely would be vacated with instructions to dismiss, its ruling and guidance also then erased. Rights and privileges of hundreds of thousands of persons would be adversely affected, pending a case in which all pruden-tial concerns about justiciability are absent. [In] these unusual and urgent circumstances, the very term "prudential" counsels that it is a proper exer-cise of the Court's responsibility to take jurisdiction. For these reasons, the prudential and Article III requirements are met here; and, as a consequence, the Court need not decide whether BLAG would have standing to challenge the District Court's ruling and its affirmance in the Court of Appeals on BLAG's own authority.

Justice Scalia (joined by Chief Justice Roberts and Justice Thomas) dissented. He wrote that "the plaintiff and the Government agree entirely on what should happen in this lawsuit. They agree that the court below got it right; and they agreed in the court below that the court below that one got it right as well. What, then, are we *doing* here?" He added:

> What the petitioner United States asks us to do in the case before us is exactly what the respondent Windsor asks us to do: not to provide relief from the judgment below but to say that that judgment was correct. And the same was true in the Court of Appeals: Neither party sought to undo the judgment for Windsor, and so that court should have dismissed the appeal (just as we should dismiss) for lack of jurisdiction. Since both parties agreed with the judgment of the District Court for the Southern District of New York, the suit should have ended there. The further proceedings have been a contrivance, having no object in mind except to elevate a District Court judgment that has no precedential effect in other courts, to one that has precedential effect throughout the Second Circuit, and then (in this Court) precedential effect throughout the United States.

In a separate dissenting opinion, Justice Alito essentially agreed with Justice Scalia with respect to the United States, but concluded that "the House of Representatives, which has authorized BLAG to represent its interests in this matter," suffered injury in fact, because the adverse decision had injured its ability to legislate. "In the narrow category of cases in which a court strikes down an Act of Congress and the Executive declines to defend the Act, Congress both has standing to defend the undefended statute and is a proper party to do so."

Having disposed of the standing issue, the Court reached the merits and held that DOMA was unconstitutional. This aspect of the case is considered in Chapter VI F 3 of this Supplement.

In Hollingsworth v. Perry, 133 S. Ct. 2652 (2013), the merits involved the constitutionality of a ballot initiative known as Proposition 8, which amended the California Constitution to define marriage as a union between a man and a woman. Same-sex couples, seeking to marry, filed suit in federal court, challenging Proposition 8 under the Fourteenth Amendment. After California officials (the named defendants) refused to defend the law, the district court allowed the initiative's official proponents to intervene to defend it. After a trial, the court declared Proposition 8 unconstitutional and enjoined public officials from enforcing it. Those officials elected not to appeal, but the proponents did so. The court of appeals certified to the California Supreme Court the question whether official proponents of a ballot initiative have authority to assert the State's interest in defending the constitutionality of the initiative when public officials refuse to do so. The California Supreme Court answered that they did.

Notwithstanding that answer, the Court concluded that the requirements of Article III were not met. Chief Justice Roberts (joined by Justices Scalia, Ginsburg, Breyer, and Kagan) explained that the proponents of the law had only a generalized grievance and no "direct stake" in the case. "Their only interest in having the District Court order reversed was to vindicate the constitutional validity of a generally applicable California law." To be sure, the proponents of a ballot proposition have a particular interest under California law, "but only when it comes to the process of enacting the law." After enactment, they "have no 'personal stake' in defending its enforcement that is distinguishable from the general interest of every citizen of California."

The Court acknowledged the proponents' argument that "even if they have no cognizable interest in appealing the District Court's judgment, the State of California does, and they may assert that interest on the State's behalf." But the Court responded that it is "a 'fundamental restriction on our authority' that '[i]n the ordinary course, a litigant must assert his or her own legal rights and interests, and cannot rest a claim to relief on the legal rights or interests of third parties.'" Exceptions to that presumption could not be found here. To the argument that California itself recognized a right here, the Court said that "no matter its reasons, the fact that a State thinks a private party should have standing to seek relief for a generalized grievance cannot override our settled law to the contrary. [We] have never before upheld the standing of a private party to defend the constitutionality of a state statute when state officials have chosen not to. We decline to do so for the first time here."

In dissent, Justice Kennedy (writing for himself and for Justices Thomas, Alito, and Sotomayor) emphasized that "[under] California law, a proponent has the authority to appear in court and assert the State's interest in defending an enacted initiative when the public officials charged with that duty refuse to do so." In his view, that authority is akin to a property right, one that gives rise to injury in fact. "Proponents' authority under state law is not a contrivance. It is not a fictional construct. It is the product of the California Constitution and the California Elections Code." As a matter of state law, the purpose of the initiative process "is undermined if the very officials the initiative process seeks to circumvent are the only parties who can defend an enacted initiative when it is challenged in a legal proceeding."

Is the Court's majority saying that a state lacks the constitutional power to create a legal right to defend the outcome of a referendum? If so, how is its decision consistent with *Akins*? Is *Windsor* consistent with *Perry*?

33

II
FEDERALISM AT WORK: CONGRESS AND THE NATIONAL ECONOMY

A. The Values of Federalism and Some Techniques for Implementing Them

Page 160. Before section 2 of the Note, add the following:

1a. *Inherent presidential powers and enumerated congressional powers.* In Zivotofsky v. Kerry, 192 L.Ed. 2d 83 (2015), discussed in more detail in Chapter IV below, dealing with a statute requiring that passports for U.S. citizens born in Jerusalem state that the passport holder was born in Israel, Justice Thomas's separate opinion found that the President had inherent executive power to regulate the passport document itself, a consequence of the Framers' decision to allocate all "residual" foreign affairs powers — those not given to Congress — to the President. He also concluded that Congress had no enumerated power enabling it to so require: The requirement was not one dealing with foreign commerce, nor one dealing with naturalization.

Page 165. After section 9 of the Note, add the following:

10. *Cooperative federalism.* A substantial literature on cooperative federalism is summarized in Erin Ryan, Negotiating Federalism and the Structural Constitution: Navigating the Separation of Powers Both Vertically and Horizontally, 115 Colum. L. Rev. Sidebar 4 (April 2015). Cooperative federalism takes many forms, but all involve sustained interactions in the development, implementation, and

enforcement of policy nominally determined by the national government. Cooperative federalism is sometimes suggested as a way of avoiding the problems associated with a constitutional federalism whose defining characteristic is the allocation of powers between the nation and the states. Are there any constitutional objections to truly cooperative federalism? Note that sometimes states may object that their cooperation has been coerced.

B. Doctrinal Fundamentals: Federalism and Judicial Review

Page 175.   At the end of section 2 of the Note, add the following:

For a collection of essays whose general thrust is to update Wechsler's argument by drawing on more recent studies of the actual functioning of Congress, see Feature, Federalism as the New Nationalism, 123 Yale L.J. 1888 (2014).

Page 178.   After section 7 of the Note, add the following:

To what extent should understandings of the Constitution or constitutional doctrine be shaped by an analysis of contemporary political realities, such as the existence of divided or unified government, or the state of parties as coalitions or ideologically unified? For a relevant discussion, see Pildes, Romanticizing Democracy, Political Fragmentation, and the Decline of American Government, 124 Yale L. J. 804 (2014). Note (a) that those political realities change from time to time, (b) that accurately describing them can be controversial, and (c) the normative implications of even agreed upon descriptions may be controversial. Consider the possibility that such realities might be relevant to understanding the Constitution but not to the development of constitutional doctrine.

C. The Evolution of the Commerce Clause Doctrine

Page 185.   After section 2 of the Note, add the following:

2a. *Regulation or prohibition.* Consider the suggestion in Friedman & Lakier, "To Regulate," Not "To Prohibit": Limiting the Commerce Power, 2012 Sup. Ct. Rev. 255, 261-262 (2013):

[In light of] Framing-era understandings of the proper division between the national and state government [and] modern economic analysis of the values of federalism, [the] only conceivable justification for allowing Congress to ban markets [is] to control the spillover costs of state diversity. [This] rationale standing alone is insufficient justification to allow Congress to prohibit commerce. [But Congress] would still be able to ban goods when doing so serves [interstate] markets. [Because "in-service" laws do] not work to shut interstate commerce down, but instead typically help enforce rules by which interstate commerce operates, they do not represent prohibition of commerce. [Congress] would also have the power to adopt "helper" statutes [that] lend federal enforcement authority to states that have chosen through their own democratic processes to ban certain goods.

Page 199.   At the end of section 4 of the Note, add the following:

The Chemical Weapons Convention Implementation Act prohibits the use of "any chemical weapon." The statute defines a chemical weapon as "[a] toxic chemical," and defines a toxic chemical as "any chemical which through its chemical action on life processes can cause death, temporary incapacitation or permanent harm to humans or animals. The term includes all such chemicals[.]" In Bond v. United States, 134 S. Ct. 2077 (2014), a defendant was prosecuted under the Act for spreading two chemicals on the car handles and mailbox of a woman who had become pregnant after intercourse with the defendant's husband. The chemicals "are toxic to humans and, in high enough doses, potentially lethal." The defendant challenged the constitutionality of the Act. Chief Justice Roberts for a six-person majority did not address the constitutional claims, but held that the Act did not apply to the defendant's actions. (For a discussion of the constitutional arguments, see page 44 of this Supplement, infra.) The majority "doubt[ed] that a treaty about *chemical weapons* has anything to do with Bond's conduct." The statute "must be read consistent with principles of [federalism]," which make it "appropriate to refer to basic principles of federalism [to] resolve ambiguity in a federal statute. In this case, the ambiguity derives from the improbably broad reach of the key statutory definition given the term— 'chemical weapon'— being defined; the deeply serious consequences of adopting such a boundless reading; and the lack of any apparent need to do so in light of the context from which the statute arose—a treaty about chemical warfare and terrorism." Justices Scalia, Thomas, and Alito each filed separate opinions concurring in the result. Each of them found that the statute covered the alleged conduct, but that it was unconstitutional.

Page 215.   At the end of section 1 of the Note, add the following:

(In United States v. Windsor, 133 S. Ct. 2675 (2013), Justice Kennedy's opinion for the Court observed that the Defense of Marriage Act, held unconstitutional on equal protection grounds, was "an unusual deviation from the usual tradition of recognizing and accepting state definitions of marriage[, which] is strong evidence of a law having the purpose and effect of disapproval of that class." That "purpose and effect" were what rendered the statute unconstitutional as a violation of equality. *Windsor* is excerpted at greater length in Chapter VI F 3 of this Supplement.)

Page 216.   At the end of section 3 of the Note, add the following:

See Taylor v. United States, 136 S.Ct. 2074 (2016) (relying on *Raich* to hold that the Hobbs Act, which makes it a federal crime to "affect commerce" by robbery, extends to robbing marijuana dealers of drugs or drug proceeds, and the fact that some of the drugs may have been produced by the victim for individual use is irrelevant) (per Alito, J., with Thomas, J., dissenting).

Page 217.   At the end of section 4 of the Note, add the following:

For additional discussion of the necessary and proper clause, see United States v. Kebodeaux, 133 S. Ct. 2496 (2013).

Page 239.   After section 5 of the Note, add the following:

6. *The "antinovelty" principle.* Relying on *NFIB* and *Printz* (discussed in Section III-C below), Schmidt, Active Avoidance: The Modern Supreme Court and Legal Change, 128 Harv. L. Rev. 2109, 2139-49 (2015), discuss the emergence of an "antinovelty" doctrine, according to which "a law without historical precedent is constitutionally suspect." What grounds might there be for such a doctrine? If the exercise of the asserted power is "attractive" in principle, perhaps the fact that Congress's in the past refrained from seeking to justify statutes with reference to the power might be taken as evidence of a congressional understanding that the

Constitution did not in fact confer the power on it. Yet, if the problem Congress addresses is itself novel, why should novelty in the exercise of an enumerated power count against constitutionality, in a Constitution designed to endure for ages to come, as McCulloch v. Maryland put it? Katyal and Schmidt argue that the antinovelty principle is inconsistent with the presumption of constitutionality because it places the burden on the government to justify the exercise of congressional power. Id. at 2139-40. Note that whether an exercise of power counts as novel will depend on the specificity with which the exercise is described.

7. *Why search for limits?* Rosen & Schmidt, Why Broccoli?: Limiting Principles and Popular Constitutionalism in the Health Care Case, 61 UCLA L. Rev. 66, 70, 71 (2013), argue that "a survey of constitutional history shows that when confronted with novel constitutional questions, the Court almost always declines to provide limiting principles that define the metes and bounds of the constitutional power or right at issue. Instead, [it] typically answers the question in a narrow [fashion] that analyzes [the] constitutionality of only the governmental action that is before the Court. Indeed, the Court typically avoids any attempt at identifying a limiting principle until it has considered the constitutional question many times, and not infrequently it declines to *ever* identify a limiting principle." Rosen and Schmidt connect the case to ideas about popular constitutionalism, and argue that the *NFIB* Court sought a limiting principle even though the constitutional question was novel because "popular constitutional demands [structured] public expectations about the stakes of the ACA challenge to such a degree that it would have been notable had the Court chosen not to go beyond the facts of the case to engage with the limits of congressional power."

For a collection of essays on *NFIB*, see Persilly, Metzger, & Morrison, eds., The Health Care Case: The Supreme Court's Decision and Its Implications (2013).

D. State Regulation of Interstate Commerce

Page 263. At the end of section 2 of the Note, add the following:

e. For a recent discussion of the privileges and immunities clause and the dormant commerce clause, see McBurney v. Young, 133 S. Ct. 1709 (2013), holding that a Virginia freedom of information statute limiting its use to state citizens is constitutional. According to the Court, statutory access to state-held information is not a "fundamental" right protected by the privileges and immunities clause, the distinction was not drawn to provide economic protection to citizens engaged in businesses using state-held information, and Virginia provided reasonable alternative methods by which out-of-state citizens could get access to information about judicial and other public proceedings. Questioning whether the statute triggered dormant commerce clause scrutiny (because the statute did not prohibit access to an interstate market or unduly burden such access), the Court held that the market-participant doctrine permitted the distinction because the state had created the market for information subject to the freedom of information act.

Page 282.   After the second full paragraph, add the following:

Comptroller of the Treasury of Maryland v. Wynne, 135 S. Ct. 1787 (2015), held unconstitutional portions of Maryland's income tax statute because it might lead to double taxation, and therefore violated the dormant commerce clause's ban on taxes that discriminated against interstate commerce.

E.   Preemption

Page 290.   At the end of section 7 of the Note, add the following:

For an argument that Arizona v. United States exemplifies a distinctive form of "plenary power preemption," see Abrams, Plenary Power Preemption, 99 Va. L. Rev. 601 (2013). What subjects might be covered by such a doctrine, in addition to immigration/alienage and foreign affairs? In what sense is national power over such subjects "plenary" while national power over interstate commerce is not? How might "plenary power preemption" differ from "field preemption"?

III
THE SCOPE OF CONGRESS'S POWERS: TAXING AND SPENDING, WAR POWERS, INDIVIDUAL RIGHTS, AND STATE AUTONOMY

A. Regulation Through Taxing, Spending, and the War Power

Page 316.   Replace "[The joint dissent concluded that the Medicaid expansion was inseverable from the Medicaid extension, and that the entire expansion, including the option for states to participate, therefore had to fall.]" with the following:

[The joint dissent concluded that the penalty for not participating in the Medicaid expansion was inseverable from the entire scheme of Medicaid expansion, and that the entire expansion, including the option for states to participate, therefore had to fall.]

B. Congress's Enforcement Powers under the Reconstruction Amendments

Page 335.   After section 3 of the Note, add the following:

3a. *Justifying "current burdens" by "current needs."* The Voting Rights Act of 1965 (VRA) adopted an aggressive remedy for protection of voting rights. Section 4 of the Act provided a "coverage formula" that singled out several states and political subdivisions that used literacy tests or similar devices as a prerequisite to voting and where registration or turnout in the 1964 election was significantly below the national average. The formula was amended in 1970 and 1975 to cover jurisdictions with low participation in either or both the 1968 or 1972 election. Those covered jurisdictions were required, under section 5 of the Act, to obtain federal approval before making changes in their voting laws. In 1982 and 2006, Congress extended section 5's "preclearance requirement" without changing the coverage formula.

In Shelby County v. Holder, 133 S. Ct. 2612 (2013), the Supreme Court, in an opinion by Chief Justice Roberts, held that the coverage formula of section 4 was unconstitutional and could no longer be used to subject jurisdictions to the preclearance regime of section 5.

Referring to its decision in Northwest Austin Municipal Utility District No. 1 v. Holder, 557 U.S. 193 (2009), the Court emphasized that "the Act imposes current burdens and must be justified by current needs." It saw the Act's preclearance regime as a departure from baseline constitutional principles because the Act "suspends 'all changes to state election law'—however innocuous—until they have been precleared by federal authorities in Washington, D.C.," requiring states to "beseech the Federal Government for permission to implement laws that they would otherwise have the right to enact and execute on their own," and because, "despite the tradition of equal sovereignty, the Act applies to only nine States (and several additional counties)." While "these departures from the basic features of our system of government" may have been justified by the pervasive discrimination that existed in 1965, they were no longer justified: "Nearly 50 years later, things have changed dramatically":

> When upholding the constitutionality of the coverage formula in 1966, we concluded that it was "rational in both practice and theory." The formula looked to cause (discriminatory tests) and effect (low voter registration and turnout), and tailored the remedy (preclearance) to those jurisdictions exhibiting both.
>
> By 2009, however, we concluded that the "coverage formula raise[d] serious constitutional questions." As we explained, a statute's "current

burdens" must be justified by "current needs," and any "disparate geographic coverage" must be "sufficiently related to the problem that it targets." The coverage formula met that test in 1965, but no longer does so.

Coverage today is based on decades-old data and eradicated practices. The formula captures States by reference to literacy tests and low voter registration and turnout in the 1960s and early 1970s. But such tests have been banned nationwide for over 40 years. And voter registration and turnout numbers in the covered States have risen dramatically in the years since. Racial disparity in those numbers was compelling evidence justifying the preclearance remedy and the coverage formula. There is no longer such a disparity.

In 1965, the States could be divided into two groups: those with a recent history of voting tests and low voter registration and turnout, and those without those characteristics. Congress based its coverage formula on that distinction. Today the Nation is no longer divided along those lines, yet the Voting Rights Act continues to treat it as if it were.

Justice Ginsburg, joined by Justices Breyer, Sotomayor, and Kagan, dissented. Their view was that Congress, rather than the Court, should decide whether the coverage formula remains appropriate:

It is well established that Congress' judgment regarding exercise of its power to enforce the Fourteenth and Fifteenth Amendments warrants substantial deference. The VRA addresses the combination of race discrimination and the right to vote, which is "preservative of all rights." Yick Wo v. Hopkins, 118 U.S. 356, 370 (1886). When confronting the most constitutionally invidious form of discrimination, and the most fundamental right in our democratic system, Congress' power to act is at its height.

The basis for this deference is firmly rooted in both constitutional text and precedent. The Fifteenth Amendment, which targets precisely and only racial discrimination in voting rights, states that, in this domain, "Congress shall have power to enforce this article by appropriate legislation." . . .

It cannot tenably be maintained that the VRA, an Act of Congress adopted to shield the right to vote from racial discrimination, is inconsistent with the letter or spirit of the Fifteenth Amendment, or any provision of the Constitution read in light of the Civil War Amendments. Nowhere in today's opinion [is] there clear recognition of the transformative effect the Fifteenth Amendment aimed to achieve. . . .

The stated purpose of the Civil War Amendments was to arm Congress with the power and authority to protect all persons within the Nation from violations of their rights by the States. In exercising that power, then,

Congress may use "all means which are appropriate, which are plainly adapted" to the constitutional ends declared by these Amendments. McCulloch, 4 Wheat., at 421. So when Congress acts to enforce the right to vote free from racial discrimination, we ask not whether Congress has chosen the means most wise, but whether Congress has rationally selected means appropriate to a legitimate end. "It is not for us to review the congressional resolution of [the need for its chosen remedy]. It is enough that we be able to perceive a basis upon which the Congress might resolve the conflict as it did." Katzenbach v. Morgan, 384 U.S. 641, 653 (1966). . . .

For three reasons, legislation reauthorizing an existing statute is especially likely to satisfy the minimal requirements of the rational-basis test. First, when reauthorization is at issue, Congress has already assembled a legislative record justifying the initial legislation. Congress is entitled to consider that preexisting record as well as the record before it at the time of the vote on reauthorization. . . .

Second, the very fact that reauthorization is necessary arises because Congress has built a temporal limitation into the Act. . . .

Third, a reviewing court should expect the record supporting reauthorization to be less stark than the record originally made. Demand for a record of violations equivalent to the one earlier made would expose Congress to a catch-22. If the statute was working, there would be less evidence of discrimination, so opponents might argue that Congress should not be allowed to renew the statute. In contrast, if the statute was not working, there would be plenty of evidence of discrimination, but scant reason to renew a failed regulatory regime.

C.   The Tenth Amendment as a Federalism-Based Limitation on Congressional Power

Page 348.   After section 1 of the Note, add the following:

1a. *Constitutional limits on the power to implement treaties.* Bond v. United States, 134 S. Ct. 2077 (2014), involved a federal statute implementing the International Convention on the Prohibition of the Development, Production, Storage, Stockpiling, and Use of Chemical Weapons, a treaty ratified in 1997. A majority of the Court held that the statute did not apply to the defendant's actions. (See page 34 of this Supplement, supra.) Justice Scalia, concurring in the judgment, argued that the statute was unconstitutional because its only textual foundation was the necessary and proper clause. That clause gave Congress the power to make laws necessary and proper for carrying into execution" the "Power [to] make Treaties." It did not grant to Congress a "power to execute the treaties themselves." It gave Congress the power to "appropriate[ ] money for hiring treaty negotiators, [or to pay] for a bevy of spies to monitor the treaty-related deliberations of other potential signatories. [A] power to help the President *make* treaties is not a power to *implement* treaties already made. [To] legislate compliance with the United States' treaty obligations, Congress must rely upon its independent [Article] I, §8, powers." Justice Thomas joined this part of Justice Scalia's opinion.

Justice Thomas, joined by Justice Scalia and in substantial part by Justice Alito, also concurred in the result, "suggest[ing] that the Treaty Power is [a] limited federal power," which "can be used to arrange intercourse with other nations, but not to regulate purely domestic affairs." He did not offer a definition of "intercourse with other nations," but used the term to refer to treaties "dealing with conditions of commerce, with mutual defense, with belligerent relations, with rights of passage [etc.]." He quoted Madison: "The Federal Government's powers ['will'] be exercised principally on external objects, as war, peace, negotiation, and foreign commerce—the traditional subjects of treaty-making." He acknowledged that "the Federal Government needed the ability to respond to unforeseeable varieties of intercourse with other nations," but, again quoting Madison, any exercise of the Treaty Power " 'must be consistent with the object of the delegation,' which is 'the regulation of intercourse with foreign nations.'"

IV
THE DISTRIBUTION OF NATIONAL POWERS

A. Introduction

Page 370.   At the end of the Note, add the following:

Consider whether judicial abstention is especially appropriate in an age of partisan gridlock and political malfunction. In Pozen, Self-Help and the Separation of Powers, 124 Yale L. J. 2, 8 (2014), the author argues that in this environment "many of the most pointed ways in which Congress and the President challenge one another can plausibly and profitably be modeled as self-help rather than self-aggrandizement, as efforts to enforce constitutional settlements rather than to circumvent them." Compare Marshall, Warning!: Self-Help and the Presidency, 124 Yale L. J. Forum 95, 98 (2014): "The last thing American constitutional law needs is another rationale that could be used to justify an expansive exercise of executive branch power, particularly when that exercise is based on little more than a President's own conclusion that Congress has somehow engaged in constitutional wrongdoing when it aggressively seeks to frustrate her agenda." Consider the view that judicial intervention is *more* justified in this environment so as to avoid an endless tit-for-tat pattern between the political branches.

C. Foreign Affairs

Page 388.   Before the Note, add the following:

Zivotofsky v. Kerry, 135 S.Ct. 2076 (2015). For many years, Presidents of both parties have refused to recognize Israeli sovereignty over Jerusalem and have instead insisted that the status of Jerusalem should be determined by negotiations between the parties. The Foreign Relations Authorization Act for the 2003 fiscal year provided that "[for] purposes of the registration of birth, certification of nationality, or issuance of a passport of a United States citizen, born in the city of Jerusalem, the Secretary shall, upon the request of the citizen or the citizen's legal guardian, record the place of birth as Israel." Although President George W. Bush signed the Act into law, he issued a signing statement stating that if the measure was construed as mandatory, it impermissible interfered with the President's constitutional authority in the field of international affairs.

Petitioner was born to United States citizens living in Jerusalem, and his mother requested that his passport and the consular report of his birth list his place of birth as Jerusalem, Israel. The State Department refused to comply with the request, and petitioner brought this action. The trial court dismissed the case on the ground that it constituted a nonjusticiable political question, but the Supreme Court reversed. (This aspect of the litigation is discussed at Page 132 of the Main Volume). On remand, the Court of Appeals held that the statute was unconstitutional, and the Supreme Court affirmed.

Justice Kennedy wrote the opinion for the Court. He began his analysis by asserting that petitioner had waived his argument that the consular report of birth abroad should be treated differently from the passport. Accordingly, the opinion addressed only the passport issue. With regard to that issue, the Court noted that under Justice Jackson's tripartite analysis in *Youngstown*, the President was acting in contravention of the views of Congress and that his power was therefore "at its lowest ebb" and his claim must be "scrutinized with caution."

Nonetheless, the Court held that the passport requirement implicated the power to recognize a foreign government and that this power belonged to the President. Although the power was not expressly mentioned in the Constitution, it was a "logical and proper inference" from the power to "receive Ambassadors and other public Ministers" which is granted in Article II. This inference was reinforced by the Article II powers to make treaties and appoint ambassadors with the advice and consent of the Senate.

"Beyond that, the President himself has the power to open diplomatic channels simply by engaging in direct diplomacy with foreign heads of state and their ministers. The Constitution thus assigns the President means to effect recognition on his own initiative. Congress, by contrast, has no constitutional power that would enable it to initiate diplomatic relations with a foreign nation. Because these specific Clauses confer the recognition power on the President, the Court need not consider whether or to what extent the Vesting Clause, which provides that the 'executive Power' shall be vested in the President, provides further support for the President's action here."

Having found that the President had the recognition power, the Court then proceeded to determine whether the power was exclusive. It held that it was. "The various ways in which the President may unilaterally effect recognition—and the lack of any similar power vested in Congress—suggest that [the power is exclusive]. So, too, do functional considerations. Put simply, the Nation must have a single policy regarding which governments are legitimate in the eyes of the United States and which are not."

The Court then discussed the historical practice, finding that Presidents since the founding had exercised unilateral power to recognize new states and that the Court had endorsed the practice.

In the Court's view, it remained "true [that] many decisions affecting foreign relations—including decisions that may determine the course of our relations with recognized countries—require congressional action. . . .

"If Congress disagrees with the President's recognition policy, there may be consequences. Formal recognition may seem a hollow act if it is not accompanied by the dispatch of an ambassador, the easing of trade restrictions, and the conclusion of treaties. And those decisions require action by the Senate or the whole Congress.

"In practice, then, the President's recognition determination is just one part of a political process that may require Congress to make laws. The President's exclusive recognition power encompasses the authority to acknowledge, in a formal sense, the legitimacy of other states and governments, including their territorial bounds. Albeit limited, the exclusive recognition power is essential to the conduct of Presidential duties."

Finally, the Court held that the passport requirement contained in the Act infringed on the President's recognition power. "If Congress may not pass a law, speaking in its own voice, that effects formal recognition, then it follows that it may not force the President himself to contradict his earlier statement. That congressional command would not only prevent the Nation from speaking with one voice but also prevent the Executive itself from doing so in conducting foreign relations.

"Although the statement required by [the Act] would not itself constitute a formal act of recognition, it is a mandate that the Executive contradict his prior recognition determination in an official document issued by the Secretary of State. As a result, it is unconstitutional."

In an opinion concurring in part and dissenting in part, Justice Thomas argued that the passport requirement violated the vesting clause of Article II which, in his view, vested residual foreign affairs powers not specifically enumerated in the Constitution, in the President. In contrast, he would have upheld that statute insofar as it applied to consular reports of births abroad because this portion of the statute effectuated naturalization laws and therefore falls within Congress' enumerated powers under the naturalization and necessary and proper clauses of Article I.

Justice Thomas also argued that the passport requirement was not justified by any of Congress' enumerated powers. (This aspect of his opinion is discussed in the supplement to Page 162 of the Main Volume).

Justice Scalia, joined by Chief Justice Roberts and Justice Alito, dissented. In his view, the passport requirement was an appropriate exercise of Congress' naturalization power because the power "enables Congress to furnish the people it makes citizens with papers verifying their citizenship." With regard to the President's recognition power, he "[agreed] that the Constitution *empowers* the President to extend recognition on behalf of the United States, but [found] it a much harder question whether it makes that power exclusive. [Fortunately], I have no need to confront these matters today—nor does the Court—because [the Act] plainly does not concern recognition. . . .

"[The Act] does not require the Secretary to make a formal declaration about Israel's sovereignty over Jerusalem. And nobody suggests that international custom infers acceptance of sovereignty from the birth place designation on a passport or birth report, as it does from bilateral treaties or exchanges of ambassadors."

Chief Justice Roberts filed a separate dissenting opinion. Justice Breyer filed a brief concurrence.

* * *

Note that the Court's opinion, unlike the opinion of Justice Thomas, does not argue that the Act was beyond Congress' enumerated powers. Suppose, then, that the President decides to recognize the present government of Cuba, but Congress fails to appropriate money to operate an embassy there or to confirm an ambassador. Are these actions constitutional? Would it be constitutional for Congress to pass a "sense of Congress resolution" stating that in the opinion of Congress, Jerusalem is the capital of Israel?

In considering the impact of Zivotofsy, note that most constitutional disputes about the President's foreign affairs powers never reach the courts. See Goldsmith, Zivotofsky II as Precedent in the Executive Branch, 129 Harv. L. Rev. 112, 114 (2015):

One can read [Zivotofsky] narrowly, and future courts might do so if given the chance. But executive branch lawyers, who are governed by different principles and incentives than judges, won't read the decision narrowly. They will read it generously in favor the President in resolving everyday foreign policy disputes between the political branches. In this respect, [Zivotofsky] is a reminder that the impact of a Supreme Court decision depends very much on the institution that interprets and applies it.

Page 388.   At the end of section 1 of the Note, add the following:

In Sitaraman & Wuerth, The Normalization of Foreign Relations Law, 128 Harv. L. Rev. 1897, 1901 (2015), the authors argue that since the end of the Cold War, the "foreign policy exceptionalism"reflected in *Curtiss-Wright* has eroded.

> Over the last twenty-five years, [the] Supreme Court has rejected the idea that foreign affairs are different from domestic affairs Instead, the Court has treated foreign relations issues as if they were run-of-the-mill separation of powers and statutory interpretation principles. The result is that foreign relations law is being normalized.

Are these claims consistent with the *Zivotosky*. Consider Goldsmith, supra at 130: "[*Zivotofsky*] defied the claims one month after they were published, when it made clear that the Court had not in fact rejected functional considerations as a basis for measuring presidential power in foreign relations and could switch back to it on a dime."

If the claims are nonetheless correct, is the Court's shift in focus desirable? Sitaraman and Wuerth argue that

> analyzing foreign relations law as ordinary law is not so threatening. [The] considerations that are often cited to support exceptionalism—flexibility, speed, secrecy, the nature of the subject matter, error costs, and the like—all operate at far too high a level of generality. The foreign versus domestic divide is hardly justifiable on its own terms as narrowly tailored to these underlying values, and exceptionalism is both over- and under-inclusive as a proxy for these underlying functional values.

Id. at 1903. Do you agree?

Page 389.   At the end of section 2 of the Note, add the following:

Consider also Bradley & Morrison, Historical Gloss and the Separation of Powers, 126 Harv. L. Rev. 411, 414-415 (2012):

> [The] concept of institutional acquiescence needs to be tied more closely to the reality of how the political branches actually interact. Claims about acquiescence are typically based on a Madisonian conception of interbranch

competition pursuant to which Congress and the Executive are each assumed to have the tools and motivation to guard against encroachments on their authority. It has become apparent from political science scholarship, however, that the Madisonian model does not accurately reflect the dynamics of modern congressional-executive relations. [Although] Congress and the President may disagree about particular policies, Congress as a body does not systematically seek to protect its prerogatives against presidential encroachment.

Bradley and Morrison conclude that this fact argues "not so much for rejecting the idea of acquiescence altogether as for being more cautious about treating apparently legislative inaction as acquiescence, and for looking beyond formal enactments when assessing whether any given case actually involves acquiescence or nonacquiescence." In particular, a finding of acquiescence may be more defensible "when the practice in question is not only long standing but also the product of bipartisan choices." Id.

D. Domestic Affairs

Page 423.   After the first paragraph of section 3 of the Note, add the following:

For a discussion of the extent to which, and methods by which, the president is controlled by law rather than politics, see Bradley & Morrison, Presidential Power, Historical Practice, and Legal Constraint, 113 Colum. L. Rev. 1097 (2013). For arguments that legal constraints on the executive have mostly collapsed, see B. Ackerman, The Decline and Fall of the American Republic (2010); E. Posner & A. Vermeule, The Executive Unbound: After the Madisonian Republic (2010).

Page 427.   Before subsection c of the Note, add the following:

Consider the possibility that advocates of reviving the nondelegation doctrine view it as "a second-best enterprise – an attempt to compensate for perceived departures during the New Deal from the baseline of the original constitutional order." Sunstein & Vermeule, Libertarian Constitutional Law, 82 U. Chi. L. Rev. 393, 399 (2015).

Suppose that [one believes] that a central goal of the Constitution is to safeguard private liberty, and that it should do so by constraining the influence of private factions. If so, then there is a plausible argument for the nondelegation doctrine as a way of achieving that goal. It might well be thought that, by requiring members of Congress to surmount the difficulty of agreement on a specific form of words and by forbidding legislation that lacks such agreement, the nondelegation doctrine reduces the likelihood that law will be enacted at all. If national law itself is seen as potentially a threat to liberty, this constraint will seem appealing.

Id. at 416.

Does the granting of significant law-making authority to private entities unconstitutionally delegate *executive* power in violation of the vesting clause of Article II? For an exploration of the issue, see Mishra, An Executive-Power Non-Delegation Doctrine for the Private Administration of Federal Law, 68 Vand. L. Rev. 1509 (2015).

Page 428.   Before section 5 of the Note, add the following:

For a broad based critique of modern antidelegation doctrine, see Justice Thomas's concurring opinion in Department of Transportation v. Association of American Railroads, 135 S. Ct.1225 (2015):

> We have held that the Constitution categorically forbids Congress to delegate its legislative power to any other body, but it has become increasingly clear to me that the test we have applied to distinguish legislative from executive power largely abdicates our duty to enforce that prohibition. Implicitly recognizing that the power to fashion legally binding rules is legislative, we have nevertheless classified rulemaking as executive (or judicial) power when the authorizing statute sets out "an intelligible principle" to guide the rulemaker's discretion. Although the Court may never have intended the boundless standard the "intelligible principle" test has become, it is evident that it does not adequately reinforce the Constitution's allocation of legislative power. I would return to the original understanding of the federal legislative power and require that the Federal Government create generally applicable rules of private conduct only through the constitutionally prescribed legislative process.

Page 435.   At the end of section 1 of the Note, add the following:

Consider the "Regulation from the Executive in Need of Scrutiny Act of 2011," passed by the House of Representatives in 2011, REINS Act, H.R. 10, 112th

Cong., § 3, which provides that a "major rule [promulgated by an administrative agency] shall not take effect unless the Congress enacts a joint resolution of approval." The Senate has not passed the Act. If it were enacted into law, would it be constitutional? Compare Statement of Rep. John Conyers, Jr., Ranking Member, H. Comm. on the Judiciary, REINS Act—Promoting Jobs and Expanding Freedom by Reducing Needless Regulations: Hearings Before the Subcomm. on Courts, Commercial & Admin. Law of the H. Comm. on the Judiciary, 112th Cong. 8 (2011) (arguing that the Act would violate *Chadha* because if an agency promulgated a rule, either House of Congress acting alone could block it by not passing a resolution of approval), with Siegel, The REINS Act and the Struggle to Control Agency Rulemaking, 16 N.Y.U. J. Legis. & Pub. Pol'y 131, 185 (2013) (arguing that the Act is "a bad idea" because Congress lacks the time and expertise to decide these questions but that it is "perfectly constitutional" because it "merely reclaim[s] the power that Congress has ceded over time").

Page 451.   After section 4 of the Note, add the following:

Many statutes establish "partisan balance requirements" for administrative agencies. These provisions require the President to appoint some members of the other party to important positions within the agency. Suppose that you were a lawyer tasked with attacking the constitutionality of these requirements. How might you use *Free Enterprise Fund* to mount such an attack? *See generally* Krotoszynski, Hodge, & Wintermyer, Partisan Balance Requirements in the Age of New Formalism, 90 Notre Dame L. Rev. 941 (2015).

4a. *Recess appointments.* Article II, section 2, clause 2 of the Constitution requires the advice and consent of the Senate for most presidential appointments, but Article II, section 2, clause 3 provides that "[the] President shall have the Power to fill up all Vacancies that may happen during the Recess of the Senate, by granting Commissions which shall expire at the End of [Congress's] next session. In National Labor Relations Board v. Noel Canning, 134 S. Ct. 2550 (2014), the Supreme Court for the first time adjudicated a case concerning the scope of this power.

The case arose amidst intense political controversy over the use of the Senate filibuster to block presidential appointments (sometimes because of opposition to the existence of the agency in question rather than because of opposition to the particular nominee) and over the President's attempt to circumvent filibusters by making recess appointments. When the Senate delayed the confirmation of three members of the National Labor Relations Board, President Obama used his recess appointments power to place them on the Board. He made the appointments after the Senate adopted a resolution providing that it would take a series of brief recesses beginning on December 17, 2011. The resolution provided that the Senate would hold "pro forma" sessions every Tuesday and Friday until it returned to ordinary business on January 23, 2012. President Obama made the appointments on January 4, between the January 3 and January 6 pro forma sessions.

Noel Canning, which had been found by the Board to have violated the labor laws, claimed that the Board lacked a quorum to act because three of the Board's five members had been illegally appointed.

The Court of Appeals agreed with Noel Canning that the appointments were illegal because, in its view, the words "the recess of the Senate" referred only to Congress's annual inter-session recess, not to its more frequent intra-session recesses, and because the words "vacancies that may happen during the recess" referred only to vacancies that come into existence during the recess, not to vacancies that occur earlier but that remain unfilled during a recess.

By a vote of five to four, the Court, per Justice Breyer, rejected both of these arguments. It nonetheless held that the appointments were illegal. The Court reasoned that the *pro forma* sessions brought to a close the recesses between them. This meant that the appointments occurred during a three-day recess, and the Court held that a "recess of [less] than 10 days is presumptively too short to fall within the Clause. We add the word 'presumptively' to leave open the possibility that some very unusual circumstance—a national catastrophe, for instance, that renders the Senate unavailable but calls for an urgent response—could demand the exercise of the recess-appointment power during a shorter break."

In reaching these conclusions, the Court emphasized its view that the recess appointments power was not meant to "[offer] the President the authority routinely to avoid the need for Senate confirmation." It also emphasized the role of historical practice in interpreting the scope of the power. "We recognize, of course, that the separation of powers can serve to safeguard individual liberty and that it is the 'duty of the judicial department'—in a separation-of-power case as in any other—'to say what the law is' [quoting Marbury v. Madison]. But it is equally true that the longstanding 'practice of government' [quoting McCulloch v. Maryland] can inform our determination of 'what the law is.' " With regard to the second point, the Court noted that

> Presidents have made recess appointments since the beginning of the Republic. Their frequency suggests that the Senate and President have recognized that recess appointments can be both necessary and appropriate in certain circumstances. We have not previously interpreted the Clause, and, when doing so for the first time in more than 200 years, we must hesitate to upset the compromises and working arrangements that the elected branches of Government themselves have reached.

The Court then turned its attention to whether the clause permitted intra-session as well as inter-session recesses. Finding the term "the recess" ambiguous, the

Court relied on its purpose, which, it held, "[demands] the broader interpretation" because "[the] Senate is equally away during both an inter-session and an intra-session recess, and its capacity to participate in the appointments process has nothing to do with the words it uses to signal its departure." In addition, the Court cited a record of frequent intra-session appointments from the post–Civil War period to the present and opinions by the President's legal advisors supporting these appointments.

> The upshot is that restricting the Clause to inter-session recesses would frustrate its purpose. It would make the President's recess-appointment power dependent on a formalistic distinction of Senate procedure. Moreover, the President has consistently and frequently interpreted the word "recess" to apply to intra-session recesses, and has acted on that interpretation. The Senate as a body has done nothing to deny the validity of this practice for at least three-quarters of a century. And three-quarters of a century of settled practice is long enough to entitle a practice to "great weight in a proper interpretation of the constitutional provision.

The Court then considered the second ground on which the lower court had invalidated the appointment—that the vacancy had not "happened" during the recess because it did not initially occur while the Senate was in recess. Once again, the Court found that the language itself was ambiguous, but that its purpose suggested a broader interpretation. The Court reasoned that the President might not have time to fill a vacancy before the Senate went into recess and that, if the office was an important one, the inability to fill the post while the Senate was not in session could have serious adverse consequences. The Court again found that historical practice for more than 200 years supported this interpretation. While recognizing that the interpretation might be thought to allow the President to routinely avoid the confirmation process by making all appointments during recesses, the Court pointed out that this course of conduct had disadvantages, including the fact that the appointee can only serve for a limited term and her provisional status might make her less effective. "Moreover, the Senate, like the President, has institutional 'resources,' including political resources 'available to protect and assert its interests.' "

Finally, the Court turned to the issue of how to treat the "pro forma" sessions. The government argued that these sessions were periods of recess because the Senate did virtually no business during them and was therefore in recess as a functional matter. The Court disagreed:

> [The] Senate is in session when it says it is, provided that, under its own rules, it retains the capacity to transact Senate business. The Senate met that standard here.

The standard we apply is consistent with the Constitution's broad delegation of authority to the Senate to determine how and when to conduct its
business. The Constitution explicitly empowers the Senate to "determine
the Rules of its Proceedings." Art. I, § 5, cl. 2. . . .

In addition the Constitution provides the Senate with extensive control
over its schedule. . . .

We generally take at face value the Senate's own report of its actions.

Since pro forma sessions interrupted the recess, the Court was forced to decide
whether the period between these sessions was long enough to trigger the recess
appointments power. It concluded that it was not:

The Recess Appointments Clause seeks to permit the Executive Branch to
function smoothly when Congress is unavailable. And though Congress
has taken short breaks for almost 200 years, and there have been many
thousands of recess appointments in that time, we have not found a single
example of a recess appointment made during an intra-session recess that
was shorter than 10 days. . . . The lack of examples suggests that the recess
appointment power is not needed in that context.

Justice Scalia, in an opinion joined by Chief Justice Roberts and Justices
Thomas and Alito, concurred in the judgment. He would have held that the recess
appointments power arises only during the annual intermission between two formal legislative sessions and that the recess must first occur during that period. He
accused the majority of justifying its "atextual results on an adverse-possession
theory of executive authority." In Justice Scalia's view,

The Court's decision transforms the recess-appointment power from a tool
carefully designed to fill a narrow and specific need into a weapon to be
wielded by future Presidents against future Senates. To reach that result, the
majority casts aside the plain original meaning of the constitutional text in
deference to late-arising historical practices that are ambiguous at best. The
majority's insistence on deferring to the Executive's untenably broad interpretation of the power is in clear conflict with our precedent and forebodes
a diminution of this Court's role in controversies involving the separation
of powers and the structure of government.

Justice Scalia emphasized that because "separation of power exists for the protection of individual liberty," it was irrelevant that the Senate had approved of
or not objected to the encroachment. "Plainly . . . a self-aggrandizing practice
adopted by one branch well after the founding, often challenged, and never before

blessed by this Court [does] not relieve us of our duty to interpret the Constitution in light of its text, structure, and original understanding."

Moreover, Justice Scalia's review of the historical record convinced him that prior practice was "at best ambiguous."

Even if the Executive could accumulate power through adverse possession by engaging in a *consistent* and *unchallenged* practice over a long period of time, the oft-disputed practices at issue here would not meet that standard. Nor have those practices created any justifiable expectations that could be disappointed by enforcing the Constitution's original meaning. . . .

The real tragedy of today's decision is not simply the abolition of the Constitution's limits on the recess-appointment power and the substitution of a novel framework invented by this Court. It is the damage done to our separation-of-powers jurisprudence more generally. [We] should [take] every opportunity to affirm the primacy of the Constitution's enduring principles over the politics of the moment. Our failure to do so today will resonate well beyond the particular dispute at hand. Sad, but true: The Court's embrace of the adverse-possession theory of executive power [will] be cited in diverse contexts, including those presently unimagined, and will have the effect of aggrandizing the Presidency beyond its constitutional bounds and undermining respect for the separation of powers.

V

EQUALITY AND THE CONSTITUTION

C. Equal Protection Methodology: Heightened Scrutiny and the Problem of Race

Page 554.   Before *McCleskey v. Kemp*, add the following:

In Foster v. Chapman, 136 S. Ct. 2737 (2016), the Court found a *Batson* violation with respect to a capital murder trial conducted in 1987, shortly after *Batson* was decided. In using nine of its ten allotted peremptory challenges, the prosecution removed all four black venire members who were qualified to serve. (A fifth black potential juror was excused for cause.) Writing for the Court, Chief Justice Roberts found that the prosecutors' reasons for striking two of the black potential jurors were pretextual. The trial court had accepted the prosecutor's justifications for his strike. But the Chief Justice stated that the Supreme Court's "independent examination of the record" revealed "that much of the reasoning provided by [the prosecutor] has no grounding in fact." Some of the reasons were unsupported by the record. "Still other explanations given by the prosecution, while not explicitly contradicted by the record, are difficult to credit because the State willingly accepted white jurors with the same traits that supposedly rendered [one of the black venire members] an unattractive juror."

With respect to the second prospective black juror, the Court rejected both of the state's purported nonracial explanations. The first justification was that the juror's son was roughly the age of the defendant and had been convicted for "basically the same thing that this defendant is charged with." The Chief Justice responded strongly:

Nonsense. [The juror's] son had received a 12–month suspended sentence for stealing hubcaps from a car in a mall parking lot five years earlier. Foster was charged with capital murder of a 79–year–old widow after a brutal sexual assault. The "implausible" and "fantastic" assertion that the two had been charged with "basically the same thing" supports our conclusion that the focus on Hood's son can only be regarded as pretextual.

Consider the way in which facially neutral explanations regarding a juror's family members' involvement with the criminal justice system may bear more heavily on minority venire members. As for the second justification, the prosecutor claimed he had used a strike because the prospective juror belonged to the Church of Christ. The record persuaded the Court that the juror's "race, and not his religious affiliation, was [the prosecutor's] true motivation." Should religious affiliation be a legitimate reason to exercise a peremptory challenge? Is it even a race-neutral reason? The Chief Justice noted that a document with the words "*NO. No Black Church*" had been produced from the prosecutor's files.

The Chief Justice also emphasized the ways that "[the] contents of the prosecution's file . . . plainly [belied] the State's claim that it exercised its strikes in a 'color-blind' manner."

The sheer number of references to race in that file is arresting. The State, however, claims that things are not quite as bad as they seem. The focus on black prospective jurors, it contends, does not indicate any attempt to exclude them from the jury. It instead reflects an effort to ensure that the State was "thoughtful and non-discriminatory in [its] consideration of black prospective jurors [and] to develop and maintain detailed information on those prospective jurors in order to properly defend against any suggestion that decisions regarding [its] selections were pretextual." *Batson,* after all, had come down only months before Foster's trial. The prosecutors, according to the State, were uncertain what sort of showing might be demanded of them and wanted to be prepared.

This argument falls flat. To begin, it "reeks of afterthought," [Miller-El v. Dretke, 545 U.S. 213, 246 (2005)], having never before been made in the nearly 30–year history of this litigation: not in the trial court, not in the state habeas court, and not even in the State's brief in opposition to Foster's petition for certiorari.

Justice Alito concurred in the judgment. Justice Thomas dissented.

Page 598.   At the end of the page, add the following:

Are there methods of achieving the goals of affirmative action without utilizing facially racial classifications? Consider S. Cashin, Place not Race: A New Vision of Opportunity in America at xix (2014):

The rub for proponents of affirmative action is that as long as they hold on to race as the sine qua non of diversity, they stymie possibilities for transformative change. The civil rights community, for example, expends energy on a policy that primarily benefits the most advantaged children of color, while contributing to a divisive politics that makes it difficult to create quality K-12 education for all children. [The] next generation of diversity strategies should encourage rather than discourage cross-racial alliances and social mobility. [Meaningful] diversity can be achieved if institutions rethink exclusionary practices, cultivate strivers from overlooked places, and give special consideration to highly qualified applicants of all races that have had to overcome structural disadvantages like segregation.

Has the Supreme Court tightened up the narrow tailoring requirement announced in *Grutter*? The Supreme Court twice addressed that question in a case involving affirmative action in undergraduate admissions at the University of Texas.

After the Fifth Circuit held in Hopwood v. Texas, 78 F.3d 932 (1996), that the University of Texas's consideration of race in its admissions process violated the equal protection clause because it did not further a compelling government interest, the Texas legislature adopted a measure known as the Top Ten Percent Law. That statute granted automatic admission to the University (as well as other public institutions) to all students from Texas high schools who are in the top 10 percent of their class. Following the Supreme Court's decision in Grutter v. Bollinger, 539 U.S. 306 (2003), holding that racial diversity can be a compelling government interest, the University adopted an additional admissions program in which race was one factor taken into account in admitting the portion of the entering class that was not admitted under the Top Ten Percent Law.

Alison Fisher, a white student who had been denied admission to the University, brought suit, alleging that the University's consideration of race violated the equal protection clause. The district court and the court of appeals ruled in favor of the University, holding that the University was entitled to substantial deference both in deciding that racial diversity was a compelling state interest and in deciding how to achieve that diversity.

FISHER v. UNIVERSITY OF TEXAS, 133 S. Ct. 2411 (2013) (Fisher I). In an opinion by Justice Kennedy, the Supreme Court remanded the case, holding that the court of appeals had not applied "the correct standard of strict scrutiny." The Court took as given its prior decisions in Regents of University of California v. Bakke, 438 U.S. 265 (1978); *Grutter*; and Gratz v. Bollinger, 539 U.S. 244 (2003), which had found that "the interest in the educational benefits that flow from a diverse student body" was "one compelling interest that could justify the consideration of race."

"Once the University has established that its goal of diversity is consistent with strict scrutiny, however, there must still be a further judicial determination that the admissions process meets strict scrutiny in its implementation. The University must prove that the means chosen by the University to attain diversity are narrowly tailored to that goal. On this point, the University receives no deference. *Grutter* made clear that it is for the courts, not for university administrators, to ensure that '[t]he means chosen to accomplish the [government's] asserted purpose must be specifically and narrowly framed to accomplish that purpose.' True, a court can take account of a university's experience and expertise in adopting or rejecting certain admissions processes. But, as the Court said in *Grutter*, it remains at all times the University's obligation to demonstrate, and the Judiciary's obligation to determine, that admissions processes 'ensure that each applicant is evaluated as an individual and not in a way that makes an applicant's race or ethnicity the defining feature of his or her application.'

"Narrow tailoring also requires that the reviewing court verify that it is 'necessary' for a university to use race to achieve the educational benefits of diversity. *Bakke*. This involves a careful judicial inquiry into whether a university could achieve sufficient diversity without using racial classifications. Although '[N]arrow tailoring does not require exhaustion of every conceivable race-neutral alternative,' strict scrutiny does require a court to examine with care, and not defer to, a university's 'serious, good faith consideration of workable race-neutral alternatives.' See *Grutter*. Consideration by the university is of course necessary, but it is not sufficient to satisfy strict scrutiny: The reviewing court must ultimately be satisfied that no workable race-neutral alternatives would produce the educational benefits of diversity. If ' "a nonracial approach . . . could promote the substantial interest about as well and at tolerable administrative expense," ' Wygant v. Jackson Bd. of Ed., 476 U.S. 267, 280, n.6 (1986) (quoting Greenawalt, Judicial Scrutiny of "Benign" Racial Preference in Law School Admissions, 75 Colum. L. Rev. 559, 578-579 (1975)), then the university may not consider race. A plaintiff, of course, bears the burden of placing the validity of a university's adoption of an affirmative action plan in issue. But strict scrutiny imposes on the university the ultimate burden of demonstrating, before turning to racial classifications, that available, workable race-neutral alternatives do not suffice."

Justice Scalia wrote a short concurring opinion adhering to the view he expressed in *Grutter* that the Fourteenth Amendment "proscribes government discrimination on the basis of race, and state-provided education is no exception," but noting that because Fisher had not asked the Court to overrule *Grutter*, he joined the Court's opinion.

Justice Thomas wrote a lengthier concurrence, taking the position that "a State's use of race in higher education admissions decisions is categorically prohibited by the Equal Protection Clause." He saw "nothing 'pressing' or 'necessary' about obtaining whatever educational benefits may flow from racial diversity":

"[T]he educational benefits flowing from student body diversity—assuming they exist—hardly qualify as a compelling state interest. Indeed, the argument that educational benefits justify racial discrimination was advanced in support of racial segregation in the 1950's, but emphatically rejected by this Court. And just as the alleged educational benefits of segregation were insufficient to justify racial discrimination then, see Brown v. Board of Education, 347 U.S. 483 (1954), the alleged educational benefits of diversity cannot justify racial discrimination today."

He then drew a series of parallels between the arguments advanced by the University and the arguments that had been advanced in favor of racial segregation:

"The University asserts, for instance, that the diversity obtained through its discriminatory admissions program prepares its students to become leaders in a diverse society. See, e.g., Brief for Respondents 6 (arguing that student body diversity 'prepares students to become the next generation of leaders in an increasingly diverse society'). The segregationists likewise defended segregation on the ground that it provided more leadership opportunities for blacks. See, e.g., Brief for Respondents in Sweatt 96 ('[A] very large group of Northern Negroes [comes] South to attend separate colleges, suggesting that the Negro does not secure as well-rounded a college life at a mixed college, and that the separate college offers him positive advantages; that there is a more normal social life for the Negro in a separate college; that there is a greater opportunity for full participation and for the development of leadership; that the Negro is inwardly more "secure" at a college of his own people'); Brief for Appellees in Davis 25-26 ('The Negro child gets an opportunity to participate in segregated schools that I have never seen accorded to him in non-segregated schools. He is important, he holds offices, he is accepted by his fellows, he is on athletic teams, he has a full place there' (internal quotation marks omitted)). This argument was unavailing. It is irrelevant under the Fourteenth Amendment whether segregated or mixed schools produce better leaders. Indeed, no court today would accept the suggestion that segregation is permissible because historically black colleges produced Booker T. Washington, Thurgood Marshall, Martin Luther King, Jr., and other prominent leaders. Likewise, the University's racial discrimination cannot be justified on the ground that it will produce better leaders.

"The University also asserts that student body diversity improves interracial relations. See, e.g., Brief for Respondents 6 (arguing that student body diversity promotes 'cross-racial understanding' and breaks down racial and ethnic stereotypes). In this argument, too, the University repeats arguments once marshaled in support of segregation. See, e.g., Brief for Appellees in Davis 17 ('Virginia has established segregation in certain fields as a part of her public policy to prevent violence and reduce resentment. The result, in the view of an overwhelming Virginia majority, has been to improve the relationship between the different races'); id., at 25 ('If segregation be stricken down, the general welfare will be definitely harmed . . . there would be more friction developed' (internal quotation marks omitted)); Brief for Respondents in Sweatt 93 ('Texas has had no serious breaches of the peace in recent years in connection with its schools. The separation of the races has kept the conflicts at a minimum'); id., at 97-98 ('The legislative acts are based not only on the belief that it is the best way to provide education for both races, and the knowledge that separate schools are necessary to keep public support for the public schools, but upon the necessity to maintain the public peace, harmony, and welfare'); Brief for Appellees in Briggs 32 ('The southern Negro, by and large, does not want an end to segregation in itself any more than does the southern white man. The Negro in the South knows that discriminations, and worse, can and would multiply in such event' (internal quotation marks omitted)). We flatly rejected this line of arguments in McLaurin v. Oklahoma State Regents for Higher Ed., 339 U.S. 637 (1950), where we held that segregation would be unconstitutional even if white students never tolerated blacks. Id., at 641 ('It may be argued that appellant will be in no better position when these restrictions are removed, for he may still be set apart by his fellow students. This we think irrelevant. There is a vast difference—a Constitutional difference—between restrictions imposed by the state which prohibit the intellectual commingling of students, and the refusal of individuals to commingle where the state presents no such bar'). It is, thus, entirely irrelevant whether the University's racial discrimination increases or decreases tolerance.

"Finally, while the University admits that racial discrimination in admissions is not ideal, it asserts that it is a temporary necessity because of the enduring race consciousness of our society. See Brief for Respondents 53-54 ('Certainly all aspire for a colorblind society in which race does not matter. . . . But in Texas, as in America, "our highest aspirations are yet unfulfilled" '). Yet again, the University echoes the hollow justifications advanced by the segregationists. See, e.g., Brief for State of Kansas on Reargument in Brown v. Board of Education, O.T. 1953, No. 1, p. 56 ('We grant that segregation may not be the ethical or political ideal. At the same time we recognize that practical considerations may prevent realization of the ideal'); Brief for Respondents in Sweatt 94 ('The racial consciousness and feeling which exists today in the minds of many people may be regrettable and unjustified. Yet they are a reality which must be dealt with by the State if it is to preserve harmony and peace and at the same time furnish equal education to both groups'); id., at 96 (' "[T]he mores of racial relationships are such as to rule out, for the present at least, any possibility of admitting white persons and Negroes to the same institutions" '); Brief for Appellees in Briggs 26-27 ('[I]t would be unwise in administrative practice . . . to mix the two races in the same schools at the present time and under present conditions'); Brief for Appellees on Reargument in Briggs v. Elliott, O.T. 1953, No. 2, p. 79 ('It is not "racism" to be cognizant of the fact that mankind has struggled with race problems and racial tensions for upwards of sixty centuries'). But these arguments too were unavailing. The Fourteenth Amendment views racial bigotry as an evil to be stamped out, not as an excuse for perpetual racial tinkering by the State. See DeFunis v. Odegaard, 416 U.S. 312, 342 (1974) (Douglas, J., dissenting) ('The Equal Protection Clause commands the elimination of racial barriers, not their creation in order to satisfy our theory as to how society ought to be organized'). The University's arguments to this effect are similarly insufficient to justify discrimination. . . .

"The worst forms of racial discrimination in this Nation have always been accompanied by straight-faced representations that discrimination helped minorities.

"Slaveholders argued that slavery was a 'positive good' that civilized blacks and elevated them in every dimension of life. . . .

"A century later, segregationists similarly asserted that segregation was not only benign, but good for black students. They argued, for example, that separate schools protected black children from racist white students and teachers. . . .

"Following in these inauspicious footsteps, the University would have us believe that its discrimination is likewise benign. I think the lesson of history is clear enough: Racial discrimination is never benign. . . .

"While it does not, for constitutional purposes, matter whether the University's racial discrimination is benign, I note that racial engineering does in fact have insidious consequences. There can be no doubt that the University's discrimination injures white and Asian applicants who are denied admission because of their race. But I believe the injury to those admitted under the University's discriminatory admissions program is even more harmful.

"Blacks and Hispanics admitted to the University as a result of racial discrimination are, on average, far less prepared than their white and Asian classmates. In the University's entering class of 2009, for example, among the students admitted outside the Top Ten Percent plan, blacks scored at the 52d percentile of 2009 SAT takers nationwide, while Asians scored at the 93d percentile. Blacks had a mean GPA of 2.57 and a mean SAT score of 1524; Hispanics had a mean GPA of 2.83 and a mean SAT score of 1794; whites had a mean GPA of 3.04 and a mean SAT score of 1914; and Asians had a mean GPA of 3.07 and a mean SAT score of 1991. . . .

"The University admits minorities who otherwise would have attended less selective colleges where they would have been more evenly matched. But, as a result of the mismatching, many blacks and Hispanics who likely would have excelled at less elite schools are placed in a position where underperformance is all but inevitable because they are less academically prepared than the white and Asian students with whom they must compete. Setting aside the damage wreaked upon the self-confidence of these overmatched students, there is no evidence that they learn more at the University than they would have learned at other schools for which they were better prepared. Indeed, they may learn less. . . .

"[T]hese students may well drift towards less competitive majors because the mismatch caused by racial discrimination in admissions makes it difficult for them to compete in more rigorous majors.

"Moreover, the University's discrimination 'stamp[s] [blacks and Hispanics] with a badge of inferiority.' *Adarand*, 515 U.S., at 241 (opinion of Thomas, J.). It taints the accomplishments of all those who are admitted as a result of racial discrimination. Cf. J. McWhorter, Losing the Race: Self-Sabotage in Black America 248 (2000) ('I was never able to be as proud of getting into Stanford as my classmates could be. . . . [H]ow much of an achievement can I truly say it was to have been a good enough black person to be admitted, while my colleagues had been considered good enough people to be admitted'). And, it taints the accomplishments of all those who are the same race as those admitted as a result of racial discrimination. In this case, for example, most blacks and Hispanics attending the University were admitted without discrimination under the Top Ten Percent plan, but no one can distinguish those students from the ones whose race played a role in their admission. . . ."

Justice Ginsburg issued a short dissent, stating that she would have upheld the University's admissions policy:

"Petitioner urges that Texas' Top Ten Percent Law and race-blind holistic review of each application achieve significant diversity, so the University must be content with those alternatives. I have said before and reiterate here that only an ostrich could regard the supposedly neutral alternatives as race unconscious. See *Gratz*, 539 U.S., at 303-304, n.10 (dissenting opinion). As Justice Souter observed, the vaunted alternatives suffer from 'the disadvantage of deliberate obfuscation.' Id., at 297-298 (dissenting opinion).

"Texas' percentage plan was adopted with racially segregated neighborhoods and schools front and center stage. . . ." In a footnote, she added that "[t]he notion that Texas' Top Ten Percent Law is race neutral calls to mind Professor Thomas Reed Powell's famous statement: 'If you think that you can think about a thing inextricably attached to something else without thinking of the thing which it is attached to, then you have a legal mind.' T. Arnold, The Symbols of Government 101 (1935) (internal quotation marks omitted). Only that kind of legal mind could conclude that an admissions plan specifically designed to produce racial diversity is not race conscious."

"Among constitutionally permissible options, I remain convinced, 'those that candidly disclose their consideration of race [are] preferable to those that conceal it.' *Gratz*, 539 U.S., at 305, n.11 (dissenting opinion).

Justice Kagan did not participate.

On remand, the court of appeals again upheld the Texas plan.

FISHER v. UNIVERSITY OF TEXAS, 136 S. Ct. (2016) *(Fisher II).* Once again, Justice Kennedy wrote the opinion for the Court, which rejected Fisher's challenge to Texas's admissions policy. Justice Kennedy emphasized, quoting the district court's opinion, that under Texas's holistic review process "although admissions officers can consider race as a positive feature of a minority student's application, there is no dispute that race is but a 'factor of a factor of a factor' in the holistic-review calculus" and that consideration of race was not limited to underrepresented minorities, but " 'within the full context of the entire application, may be beneficial to any UT Austin applicant—including whites and Asian–Americans.' "

Justice Kennedy emphasized the distinctive posture of the case before the Court:

"Petitioner's acceptance of the Top Ten Percent Plan complicates this Court's review. In particular, it has led to a record that is almost devoid of information about the students who secured admission to the University through the [Ten Percent] Plan. The Court thus cannot know how students admitted solely based on their class rank differ in their contribution to diversity from students admitted through holistic review.

"In an ordinary case, this evidentiary gap perhaps could be filled by a remand to the district court for further factfinding. When petitioner's application was rejected, however, the University's combined percentage-plan/holistic-review approach to admission had been in effect for just three years. While studies undertaken over the eight years since then may be of significant value in determining the constitutionality of the University's current admissions policy, that evidence has little bearing on whether petitioner received equal treatment when her application was rejected in 2008. If the Court were to remand, therefore, further factfinding would be limited to a narrow 3–year sample, review of which might yield little insight. . . .

"Under the circumstances of this case, then, a remand would do nothing more than prolong a suit that has already persisted for eight years and cost the parties on both sides significant resources. Petitioner long since has graduated from another college, and the University's policy—and the data on which it first was based—may have evolved or changed in material ways.

"The fact that this case has been litigated on a somewhat artificial basis, furthermore, may limit its value for prospective guidance. The Texas Legislature, in enacting the Top Ten Percent Plan, cannot much be criticized, for it was responding to *Hopwood,* which at the time was binding law in the State of Texas. That legislative response, in turn, circumscribed the University's discretion in crafting its admissions policy. These circumstances refute any criticism that the University did not make good-faith efforts to comply with the law.

"That does not diminish, however, the University's continuing obligation to satisfy the burden of strict scrutiny in light of changing circumstances. The University engages in periodic reassessment of the constitutionality, and efficacy, of its admissions program. Going forward, that assessment must be undertaken in light of the experience the school has accumulated and the data it has gathered since the adoption of its admissions plan."

The Court rejected Fisher's argument that the University had not articulated its goals with sufficient clarity. And with respect to her argument that consideration of race was unnecessary because the University had been achieving a "critical mass" of black and Hispanic students through the Top Ten Percent Plan plus its prior race-neutral holistic review, the Court held that the record "at the time of petitioner's application," suggested otherwise:

"To start, the demographic data the University has submitted show consistent stagnation in terms of the percentage of minority students enrolling at the University from 1996 to 2002. In 1996, for example, 266 African–American freshmen enrolled, a total that constituted 4.1 percent of the incoming class. In 2003, the year *Grutter* was decided, 267 African–American students enrolled—again, 4.1 percent of the incoming class. The numbers for Hispanic and Asian–American students tell a similar story. Although demographics alone are by no means dispositive, they do have some value as a gauge of the University's ability to enroll students who can offer underrepresented perspectives.

"In addition to this broad demographic data, the University put forward evidence that minority students admitted under the *Hopwood* regime experienced feelings of loneliness and isolation.

"This anecdotal evidence is, in turn, bolstered by further, more nuanced quantitative data. In 2002, 52 percent of undergraduate classes with at least five students had no African–American students enrolled in them, and 27 percent had only one African–American student. In other words, only 21 percent of undergraduate classes with five or more students in them had more than one African–American student enrolled. Twelve percent of these classes had no Hispanic students, as compared to 10 percent in 1996. Though a college must continually reassess its need for race-conscious review, here that assessment appears to have been done with care, and a reasonable determination was made that the University had not yet attained its goals."

Building off a point made in *Parents Involved in Community Schools v. Seattle School Dist. No. 1,* 551 U.S. 701 (2007)—that there was a tension between arguing that race-conscious action is necessary and a claim that it has only a small effect—Fisher had argued that considering race was unnecessary because it affected the admissions of very few students. Justice Kennedy rejected this argument as well:

"In 2003 [prior to the use of race], 11 percent of the Texas residents enrolled through holistic review were Hispanic and 3.5 percent were African–American. In 2007, by contrast [when race was taken into account], 16.9 percent of the Texas holistic-review freshmen were Hispanic and 6.8 percent were African–American. Those increases—of 54 percent and 94 percent, respectively—show that consideration of race has had a meaningful, if still limited, effect on the diversity of the University's freshman class.

"In any event, it is not a failure of narrow tailoring for the impact of racial consideration to be minor. The fact that race consciousness played a role in only a small portion of admissions decisions should be a hallmark of narrow tailoring, not evidence of unconstitutionality."

Finally, the Court rejected the argument that there were workable race-neutral means available to the University:

"A review of the record reveals, however, that, at the time of petitioner's application, none of her proposed alternatives was a workable means for the University to attain the benefits of diversity it sought. For example, petitioner suggests that the University could intensify its outreach efforts to African–American and Hispanic applicants. But the University submitted extensive evidence of the many ways in which it already had intensified its outreach efforts to those students. The University has created three new scholarship programs, opened new regional admissions centers, increased its recruitment budget by half-a-million dollars, and organized over 1,000 recruitment events. Perhaps more significantly, in the wake of *Hopwood,* the University spent seven years attempting to achieve its compelling interest using race-neutral holistic review. None of these efforts succeeded, and petitioner fails to offer any meaningful way in which the University could have improved upon them at the time of her application.

"Petitioner also suggests altering the weight given to academic and socioeconomic factors in the University's admissions calculus. This proposal ignores the fact that the University tried, and failed, to increase diversity through enhanced consideration of socioeconomic and other factors. And it further ignores this Court's precedent making clear that the Equal Protection Clause does not force universities to choose between a diverse student body and a reputation for academic excellence.

"Petitioner's final suggestion is to uncap the Top Ten Percent Plan, and admit more—if not all—the University's students through a percentage plan. As an initial matter, petitioner overlooks the fact that the Top Ten Percent Plan, though facially neutral, cannot be understood apart from its basic purpose, which is to boost minority enrollment. Percentage plans are "adopted with racially segregated neighborhoods and schools front and center stage." *Fisher I,* 570 U.S., at —— (GINSBURG, J., dissenting). 'It is race consciousness, not blindness to race, that drives such plans.' *Ibid.* Consequently, petitioner cannot assert simply that increasing the University's reliance on a percentage plan would make its admissions policy more race neutral.

"Even if, as a matter of raw numbers, minority enrollment would increase under such a regime, petitioner would be hard-pressed to find convincing support for the proposition that college admissions would be improved if they were a function of class rank alone. That approach would sacrifice all other aspects of diversity in pursuit of enrolling a higher number of minority students. A system that selected every student through class rank alone would exclude the star athlete or musician whose grades suffered because of daily practices and training. It would exclude a talented young biologist who struggled to maintain above-average grades in humanities classes. And it would exclude a student whose freshman-year grades were poor because of a family crisis but who got herself back on track in her last three years of school, only to find herself just outside of the top decile of her class.

"These are but examples of the general problem. Class rank is a single metric, and like any single metric, it will capture certain types of people and miss others. This does not imply that students admitted through holistic review are necessarily more capable or more desirable than those admitted through the Top Ten Percent Plan. It merely reflects the fact that privileging one characteristic above all others does not lead to a diverse student body. Indeed, to compel universities to admit students based on class rank alone is in deep tension with the goal of educational diversity as this Court's cases have defined it."

Justice Thomas wrote a brief dissent restating his view that *Grutter* should be overruled.

Justice Alito, joined by the Chief Justice and Justice Thomas, wrote a lengthier dissent. He criticized the University's efforts in defense of its plan as "shifting, unpersuasive, and, at times, less than candid."

"Over the past 20 years, UT has frequently modified its admissions policies, and it has generally employed race and ethnicity in the most aggressive manner permitted under controlling precedent. . . .

"In 1997, [Texas] enacted the Top Ten Percent Plan, which mandated that UT admit all Texas seniors who rank in the top 10% of their high school classes. This facially race-neutral law served to equalize competition between students who live in relatively affluent areas with superior schools and students in poorer areas served by schools offering fewer opportunities for academic excellence. And by benefiting the students in the latter group, this plan, like the race-neutral holistic plan already adopted by UT, tended to benefit African–American and Hispanic students, who are often trapped in inferior public schools.

"Starting in 1998, when the Top Ten Percent Plan took effect, UT's holistic, race-neutral AI/PAI system continued to be used to fill the seats in the entering class that were not taken by Top Ten Percent students. The AI/PAI system was also used to determine program placement for all incoming students, including the Top Ten Percent students. . . .

"The University's revised admissions process, coupled with the operation of the Top Ten Percent Law, resulted in a more racially diverse environment at the University." By 2004—the last year under the holistic, race-neutral AI/PAI system—UT's entering class was 4.5% African–American, 17.9%

Asian–American, and 16.9% Hispanic. The 2004 entering class thus had a higher percentage of African–Americans, Asian–Americans, and Hispanics than the class that entered in 1996, when UT had last employed racial preferences.

"Notwithstanding these lauded results, UT leapt at the opportunity to reinsert race into the process. . . .

"Although UT claims that race is but a 'factor of a factor of a factor of a factor,' UT acknowledges that 'race is the only one of [its] holistic factors that appears on the cover of every application,' Tr. of Oral Arg. 54 (Oct. 10, 2012). "Because an applicant's race is identified at the front of the admissions file, reviewers are aware of it throughout the evaluation." . . . .

"Notwithstanding the omnipresence of racial classifications, UT claims that it keeps no record of how those classifications affect its process. 'The university doesn't keep any statistics on how many students are affected by the consideration of race in admissions decisions,' and it does not know how many minority students are affected in a positive manner by the consideration of race.' According to UT, it has no way of making these determinations. . . . . UT asserts that it has no idea which students were admitted as a result of its race-conscious system and which students would have been admitted under a race-neutral process. UT thus makes no effort to assess how the individual characteristics of students admitted as the result of racial preferences differ (or do not differ) from those of students who would have been admitted without them. . . .

"UT's race-conscious admissions program cannot satisfy strict scrutiny. UT says that the program furthers its interest in the educational benefits of diversity, but it has failed to define that interest with any clarity or to demonstrate that its program is narrowly tailored to achieve that or any other particular interest. By accepting UT's rationales as sufficient to meet its burden, the majority licenses UT's perverse assumptions about different groups of minority students—the precise assumptions strict scrutiny is supposed to stamp out. . . .

"When UT adopted its challenged policy, it characterized its compelling interest as obtaining a 'critical mass' of underrepresented minorities. . . .

"UT has insisted that critical mass is not an absolute number. Instead, UT prefers a deliberately malleable 'we'll know it when we see it' notion of critical mass. It defines 'critical mass' as 'an adequate representation of minority students so that the . . . educational benefits that can be derived from diversity can actually happen,' and it declares that it 'will . . . know [that] it has reached critical mass' when it 'see[s] the educational benefits happening.' In other words: Trust us.

"This intentionally imprecise interest is designed to insulate UT's program from meaningful judicial review. . . . .

"To be sure, I agree with the majority that our precedents do not require UT to pinpoint 'an interest in enrolling a certain number of minority students.' But in order for us to assess whether UT's program is narrowly tailored, the University must identify *some sort of concrete interest.* . . . .

"According to the majority, however, UT has articulated the following 'concrete and precise goals': 'the destruction of stereotypes, the promot[ion of] cross-racial understanding, the preparation of a student body for an increasingly diverse workforce and society, and the cultivat[ion of] a set of leaders with legitimacy in the eyes of the citizenry.'

"These are laudable goals, but they are not concrete or precise, and they offer no limiting principle for the use of racial preferences. For instance, how will a court ever be able to determine whether stereotypes have been adequately destroyed? Or whether cross-racial understanding has been adequately achieved? If a university can justify racial discrimination simply by having a few employees opine that racial preferences are necessary to accomplish these nebulous goals, then the narrow tailoring inquiry is meaningless. Courts will be required to defer to the judgment of university administrators, and affirmative-action policies will be completely insulated from judicial review. . . .

"[Both] UT and the majority cite demographic data as evidence that African–American and Hispanic students are 'underrepresented' at UT and that racial preferences are necessary to compensate for this underrepresentation. But neither UT nor the majority is clear about the relationship between Texas demographics and UT's interest in obtaining a critical mass.

"Does critical mass depend on the relative size of a particular group in the population of a State? For example, is the critical mass of African–Americans and Hispanics in Texas, where African–Americans are about 11.8% of the population and Hispanics are about 37.6%, different from the critical mass in neighboring New Mexico, where the African–American population is much smaller (about 2.1%) and the Hispanic population constitutes a higher percentage of the State's total (about 46.3%)?

"UT's answer to this question has veered back and forth. At oral argument in *Fisher I*, UT's lawyer indicated that critical mass 'could' vary 'from group to group' and from 'state to state.' And UT initially justified its race-conscious plan at least in part on the ground that 'significant differences between the racial and ethnic makeup of the University's undergraduate population and the state's population prevent the University from fully achieving its mission.' UT's extensive reliance on state demographics is also revealed by its substantial focus on increasing the representation of Hispanics, but not Asian–Americans, because Hispanics, but not Asian–Americans, are underrepresented at UT when compared to the demographics of the State. . . .

"To the extent that UT is pursuing parity with Texas demographics, that is nothing more than 'outright racial balancing,' which this Court has time and again held 'patently unconstitutional.' *Fisher I* . . . .

"[Even] if UT merely 'view[s] the demographic disparity as cause for concern,' Brief for United States as *Amicus Curiae* 29, and is seeking only to reduce — rather than eliminate — the disparity, that undefined goal cannot be properly subjected to strict scrutiny. In that case, there is simply no way for a court to know what specific demographic interest UT is pursuing, why a race-neutral alternative could not achieve that interest, and when that demographic goal would be satisfied. If a demographic discrepancy can serve as 'a gauge' that justifies the use of racial discrimination, then racial discrimination can be justified on that basis until demographic parity is reached. There is no logical stopping point short of patently unconstitutional racial balancing. . . . .

"The other major explanation UT offered in the Proposal was its desire to promote classroom diversity. . . .

"[The] evidence cited in support of that interest is woefully insufficient to show that UT's race-conscious plan was necessary to achieve the educational benefits of a diverse student body. As far as the record shows, UT failed to even scratch the surface of the available data before reflexively resorting to racial preferences. For instance, because UT knows which students were admitted through the Top Ten Percent Plan and which were not, as well as which students enrolled in which classes, it would seem relatively easy to determine whether Top Ten Percent students were more or less likely than holistic admittees to enroll in the types of classes where diversity was lacking. But UT never bothered to figure this out. Nor is there any indication that UT instructed admissions officers to search for African–American and Hispanic applicants who would fill particular gaps at the classroom level. Given UT's failure to present such evidence, it has not demonstrated that its race-conscious policy would promote classroom diversity any better than race-neutral options, such as expanding the Top Ten Percent Plan or using race-neutral holistic admissions.

"Moreover, if UT is truly seeking to expose its students to a diversity of ideas and perspectives, its policy is poorly tailored to serve that end. UT's own study [demonstrated] that classroom diversity was more lacking for students classified as Asian–American than for those classified as Hispanic. But the UT plan discriminates *against* Asian–American students. . . .

"Hispanics are better represented than Asian–Americans in UT classrooms. In fact, [the majority and the court of appeals] act almost as if Asian–American students do not exist. Only the District Court acknowledged the impact of UT's policy on Asian–American students. But it brushed aside this impact, concluding — astoundingly — that UT can pick and choose which racial and ethnic groups it would like to favor. According to the District Court, 'nothing in *Grutter* requires a university to give equal preference to every minority group,' and UT is allowed 'to exercise its discretion in determining which minority groups should benefit from the consideration of race.'

"This reasoning, which the majority implicitly accepts by blessing UT's reliance on the classroom study, places the Court on the 'tortuous' path of 'decid[ing] which races to favor.' *Metro Broadcasting,* 497 U.S., at 632 (KENNEDY, J., dissenting). And the Court's willingness to allow this 'discrimination against individuals of Asian descent in UT admissions is particularly troubling, in light of the long history of discrimination against Asian Americans, especially in education.' [*See, e.g.,*] *Gong Lum v. Rice,* 275 U.S. 78, 81–82 (1927) (holding that a 9–year–old Chinese–American girl could be denied entry to a 'white' school because she was 'a member of the Mongolian or yellow race'). In sum, '[w]hile the Court repeatedly refers to the preferences as favoring 'minorities,' . . . it must be emphasized that the discriminatory policies upheld today operate to exclude' Asian–American students, who 'have not made [UT's] list' of favored groups. *Metro Broadcasting* (KENNEDY, J., dissenting).

"Perhaps the majority finds discrimination against Asian–American students benign, since Asian–Americans are '*overrepresented*' at UT. But '[h]istory should teach greater humility.' . . . .

"In addition to demonstrating that UT discriminates against Asian–American students, the classroom study also exhibits UT's use of a few crude, overly simplistic racial and ethnic categories. . . .

"For example, students labeled 'Asian American,' seemingly include 'individuals of Chinese, Japanese, Korean, Vietnamese, Cambodian, Hmong, Indian and other backgrounds comprising roughly 60% of the world's population.' It would be ludicrous to suggest that all of these students have similar backgrounds and similar ideas and experiences to share. So why has UT lumped them together and concluded that it is appropriate to discriminate against Asian–American students because they are 'overrepresented' in the UT student body? UT has no good answer. And UT makes no effort to ensure that it has a critical mass of, say, 'Filipino Americans' or 'Cambodian Americans.' As long as there are a sufficient number of 'Asian Americans,' UT is apparently satisfied.

"UT's failure to provide any definition of the various racial and ethnic groups is also revealing. UT does not specify what it means to be 'African–American,' 'Hispanic,' 'Asian American,' 'Native American,' or 'White.' And UT evidently labels each student as falling into only a single racial or ethnic group, without explaining how individuals with ancestors from different groups are to be characterized. As racial and ethnic prejudice recedes, more and more students will have parents (or grandparents) who fall into more than one of UT's five groups. According to census figures, individuals describing themselves as members of multiple races grew by 32% from 2000 to 2010. A recent survey reported that 26% of Hispanics and 28% of Asian–Americans marry a spouse of a different race or ethnicity. UT's crude classification system is ill suited for the more integrated country that we are rapidly becoming. UT assumes that if an applicant describes himself or herself as a member of a particular race or ethnicity, that applicant will have a perspective that differs from that of applicants who describe themselves as members of different groups. But is this necessarily so? If an applicant has one grandparent, great-grandparent, or great-great-grandparent who was a member of a favored group, is that enough to permit UT to infer that this student's classroom contribution will reflect a distinctive perspective or set of experiences associated with that group? UT does not say. It instead relies on applicants to 'classify themselves.' This is an invitation for applicants to game the system.

"Finally, it seems clear that the lack of classroom diversity is attributable in good part to factors other than the representation of the favored groups in the UT student population. UT offers an enormous number of classes in a wide range of subjects, and it gives undergraduates a very large measure of freedom to choose their classes. UT also offers courses in subjects that are likely to have special appeal to members of the minority groups given preferential treatment under its challenged plan, and this of course diminishes the number of other courses in which these students can enroll. Having designed an undergraduate program that virtually ensures a lack of classroom diversity, UT is poorly positioned to argue that this very result provides a justification for racial and ethnic discrimination, which the Constitution rarely allows.

"UT's purported interest in intraracial diversity, or 'diversity within diversity,' also falls short. At bottom, this argument relies on the unsupported assumption that there is something deficient or at least radically different about the African–American and Hispanic students admitted through the Top Ten Percent Plan. . . .

"UT complained that the Top Ten Percent Law hinders its efforts to assemble a broadly diverse class because the minorities admitted under that law are drawn largely from certain areas of Texas where there are majority-minority schools. These students, UT argued, tend to come from poor, disadvantaged families, and the University would prefer a system that gives it substantial leeway to seek broad diversity *within* groups of underrepresented minorities. In particular, UT asserted a need for more African–American and Hispanic students from privileged backgrounds. See, *e.g.*, Brief for Respondents in No. 11–345, at 34 (explaining that UT needs race-conscious admissions in order to admit '[t]he African–American or Hispanic child of successful professionals in Dallas'); *ibid.* (claiming that privileged minorities 'have great potential for serving as a 'bridge' in promoting cross-racial understanding, as well as in breaking down racial stereotypes'); *ibid.* (intimating that the underprivileged minority students admitted under the Top Ten Percent Plan '*reinforc[e]* ' 'stereotypical assumptions'); Tr. of Oral Arg. 43–45 (Oct. 10, 2012) ('[A]lthough the percentage plan certainly helps with minority admissions, by and large, the—the minorities who are admitted tend to come from segregated, racially-identifiable schools,' and 'we want minorities from different backgrounds'). Thus, the Top Ten Percent Law is faulted for admitting *the wrong kind of African–American and Hispanic students*. . . .

"Remarkably, UT now contends that petitioner has 'fabricat[ed]' the argument that it is seeking affluent minorities. That claim is impossible to square with UT's prior statements to this Court in the briefing and oral argument in *Fisher I*.

Moreover, although UT reframes its argument, it continues to assert that it needs affirmative action to admit privileged minorities. For instance, UT's brief highlights its interest in admitting '[t]he black student with high grades from Andover.' Similarly, at oral argument, UT claimed that its 'interests in the educational benefits of diversity would not be met if all of [the] minority students were . . . coming from depressed socioeconomic backgrounds.'

"Ultimately, UT's intraracial diversity rationale relies on the baseless assumption that there is something wrong with African–American and Hispanic students admitted through the Top Ten Percent Plan, because they are 'from the lower-performing, racially identifiable schools.' [UT's] assumptions appear to be based on the pernicious stereotype that the African–Americans and Hispanics admitted through the Top Ten Percent Plan only got in because they did not have to compete against very many whites and Asian–Americans. . . . .

"In addition to relying on stereotypes, UT's argument that it needs racial preferences to admit privileged minorities turns the concept of affirmative action on its head. When affirmative action programs were first adopted, it was for the purpose of helping the disadvantaged. Now we are told that a program that tends to admit poor and disadvantaged minority students is inadequate because it does not work to the advantage of those who are more fortunate. This is affirmative action gone wild.

"It is also far from clear that UT's assumptions about the socioeconomic status of minorities admitted through the Top Ten Percent Plan are even remotely accurate. Take, for example, parental education. In 2008, when petitioner applied to UT, approximately 79% of Texans aged 25 years or older had a high school diploma, 17% had a bachelor's degree, and 8% had a graduate or professional degree. In contrast, 96% of African–Americans admitted through the Top Ten Percent Plan had a parent with a high school diploma, 59% had a parent with a bachelor's degree, and 26% had a parent with a graduate or professional degree. Similarly, 83% of Hispanics admitted through the Top Ten Percent Plan had a parent with a high school diploma, 42% had a parent with a bachelor's degree, and 21% had a parent with a graduate or professional degree. As these statistics make plain, the minorities that UT characterizes as 'coming from depressed socioeconomic backgrounds,' generally come from households with education levels exceeding the norm in Texas.

"Or consider income levels. In 2008, the median annual household income in Texas was $49,453. The household income levels for Top Ten Percent African–American and Hispanic admittees were on par: Roughly half of such admittees came from households below the Texas median, and half came from households above the median. And a large portion of these admittees are from households with income levels far exceeding the Texas median. Specifically, 25% of African–Americans and 27% of Hispanics admitted through the Top Ten Percent Plan in 2008 were raised in households with incomes exceeding $80,000. In light of this evidence, UT's actual argument is not that it needs affirmative action to ensure that its minority admittees are representative of the State of Texas. Rather, UT is asserting that it needs affirmative action to ensure that its minority students disproportionally come from families that are wealthier and better educated than the average Texas family . . . .

"[It] simply not true that Top Ten Percent minority admittees are academically inferior to holistic admittees. In fact, as UT's president explained in 2000, 'top 10 percent high school students make much higher grades in college than non-top 10 percent students,' and '[s]trong academic performance in high school is an even better predictor of success in college than standardized test scores.' Indeed, the statistics in the record reveal that, for each year between 2003 and 2007, African–American in-state freshmen who were admitted under the Top Ten Percent Law earned a higher mean grade point average than those admitted outside of the Top Ten Percent Law. The same is true for Hispanic students. These conclusions correspond to the results of nationwide studies showing that high school grades are a better predictor of success in college than SAT scores.

"It is also more than a little ironic that UT uses the SAT, which has often been accused of reflecting racial and cultural bias, as a reason for dissatisfaction with poor and disadvantaged African–American and Hispanic students who excel both in high school and in college. Even if the SAT does not reflect such bias (and I am ill equipped to express a view on that subject), SAT scores clearly correlate with wealth. . . .

"It is important to understand what is and what is not at stake in this case. *What is not at stake* is whether UT or any other university may adopt an admissions plan that results in a student body with a broad representation of students from all racial and ethnic groups. UT previously had a race-neutral plan that it claimed had 'effectively compensated for the loss of affirmative action,' and UT could have taken other steps that would have increased the diversity of its admitted students without taking race or ethnic background into account.

"*What is at stake* is whether university administrators may justify systematic racial discrimination simply by asserting that such discrimination is necessary to achieve 'the educational benefits of diversity,' without explaining — much less proving — why the discrimination is needed or how the discriminatory plan is well crafted to serve its objectives. Even though UT has never provided any coherent explanation for its asserted need to discriminate on the basis of race, and even though UT's position relies on a series of unsupported and noxious racial assumptions, the majority concludes that UT has met its heavy burden. This conclusion is remarkable — and remarkably wrong.

Justice Kagan again did not participate.

Does *Fisher II* mark a significant change in the Court's approach to race-conscious affirmative action?

Page 624. Before the Note, add the following:

SCHUETTE V. COALITION TO DEFEND AFFIRMATIVE ACTION, INTEGRATION & IMMIGRANT RIGHTS & FIGHT FOR EQUALITY BY ANY MEANS NECESSARY (BAMN)

134 S. Ct. 1623 (2014)

JUSTICE KENNEDY announced the judgment of the Court and delivered an opinion, in which [CHIEF JUSTICE ROBERTS] and JUSTICE ALITO join.

[In 2006, after the Court's decisions in *Gratz* and *Grutter,* voters of Michigan adopted Proposal 2, which amended Michigan's constitution by adding Article I, section 26. The amendment provided as follows:

[(1) The University of Michigan, Michigan State University, Wayne State University, and any other public college or university, community college, or school district shall not discriminate against, or grant preferential treatment to, any individual or group on the basis of race, sex, color, ethnicity, or national origin in the operation of public employment, public education, or public contracting.

[(2) The state shall not discriminate against, or grant preferential treatment to, any individual or group on the basis of race, sex, color, ethnicity, or national origin in the operation of public employment, public education, or public contracting.

[(3) For the purposes of this section 'state' includes, but is not necessarily limited to, the state itself, any city, county, any public college, university, or community college, school district, or other political subdivision or governmental instrumentality of or within the State of Michigan not included in sub-section 1.

[The District Court rejected an equal protection challenge to the amendment, but the Court of Appeals reversed.]

Before the Court addresses the question presented, it is important to note what this case is not about. It is not about the constitutionality, or the merits, of race-conscious admissions policies in higher education. [The] question here concerns not the permissibility of race-conscious admissions policies under the Constitution but whether, and in what manner, voters in the States may choose to prohibit the consideration of racial preferences in governmental decisions, in particular with respect to school admissions.

This Court has noted that some States have decided to prohibit race-conscious admissions policies. In *Grutter,* the Court noted: "Universities in California, Florida, and Washington State, where racial preferences in admissions are prohibited by state law, are currently engaged in experimenting with a wide variety of alternative approaches. Universities in other States can and should draw on the most promising aspects of these race-neutral alternatives as they develop." In this way, *Grutter* acknowledged the significance of a dialogue regarding this contested and complex policy question among and within States. . . .

[This] Court's decision in Reitman v. Mulkey, 387 U.S. 369 (1967), is a proper beginning point for discussing the controlling decisions. [*Mulkey* is discussed at page 1570 of the main volume.] In *Mulkey,* voters amended the California Constitution to prohibit any state legislative interference with an owner's prerogative to decline to sell or rent residential property on any basis. [The] Court agreed with the California Supreme Court that the amendment operated to insinuate the State into the decision to discriminate by encouraging that practice. The Court noted the "immediate design and intent" of the amendment was to "establis[h] a purported constitutional right to privately discriminate." The Court agreed that the amendment "expressly authorized and constitutionalized the private right to discriminate." The effect of the state constitutional amendment was to "significantly encourage and involve the State in private racial discriminations." . . .

The next precedent of relevance, Hunter v. Erickson, 393 U.S. 385 (1969), is central to the arguments the respondents make in the instant case. [*Hunter* is discussed at page 537 of the main volume.] In *Hunter*, the Court for the first time elaborated what the Court of Appeals here styled the "political process" doctrine. There, the Akron City Council found that the citizens of Akron consisted of " 'people of different race[s], . . . many of whom live in circumscribed and segregated areas, under sub-standard unhealthful, unsafe, unsanitary and overcrowded conditions, because of discrimination in the sale, lease, rental and financing of housing.' " To address the problem, Akron enacted a fair housing ordinance to prohibit that sort of discrimination. In response, voters amended the city charter to overturn the ordinance and to require that any additional antidiscrimination housing ordinance be approved by referendum. But most other ordinances "regulating the real property market" were not subject to those threshold requirements. . . .

Central to the Court's reasoning in *Hunter* was that the charter amendment was enacted in circumstances where widespread racial discrimination in the sale and rental of housing led to segregated housing, forcing many to live in " 'unhealthful, unsafe, unsanitary and overcrowded conditions.' " [The] Court found that the city charter amendment, by singling out antidiscrimination ordinances, "places special burden on racial minorities within the governmental process," thus becoming as impermissible as any other government action taken with the invidious intent to injure a racial minority. [*Hunter*] rests on the unremarkable principle that the State may not alter the procedures of government to target racial minorities. The facts in *Hunter* established that invidious discrimination would be the necessary result of the procedural restructuring. Thus, in *Mulkey* and *Hunter*, there was a demonstrated injury on the basis of race that, by reasons of state encouragement or participation, became more aggravated.

[Washington v. Seattle School District No. 1, 458 U.S. 457 (1982),] is the third case of principal relevance here. There, the school board adopted a mandatory busing program to alleviate racial isolation of minority students in local schools. Voters who opposed the school board's busing plan passed a state initiative that barred busing to desegregate. The Court first determined that, although "white as well as Negro children benefit from" diversity, the school board's plan "inures primarily to the benefit of the minority." The Court next found that "the practical effect" of the state initiative was to "remov[e] the authority to address a racial problem—and only a racial problem—from the existing decisionmaking body, in such a way as to burden minority interests" because advocates of busing "now must seek relief from the state legislature, or from the statewide electorate." The Court therefore found that the initiative had "explicitly us[ed] the racial nature of a decision to determine the decisionmaking process."

Seattle is best understood as a case in which the state action in question (the bar on busing enacted by the State's voters) had the serious risk, if not purpose, of causing specific injuries on account of race, just as had been the case in *Mulkey* and *Hunter*. Although there had been no judicial finding of *de jure* segregation with respect to Seattle's school district, it appears as though school segregation in the district in the 1940's and 1950's may have been the partial result of school board policies that "permitted white students to transfer out of black schools while restricting the transfer of black students into white schools." *Parents Involved in Community Schools v. Seattle School Dist. No. 1 (Breyer, J., dissenting)....*

As this Court held in *Parents Involved,* the school board's purported remedial action would not be permissible today absent a showing of *de jure* segregation. That holding prompted Justice Breyer to observe in dissent, as noted above, that one permissible reading of the record was that the school board had maintained policies to perpetuate racial segregation in the schools. In all events we must understand *Seattle* as *Seattle* understood itself, as a case in which neither the State nor the United States "challenge[d] the propriety of race-conscious student assignments for the purpose of achieving integration, even absent a finding of prior *de jure* segregation." In other words the legitimacy and constitutionality of the remedy in question (busing for desegregation) was assumed, and *Seattle* must be understood on that basis. *Seattle* involved a state initiative that "was carefully tailored to interfere only with desegregative busing." The *Seattle* Court, accepting the validity of the school board's busing remedy as a predicate to its analysis of the constitutional question, found that the State's disapproval of the school board's busing remedy was an aggravation of the very racial injury in which the State itself was complicit.

The broad language used in *Seattle*, however, went well beyond the analysis needed to resolve the case. [*Seattle*] stated that where a government policy "inures primarily to the benefit of the minority" and "minorities . . . consider" the policy to be " 'in their interest,' " then any state action that "place[s] effective decisionmaking authority over" that policy "at a different level of government" must be reviewed under strict scrutiny. In essence, according to the broad reading of *Seattle*, any state action with a "racial focus" that makes it "more difficult for certain racial minorities than for other groups" to "achieve legislation that is in their interest" is subject to strict scrutiny. It is this reading of *Seattle* that the Court of Appeals found to be controlling here. And that reading must be rejected.

[To] the extent *Seattle* is read to require the Court to determine and declare which political policies serve the "interest" of a group defined in racial terms, that rationale was unnecessary to the decision in *Seattle*; it has no support in precedent; and it raises serious constitutional concerns. That expansive language does not provide a proper guide for decisions and should not be deemed authoritative or controlling. . . .

[It] cannot be entertained as a serious proposition that all individuals of the same race think alike. Yet that proposition would be a necessary beginning point were the *Seattle* formulation to control, as the Court of Appeals held it did in this case. And if it were deemed necessary to probe how some races define their own interest in political matters, still another beginning point would be to define individuals according to race. But in a society in which those lines are becoming more blurred, the attempt to define race-based categories also raises serious questions of its own. Government action that classifies individuals on the basis of race is inherently suspect and carries the danger of perpetuating the very racial divisions the polity seeks to transcend. Were courts to embark upon this venture not only would it be undertaken with no clear legal standards or accepted sources to guide judicial decision but also it would result in, or at least impose a high risk of, inquiries and categories dependent upon demeaning stereotypes, classifications of questionable constitutionality on their own terms.

Even assuming these initial steps could be taken in a manner consistent with a sound analytic and judicial framework, the court would next be required to determine the policy realms in which certain groups—groups defined by race—have a political interest. That undertaking, again without guidance from any accepted legal standards, would risk, in turn, the creation of incentives for those who support or oppose certain policies to cast the debate in terms of racial advantage or disadvantage. Thus could racial antagonisms and conflict tend to arise in the context of judicial decisions as courts undertook to announce what particular issues of public policy should be classified as advantageous to some group defined by race. . . .

[In] a nation in which governmental policies are wide ranging, those who seek to limit voter participation might be tempted, were this Court to adopt the *Seattle* formulation, to urge that a group they choose to define by race or racial stereotypes are advantaged or disadvantaged by any number of laws or decisions. Tax policy, housing subsidies, wage regulations, and even the naming of public schools, highways, and monuments are just a few examples of what could become a list of subjects that some organizations could insist should be beyond the power of voters to decide, or beyond the power of a legislature to decide when enacting limits on the power of local authorities or other governmental entities to address certain subjects. Racial division would be validated, not discouraged, were the *Seattle* formulation, and the reasoning of the Court of Appeals in this case, to remain in force.

[The] holding in the instant case is simply that the courts may not disempower the voters from choosing which path to follow. In the realm of policy discussions the regular give-and-take of debate ought to be a context in which rancor or discord based on race are avoided, not invited. And if these factors are to be interjected, surely it ought not to be at the invitation or insistence of the courts.

One response to these concerns may be that objections to the larger consequences of the *Seattle* formulation need not be confronted in this case, for here race was an undoubted subject of the ballot issue. But a number of problems raised by *Seattle,* such as racial definitions, still apply. And this principal flaw in the ruling of the Court of Appeals does remain: Here there was no infliction of a specific injury of the kind at issue in *Mulkey* and *Hunter* and in the history of the Seattle schools. Here there is no precedent for extending these cases to restrict the right of Michigan voters to determine that race-based preferences granted by Michigan governmental entities should be ended. . . .

By approving Proposal 2 and thereby adding § 26 to their State Constitution, the Michigan voters exercised their privilege to enact laws as a basic exercise of their democratic power. [Michigan] voters used the initiative system to bypass public officials who were deemed not responsive to the concerns of a majority of the voters with respect to a policy of granting race-based preferences that raises difficult and delicate issues.

The freedom secured by the Constitution consists, in one of its essential dimensions, of the right of the individual not to be injured by the unlawful exercise of governmental power. [Yet] freedom does not stop with individual rights. Our constitutional system embraces, too, the right of citizens to debate so they can learn and decide and then, through the political process, act in concert to try to shape the course of their own times and the course of a nation that must strive always to make freedom ever greater and more secure. Here Michigan voters acted in concert and statewide to seek consensus and adopt a policy on a difficult subject against a historical background of race in America that has been a source of tragedy and persisting injustice. That history demands that we continue to learn, to listen, and to remain open to new approaches if we are to aspire always to a constitutional order in which all persons are treated with fairness and equal dignity.

Were the Court to rule that the question addressed by Michigan voters is too sensitive or complex to be within the grasp of the electorate; or that the policies at issue remain too delicate to be resolved save by university officials or faculties, acting at some remove from immediate public scrutiny and control; or that these matters are so arcane that the electorate's power must be limited because the people cannot prudently exercise that power even after a full debate, that holding would be an unprecedented restriction on the exercise of a fundamental right held not just by one person but by all in common. It is the right to speak and debate and learn and then, as a matter of political will, to act through a lawful electoral process. . . .

It is demeaning to the democratic process to presume that the voters are not capable of deciding an issue of this sensitivity on decent and rational grounds. The process of public discourse and political debate should not be foreclosed even if there is a risk that during a public campaign there will be those, on both sides, who seek to use racial division and discord to their own political advantage. An informed public can, and must, rise above this. The idea of democracy is that it can, and must, mature. Freedom embraces the right, indeed the duty, to engage in a rational, civic discourse in order to determine how best to form a consensus to shape the destiny of the Nation and its people. These First Amendment dynamics would be disserved if this Court were to say that the question here at issue is beyond the capacity of the voters to debate and then to determine.

These precepts are not inconsistent with the well-established principle that when hurt or injury is inflicted on racial minorities by the encouragement or command of laws or other state action, the Constitution requires redress by the courts. As already noted, those were the circumstances that the Court found present in *Mulkey, Hunter*, and *Seattle*. But those circumstances are not present here. . . .

What is at stake here is not whether injury will be inflicted but whether government can be instructed not to follow a course that entails, first, the definition of racial categories and, second, the grant of favored status to persons in some racial categories and not others. The electorate's instruction to governmental entities not to embark upon the course of race-defined and race-based preferences was adopted, we must assume, because the voters deemed a preference system to be unwise, on account of what voters may deem its latent potential to become itself a source of the very resentments and hostilities based on race that this Nation seeks to put behind it. Whether those adverse results would follow is, and should be, the subject of debate. Voters might likewise consider, after debate and reflection, that programs designed to increase diversity — consistent with the Constitution — are a necessary part of progress to transcend the stigma of past racism.

This case is not about how the debate about racial preferences should be resolved. It is about who may resolve it. There is no authority in the Constitution of the United States or in this Court's precedents for the Judiciary to set aside

Michigan laws that commit this policy determination to the voters. Deliberative debate on sensitive issues such as racial preferences all too often may shade into rancor. But that does not justify removing certain court-determined issues from the voters' reach. Democracy does not presume that some subjects are either too divisive or too profound for public debate. . . .

JUSTICE KAGAN took no part in the consideration or decision of this case.

CHIEF JUSTICE ROBERTS, concurring.

The dissent devotes 11 pages to expounding its own policy preferences in favor of taking race into account in college admissions, while nonetheless concluding that it "do[es] not mean to suggest that the virtues of adopting race-sensitive admissions policies should inform the legal question before the Court." The dissent concedes that the governing boards of the State's various universities could have implemented a policy making it illegal to "discriminate against, or grant preferential treatment to," any individual on the basis of race. On the dissent's view, if the governing boards conclude that drawing racial distinctions in university admissions is undesirable or counterproductive, they are permissibly exercising their policymaking authority. But others who might reach the same conclusion are failing to take race seriously.

The dissent states that "[t]he way to stop discrimination on the basis of race is to speak openly and candidly on the subject of race." And it urges that "[r]ace matters because of the slights, the snickers, the silent judgments that reinforce that most crippling of thoughts: 'I do not belong here.'" But it is not "out of touch with reality" to conclude that racial preferences may themselves have the debilitating effect of reinforcing precisely that doubt, and—if so—that the preferences do more harm than good. To disagree with the dissent's views on the costs and benefits of racial preferences is not to "wish away, rather than confront" racial inequality. People can disagree in good faith on this issue, but it similarly does more harm than good to question the openness and candor of those on either side of the debate.

JUSTICE SCALIA, with whom JUSTICE THOMAS joins, concurring in the judgment.

It has come to this. Called upon to explore the jurisprudential twilight zone between two errant lines of precedent, we confront a frighteningly bizarre question: Does the Equal Protection Clause of the Fourteenth Amendment *forbid* what its text plainly *requires*? Needless to say (except that this case obliges us to say it), the question answers itself. "The Constitution proscribes government discrimination on the basis of race, and state-provided education is no exception." [*Grutter* (Scalia, J., concurring in part and dissenting in part)]. It is precisely this understanding—the correct understanding—of the federal Equal Protection Clause that the people of the State of Michigan have adopted for their own fundamental law. By adopting it, they did not simultaneously *offend* it.

Even taking this Court's sorry line of race-based-admissions cases as a given, I find the question presented only slightly less strange: Does the Equal Protection Clause forbid a State from banning a practice that the Clause barely—and only provisionally—permits? Reacting to those race-based-admissions decisions, some States—whether deterred by the prospect of costly litigation; aware that *Grutter*'s bell may soon toll; or simply opposed in principle to the notion of "benign" racial discrimination—have gotten out of the racial-preferences business altogether. And with our express encouragement: "Universities in California, Florida, and Washington State, where racial preferences in admissions are prohibited by state law, are currently engaging in experimenting with a wide variety of alternative approaches. Universities in other States can *and should* draw on the most promising aspects of these race-neutral alternatives as they develop." (emphasis added). Respondents seem to think this admonition was merely in jest. The experiment, they maintain, is not only over; it never rightly began. Neither the people of the States nor their legislatures ever had the option of directing subordinate public-university officials to cease considering the race of applicants, since that would deny members of those minority groups the option of enacting a policy designed to further their interest, thus denying them the equal protection of the laws. Never mind that it is hotly disputed whether the practice of race-based admissions is *ever* in a racial minority's interest. And never mind that, were a public university to stake its defense of a race-based-admissions policy on the ground that it was *designed* to benefit primarily minorities (as opposed to all students, regardless of color, by enhancing diversity), *we would hold the policy unconstitutional.*

But the battleground for this case is not the constitutionality of race-based admissions—at least, not quite. Rather, it is the so-called political-process doctrine, derived from this Court's opinions in *Washington v. Seattle School Dist. No. 1, and Hunter v. Erickson.* I agree with those parts of the plurality opinion that repudiate this doctrine. But I do not agree with its reinterpretation of *Seattle* and *Hunter*, which makes them stand in part for the cloudy and doctrinally anomalous proposition that whenever state action poses "the serious risk . . . of causing specific injuries on account of race," it denies equal protection. I would instead reaffirm that the "ordinary principles of our law [and] of our democratic heritage" require "plaintiffs alleging equal protection violations" stemming from facially neutral acts to "prove intent and causation and not merely the existence of racial disparity." Freeman v. Pitts, 503 U.S. 467, 506 (Scalia, J., concurring) (citing Washington v. Davis, 426 U.S. 229 (1976)). I would further hold that a law directing state actors to provide equal protection is (to say the least) facially neutral, and cannot violate the Constitution. Section 26 of the Michigan Constitution (formerly Proposal 2) rightly stands. . . .

[*Hunter,*] *Seattle,* and, I think, the plurality endorse a version of the proposition that a facially neutral law may deny equal protection solely because it has a disparate racial impact. Few equal-protection theories have been so squarely and soundly rejected. . . .

Notwithstanding our dozens of cases confirming the exceptionless nature of the *Washington v. Davis* rule, the plurality opinion leaves ajar an effects-test escape hatch modeled after *Hunter* and *Seattle*, suggesting that state action denies equal protection when it "ha[s] the *serious risk,* if not purpose, of causing specific injuries on account of race," or is either "designed to be used, or . . . *likely to be used,* to encourage infliction of injury by reason of race." (emphasis added). Since these formulations enable a determination of an equal-protection violation where there is no discriminatory intent, they are inconsistent with the long *Washington v. Davis* line of cases. . . .

Thus, the question in this case, as in every case in which neutral state action is said to deny equal protection on account of race, is whether the action reflects a racially discriminatory purpose. *Seattle* stresses that "singling out the political processes affecting racial issues for uniquely disadvantageous treatment inevitably raises dangers of impermissible motivation." True enough, but that motivation must be proved. And respondents do not have a prayer of proving it here. The District Court noted that, under "conventional equal protection" doctrine, the suit was "doom[ed]." Though the Court of Appeals did not opine on this question, I would not leave it for them on remand. In my view, any law expressly requiring state actors to afford all persons equal protection of the laws (such as Initiative 350 in *Seattle*, though not the charter amendment in *Hunter*) does not — *cannot* — deny "to any person . . . equal protection of the laws," U.S. Const., Amdt. 14, § 1, regardless of whatever evidence of seemingly foul purposes plaintiffs may cook up in the trial court.

* * *

As Justice Harlan observed over a century ago, "[o]ur Constitution is color-blind, and neither knows nor tolerates classes among citizens." (dissenting opinion). The people of Michigan wish the same for their governing charter. It would be shameful for us to stand in their way.[11]

JUSTICE BREYER, concurring in the judgment. . . .

I agree with the plurality that the amendment is consistent with the Federal Equal Protection Clause. But I believe this for different reasons.

---

11. And doubly shameful to equate "the majority" behind § 26 with "the majority" responsible for Jim Crow. (Sotomayor, J., dissenting).

[We] do not address the amendment insofar as it forbids the use of race-conscious admissions programs designed to remedy past exclusionary racial discrimination or the direct effects of that discrimination. Application of the amendment in that context would present different questions which may demand different answers. . . .

I continue to believe that the Constitution permits, though it does not require, the use of the kind of race-conscious programs that are now barred by the Michigan Constitution. . . .

The Constitution allows local, state, and national communities to adopt narrowly tailored race-conscious programs designed to bring about greater inclusion and diversity. But the Constitution foresees the ballot box, not the courts, as the normal instrument for resolving differences and debates about the merits of these programs.

[Cases] such as *Hunter v. Erickson and Washington v. Seattle School Dist. No. 1* reflect an important principle, namely, that an individual's ability to participate meaningfully in the political process should be independent of his race. Although racial minorities, like other political minorities, will not always succeed at the polls, they must have the same opportunity as others to secure through the ballot box policies that reflect their preferences. In my view, however, neither *Hunter* nor *Seattle* applies here. And the parties do not here suggest that the amendment violates the Equal Protection Clause if not under the *Hunter-Seattle* doctrine.

[*Hunter* and *Seattle*] involved a restructuring of the political process that changed the political level at which policies were enacted. In *Hunter*, decisionmaking was moved from the elected city council to the local electorate at large. And in *Seattle*, decisionmaking by an elected school board was replaced with decisionmaking by the state legislature and electorate at large.

This case, in contrast, does not involve a reordering of the *political* process; it does not in fact involve the movement of decisionmaking from one political level to another. Rather, here, Michigan law delegated broad policymaking authority to elected university boards, but those boards delegated admissions-related decisionmaking authority to unelected university faculty members and administrators. Although the boards unquestionably retained the *power* to set policy regarding race-conscious admissions, in *fact* faculty members and administrators set the race-conscious admissions policies in question. [Thus], unelected faculty members and administrators, not voters or their elected representatives, adopted the race-conscious admissions programs affected by Michigan's constitutional amendment. The amendment took decisionmaking authority away from these unelected actors and placed it in the hands of the voters.

[The] doctrine set forth in *Hunter* and *Seattle* does not easily fit this case. In those cases minorities had participated in the political process and they had won. The majority's subsequent reordering of the political process repealed the

87

minority's successes and made it more difficult for the minority to succeed in the future. [But] one cannot as easily characterize the movement of the decision-making mechanism at issue here—from an administrative process to an electoral process—as diminishing the minority's ability to participate meaningfully in the *political* process. There is no prior electoral process in which the minority participated.

For another thing, to extend the holding of *Hunter* and *Seattle* to reach situations in which decisionmaking authority is moved from an administrative body to a political one would pose significant difficulties. The administrative process encompasses vast numbers of decisionmakers answering numerous policy questions in hosts of different fields. Administrative bodies modify programs in detail, and decisionmaking authority within the administrative process frequently moves around—due to amendments to statutes, new administrative rules, and evolving agency practice. It is thus particularly difficult in this context for judges to determine when a change in the locus of decisionmaking authority places a comparative structural burden on a racial minority. And to apply *Hunter* and *Seattle* to the administrative process would, by tending to hinder change, risk discouraging experimentation, interfering with efforts to see when and how race-conscious policies work.

Finally, the principle that underlies *Hunter* and *Seattle* runs up against a competing principle, discussed above. This competing principle favors decisionmaking [through] the democratic process. Just as this principle strongly supports the right of the people, or their elected representatives, to adopt race-conscious policies for reasons of inclusion, so must it give them the right to vote not to do so. . . .

Justice Sotomayor, with whom Justice Ginsburg joins, dissenting.

We are fortunate to live in a democratic society. But without checks, democratically approved legislation can oppress minority groups. For that reason, our Constitution places limits on what a majority of the people may do. This case implicates one such limit: the guarantee of equal protection of the laws. Although that guarantee is traditionally understood to prohibit intentional discrimination under existing laws, equal protection does not end there. Another fundamental strand of our equal protection jurisprudence focuses on process, securing to all citizens the right to participate meaningfully and equally in self-government. That right is the bedrock of our democracy, for it preserves all other rights.

Yet to know the history of our Nation is to understand its long and lamentable record of stymieing the right of racial minorities to participate in the political process. At first, the majority acted with an open, invidious purpose. Notwithstanding the command of the Fifteenth Amendment, certain States shut racial minorities out of the political process altogether by withholding the right to vote. This Court intervened to preserve that right. The majority tried again, replacing outright bans on voting with literacy tests, good character requirements, poll taxes, and gerrymandering. The Court was not fooled; it invalidated those measures, too. The majority persisted. This time, although it allowed the minority access to the political process, the majority changed the ground rules of the process so as to make it more difficult for the minority, and the minority alone, to obtain policies designed to foster racial integration. Although these political restructurings may not have been discriminatory in purpose, the Court reaffirmed the right of minority members of our society to participate meaningfully and equally in the political process.

This case involves this last chapter of discrimination: A majority of the Michigan electorate changed the basic rules of the political process in that State in a manner that uniquely disadvantaged racial minorities.[1] Prior to the enactment of the constitutional initiative at issue here, all of the admissions policies of Michigan's public colleges and universities — including race-sensitive admissions policies — were in the hands of each institution's governing board. The members of those boards are nominated by political parties and elected by the citizenry in statewide elections. After over a century of being shut out of Michigan's institutions of higher education, racial minorities in Michigan had succeeded in persuading the elected board representatives to adopt admissions policies that took into account the benefits of racial diversity. And this Court twice blessed such efforts — first in *Regents of Univ. of Cal. v. Bakke,* and again in *Grutter v. Bollinger,* a case that itself concerned a Michigan admissions policy.

In the wake of *Grutter,* some voters in Michigan set out to eliminate the use of race-sensitive admissions policies. Those voters were of course free to pursue this end in any number of ways. For example, they could have persuaded existing board members to change their minds through individual or grassroots lobbying efforts, or through general public awareness campaigns. Or they could have mobilized efforts to vote uncooperative board members out of office, replacing them with members who would share their desire to abolish race-sensitive admissions policies. When this Court holds that the Constitution permits a particular policy, nothing prevents a majority of a State's voters from choosing not to adopt that policy. Our system of government encourages — and indeed, depends on — that type of democratic action.

---

1. I of course do not mean to suggest that Michigan's voters acted with anything like the invidious intent, of those who historically stymied the rights of racial minorities. Contra, n. 11 (Scalia, J., concurring in judgment). But like earlier chapters of political restructuring, the Michigan amendment at issue in this case changed the rules of the political process to the disadvantage of minority members of our society.

But instead, the majority of Michigan voters changed the rules in the middle of the game, reconfiguring the existing political process in Michigan in a manner that burdened racial minorities. They did so in the 2006 election by amending the Michigan [Constitution].

As a result of § 26, there are now two very different processes through which a Michigan citizen is permitted to influence the admissions policies of the State's universities: one for persons interested in race-sensitive admissions policies and one for everyone else. A citizen who is a University of Michigan alumnus, for instance, can advocate for an admissions policy that considers an applicant's legacy status by meeting individually with members of the Board of Regents to convince them of her views, by joining with other legacy parents to lobby the Board, or by voting for and supporting Board candidates who share her position. The same options are available to a citizen who wants the Board to adopt admissions policies that consider athleticism, geography, area of study, and so on. The one and only policy a Michigan citizen may not seek through this long-established process is a race-sensitive admissions policy that considers race in an individualized manner when it is clear that race-neutral alternatives are not adequate to achieve diversity. For that policy alone, the citizens of Michigan must undertake the daunting task of amending the State Constitution.

Our precedents do not permit political restructurings that create one process for racial minorities and a separate, less burdensome process for everyone else. . . .

Today, disregarding *stare decisis,* a majority of the Court effectively discards those precedents. The plurality does so, it tells us, because the freedom actually secured by the Constitution is the freedom of self-government — because the majority of Michigan citizens "exercised their privilege to enact laws as a basic exercise of their democratic power." It would be "demeaning to the democratic process," the plurality concludes, to disturb that decision in any way. This logic embraces majority rule without an important constitutional limit.

The plurality's decision fundamentally misunderstands the nature of the injustice worked by § 26. This case is not, as the plurality imagines, about "who may resolve" the debate over the use of race in higher education admissions. I agree wholeheartedly that nothing vests the resolution of that debate exclusively in the courts or requires that we remove it from the reach of the electorate. Rather, this case is about *how* the debate over the use of race-sensitive admissions policies may be resolved — that is, it must be resolved in constitutionally permissible ways. While our Constitution does not guarantee minority groups victory in the political process, it does guarantee them meaningful and equal access to that process. It guarantees that the majority may not win by stacking the political process against minority groups permanently, forcing the minority alone to surmount unique obstacles in pursuit of its goals — here, educational diversity that cannot reasonably be accomplished through race-neutral measures. Today, by permitting a majority of the voters in Michigan to do what our Constitution forbids, the Court ends the debate over race-sensitive admissions policies in Michigan in a manner that contravenes constitutional protections long recognized in our precedents.

Like the plurality, I have faith that our citizenry will continue to learn from this Nation's regrettable history; that it will strive to move beyond those injustices towards a future of equality. And I, too, believe in the importance of public discourse on matters of public policy. But I part ways with the plurality when it suggests that judicial intervention in this case "impede[s]" rather than "advance[s]" the democratic process and the ultimate hope of equality. I firmly believe that our role as judges includes policing the process of self-government and stepping in when necessary to secure the constitutional guarantee of equal protection. Because I would do so here, I respectfully dissent. . . .

Section 26 has a "racial focus." *Seattle.* That is clear from its text, which prohibits Michigan's public colleges and universities from "grant[ing] preferential treatment to any individual or group on the basis of race." Like desegregation of public schools, race-sensitive admissions policies "inur[e] primarily to the benefit of the minority," [*Seattle,*] as they are designed to increase minorities' access to institutions of higher education.

Petitioner argues that race-sensitive admissions policies cannot "inur[e] primarily to the benefit of the minority," as the Court has upheld such policies only insofar as they further "the educational benefits that flow from a diverse student body," [*Grutter.*] But there is no conflict between this Court's pronouncement in *Grutter* and the common-sense reality that race-sensitive admissions policies benefit minorities. Rather, race-sensitive admissions policies further a compelling state interest in achieving a diverse student body precisely because they increase minority enrollment, which necessarily benefits minority groups. In other words, constitutionally permissible race-sensitive admissions policies can both serve the compelling interest of obtaining the educational benefits that flow from a diverse student body, and inure to the benefit of racial minorities. . . .

Section 26 restructures the political process in Michigan in a manner that places unique burdens on racial minorities. It establishes a distinct and more burdensome political process for the enactment of admissions plans that consider racial diversity. . . .

The plurality sees it differently. [According] to the plurality, the *Hunter* and *Seattle* Courts were not concerned with efforts to reconfigure the political process to the detriment of racial minorities; rather, those cases invalidated governmental actions merely because they reflected an invidious purpose to discriminate. This is not a tenable reading of those cases.

The plurality identifies "invidious discrimination" as the "necessary result" of the restructuring in *Hunter*. It is impossible to assess whether the housing amendment in *Hunter* was motivated by discriminatory purpose, for the opinion does not discuss the question of intent. What is obvious, however, is that the possibility of invidious discrimination played no role in the Court's reasoning. We ordinarily understand our precedents to mean what they actually say, not what we later think they could or should have said. The *Hunter* Court was clear about why it invalidated the Akron charter amendment: It was impermissible as a restructuring of the political process, not as an action motivated by discriminatory intent.

Similarly, the plurality disregards what *Seattle* actually says and instead opines that "the political restriction in question was designed to be used, or was likely to be used, to encourage infliction of injury by reason of race." Here, the plurality derives its conclusion not from *Seattle* itself, but from evidence unearthed more than a quarter-century later in *Parents Involved in Community Schools v. Seattle School Dist. No. 1.* . . .

Not once did the [*Seattle*] Court suggest the presence of *de jure* segregation in Seattle. Quite the opposite: The opinion explicitly suggested the desegregation plan was adopted to remedy *de facto* rather than *de jure* segregation. The Court, moreover, assumed that no "constitutional violation" through *de jure* segregation had occurred. And it unmistakably rested its decision on *Hunter*, holding Seattle's initiative invalid because it "use[d] the racial nature of an issue to define the governmental decisionmaking structure, and thus impose[d] substantial and unique burdens on racial minorities." . . .

[Justice] Scalia disagrees with "the proposition that a facially neutral law may deny equal protection solely because it has a disparate racial impact." (opinion concurring in judgment). He would acknowledge, however, that an act that draws racial distinctions or makes racial classifications triggers strict scrutiny regardless of whether discriminatory intent is shown. That should settle the matter: Section 26 draws a racial distinction. As the *Seattle* Court explained, "when the political process or the decisionmaking mechanism used to *address* racially conscious legislation—and only such legislation—is singled out for peculiar and disadvantageous treatment, the governmental action plainly rests on 'distinctions based on race.'" . . .

My colleagues are of the view that we should leave race out of the picture entirely and let the voters sort it out. We have seen this reasoning before. See *Parents Involved* ("The way to stop discrimination on the basis of race is to stop discriminating on the basis of race"). It is a sentiment out of touch with reality, one not required by our Constitution, and one that has properly been rejected as "not sufficient" to resolve cases of this nature. Id. (Kennedy, J., concurring in part and concurring in judgment). While "[t]he enduring hope is that race should not matter[,] the reality is that too often it does." Id. "[R]acial discrimination . . . [is] not ancient history." Bartlett v. Strickland, 556 U.S. 1, 25 (2009) (plurality opinion).

Race matters. Race matters in part because of the long history of racial minorities' being denied access to the political process. And although we have made great strides, "voting discrimination still exists; no one doubts that." [Shelby Cnty. v. Holder, 133 S. Ct. 2612, 2619 (2012)].

Race also matters because of persistent racial inequality in society—inequality that cannot be ignored and that has produced stark socioeconomic disparities. . . .

And race matters for reasons that really are only skin deep, that cannot be discussed any other way, and that cannot be wished away. Race matters to a young man's view of society when he spends his teenage years watching others tense up as he passes, no matter the neighborhood where he grew up. Race matters to a young woman's sense of self when she states her hometown, and then is pressed, "No, where are you *really* from?", regardless of how many generations her family has been in the country. Race matters to a young person addressed by a stranger in a foreign language, which he does not understand because only English was spoken at home. Race matters because of the slights, the snickers, the silent judgments that reinforce that most crippling of thoughts: "I do not belong here."

In my colleagues' view, examining the racial impact of legislation only perpetuates racial discrimination. This refusal to accept the stark reality that race matters is regrettable. The way to stop discrimination on the basis of race is to speak openly and candidly on the subject of race, and to apply the Constitution with eyes open to the unfortunate effects of centuries of racial discrimination. As members of the judiciary tasked with intervening to carry out the guarantee of equal protection, we ought not sit back and wish away, rather than confront, the racial inequality that exists in our society. It is this view that works harm, by perpetuating the facile notion that what makes race matter is acknowledging the simple truth that race *does* matter. . . .

V

Although the only constitutional rights at stake in this case are process-based rights, the substantive policy at issue is undeniably of some relevance to my colleagues. I will therefore speak in response. . . .

[Justice Sotomayor outlines the history of segregation in Michigan's colleges and universities, the growing diversity of the student population during the period when the state used "race-sensitive" admissions policies, and the decline in diversity in Michigan and elsewhere after abandonment of "race-sensitive" policies.]

These statistics may not influence the views of some of my colleagues, as they question the wisdom of adopting race-sensitive admissions policies and would prefer if our Nation's colleges and universities were to discard those policies altogether. See (Roberts, C.J., concurring) (suggesting that race-sensitive admissions policies might "do more harm than good"); (Scalia, J., concurring in judgment); *Grutter* (Thomas, J., concurring in part and dissenting in part); id. (Scalia, J., concurring in part and dissenting in part). That view is at odds with our recognition in *Grutter,* and more recently in *Fisher v. University of Texas at Austin,* that race-sensitive admissions policies are necessary to achieve a diverse student body when race-neutral alternatives have failed. More fundamentally, it ignores the importance of diversity in institutions of higher education and reveals how little my colleagues understand about the reality of race in America. . . .

To be clear, I do not mean to suggest that the virtues of adopting race-sensitive admissions policies should inform the legal question before the Court today regarding the constitutionality of § 26. But I cannot ignore the unfortunate outcome of today's decision: Short of amending the State Constitution, a Herculean task, racial minorities in Michigan are deprived of even an opportunity to convince Michigan's public colleges and universities to consider race in their admissions plans when other attempts to achieve racial diversity have proved unworkable, and those institutions are unnecessarily hobbled in their pursuit of a diverse student body. . . .

Today's decision eviscerates an important strand of our equal protection jurisprudence. For members of historically marginalized groups, which rely on the federal courts to protect their constitutional rights, the decision can hardly bolster hope for a vision of democracy that preserves for all the right to participate meaningfully and equally in self-government.

I respectfully dissent.

Page 628.   Before section 4 of the Note, add the following:

3a. *Affirmative action, democracy, and the standard of review.* Note the *Schuette* Court's view that "[it] is demeaning to the democratic process to presume that the voters are not capable of deciding an issue of this sensitivity on decent and rational grounds" and that "[freedom] embraces the right, indeed the duty, to engage in a rational, civic discourse in order to determine how best to form a consensus to shape the destiny of the Nation and its people." Is this position consistent with the Court's insistence on strictly scrutinizing decisions by the political branches to adopt affirmative action programs? Is the Court's insistence on strict scrutiny for these programs, even when their purpose is benign, consistent with its use of rational basis review when a facially neutral statute harms racial minorities for benign purposes?

Siegel, Foreword: Equality Divided, 127 Harv. L. Rev. 1, 50 (2013), argues that "[equal] protection doctrine governing affirmative action worries about the racial meaning and impact of state action even when the government has compelling purposes; but the [illegitimate purpose framework for *Feeney* (discussed at page 544 of the main volume)] makes the impact of state action on adversely affected communities immaterial unless the plaintiffs can show that the government acted, at least in part, for the purpose of inflicting the adverse impact on them." Siegel concludes that the Court has thereby turned its traditional *Carolene Products* approach inside out to create "a form of judicial review that cares more about protecting members of majority groups from actions of representative government that promote minority opportunities than it cares about protecting 'discrete and insular minorities' from actions of representative government that reflect 'prejudice.' " Does this approach place too little weight on the fact that affirmative action programs make facial distinctions whereas programs like the one upheld in *Feeney* are facially neutral? If so, why is this difference so significant?

Page 629.   At the end of the Note, add the following:

6. *Disproportionate impact.* In light of *Parents Involved*, are antidiscrimination laws that make actions illegal when they produce a disproportionate impact unconstitutional? In Texas Department of Housing and Community Affairs v. Inclusive Communities Project, Inc., 135 S. Ct. 2507 (2015), the Court, in an opinion by Justice Kennedy, interpreted the Fair Housing Act of 1968 to prohibit not just actions that had a discriminatory intent, but also actions that had a disproportionately adverse effect on minorities and are otherwise unjustified by a legitimate rationale. The Court noted however, that remedial orders issued under a disparate impact theory "must be consistent with the Constitution." In order to meet this requirement, courts "should concentrate on the elimination of the offending practice that 'arbitrar[ily] . . . operate[s] invidiously to discriminate on the basis of rac[e].' If additional measures are adopted, courts should strive to design them to eliminate racial disparities through race-neutral means. [Remedial] orders that impose racial targets or quotas might raise more difficult constitutional questions." Nonetheless, the Court observed, race "may be considered in certain circumstances and in a proper fashion. [When] setting their larger goals, local housing authorities may choose to foster diversity and combat racial isolation with race-neutral tools, and mere awareness of race in attempting to solve the problems facing inner cities does not doom that endeavor at the outset."

Justice Thomas, and Justice Alito, joined by Chief Justice Roberts and Justices Scalia and Thomas, wrote opinions dissenting on the statutory construction question.

E.   The Problem of Sexual Orientation

Page 689.   At the end of the block quote, add the following:

The Supreme Court affirmed *Windsor* in United States v. Windsor, 133 S. Ct. 2675 (2013). The opinions in the case are excerpted in Chapter VI F 3 of this

Supplement. Justice Kennedy, writing for the Court's majority, stated that "[t]he liberty protected by the Fifth Amendment's Due Process Clause contains within it the prohibition against denying to any person the equal protection of the laws. While the Fifth Amendment itself withdraws from Government the power to degrade or demean in the way this law does, the equal protection guarantee of the Fourteenth Amendment makes that Fifth Amendment right all the more specific and all the better understood and preserved." The majority opinion does not discuss the appropriate standard of review. Consider the following excerpt from Justice Alito's dissenting opinion:

> Our equal protection framework, upon which Windsor and the United States rely, is a judicial construct that provides a useful mechanism for analyzing a certain universe of equal protection cases. But that framework is ill suited for use in evaluating the constitutionality of laws based on the traditional understanding of marriage, which fundamentally turn on what marriage is. . . .
>
> In asking the Court to determine that § 3 of DOMA is subject to and violates heightened scrutiny, Windsor and the United States thus ask us to rule that the presence of two members of the opposite sex is as rationally related to marriage as white skin is to voting or a Y-chromosome is to the ability to administer an estate. That is a striking request and one that unelected judges should pause before granting. Acceptance of the argument would cast all those who cling to traditional beliefs about the nature of marriage in the role of bigots or superstitious fools.
>
> By asking the Court to strike down DOMA as not satisfying some form of heightened scrutiny, Windsor and the United States are really seeking to have the Court resolve a debate between two competing views of marriage.
>
> The first and older view, which I will call the "traditional" or "conjugal" view, sees marriage as an intrinsically opposite-sex institution. BLAG notes that virtually every culture, including many not influenced by the Abrahamic religions, has limited marriage to people of the opposite sex. And BLAG attempts to explain this phenomenon by arguing that the institution of marriage was created for the purpose of channeling heterosexual intercourse into a structure that supports child rearing. Others explain the basis for the institution in more philosophical terms. They argue that marriage is essentially the solemnizing of a comprehensive, exclusive, permanent union that is intrinsically ordered to producing new life, even if it does not always do so. While modern cultural changes have weakened the link between marriage and procreation in the popular mind, there is no doubt that, throughout human history and across many cultures, marriage has been viewed as an exclusively opposite-sex institution and as one inextricably linked to procreation and biological kinship.

The other, newer view is what I will call the "consent-based" vision of marriage, a vision that primarily defines marriage as the solemnization of mutual commitment—marked by strong emotional attachment and sexual attraction—between two persons. At least as it applies to heterosexual couples, this view of marriage now plays a very prominent role in the popular understanding of the institution. Indeed, our popular culture is infused with this understanding of marriage. Proponents of same-sex marriage argue that because gender differentiation is not relevant to this vision, the exclusion of same-sex couples from the institution of marriage is rank discrimination.

The Constitution does not codify either of these views of marriage (although I suspect it would have been hard at the time of the adoption of the Constitution or the Fifth Amendment to find Americans who did not take the traditional view for granted). The silence of the Constitution on this question should be enough to end the matter as far as the judiciary is concerned. Yet, Windsor and the United States implicitly ask us to endorse the consent-based view of marriage and to reject the traditional view, thereby arrogating to ourselves the power to decide a question that philosophers, historians, social scientists, and theologians are better qualified to explore. Because our constitutional order assigns the resolution of questions of this nature to the people, I would not presume to enshrine either vision of marriage in our constitutional jurisprudence. . . .

Page 696.   Before Section F, add the following:

In Obergefell v. Hodges, 135 S. Ct. 2584 (2015), the Court relied on both the due process clause and the equal protection clause to invalidate state laws that prohibited gay marriage. The Court's discussion of the equal protection clause did not specify the standard of review that it was utilizing. The case is excerpted at the supplement to Page 932 of the Main Volume.

F.   Other Candidates for Heightened Scrutiny

Page 719.   At the end of the Note, add the following:

Consider Pollvogt, Beyond Suspect Classifications, 16 U. Pa. J. Const. L. 739, 798 (2014): "[Suspect] classification analysis asks the wrong question and scrutinizes the wrong actor. [The] approach relies on a questionable assumption that the Court can properly identify social and political marginalization, and [contemporary] prejudices." Instead of asking questions about group marginalization, prejudice, and political power, Pollvogt suggests the following test for all classifications: "Where a law or other government action relies on a facial classification of persons the burden is on the government to prove an affirmative connection between the trait that defines the targeted group and the governmental and individual interests being regulated." Note that this test does not specify the necessary degree of fit between the classification and the trait or how heavy the government's burden should be. Does answering those questions lead back to suspect classification analysis?

VI
IMPLIED FUNDAMENTAL RIGHTS

A. *Introduction*

Page 725. Before subsection c of the Note, add the following:

In Fallon, The Meaning of Legal "Meaning" and Its Implications for Theories of Legal Interpretation, 82 U. Chi. L. Rev. 1235, 1239, 1241, 1255-1263 (2015), the author challenges the assumption that "constitutional provisions have uniquely correct meanings that exist as a matter of prelegal, linguistic fact," and claims that "[in] nonlegal as much as in legal conversation, there are frequently multiple candidates to furnish the meaning of prescriptive utterances." Among the competing candidates are semantic or literal meaning, contextual meaning, real conceptual meaning, intended meaning, reasonable meaning, and interpreted meaning.

To illustrate the various possibilities, Fallon imagines a wealthy owner of a large tract of land who voluntarily allows some members of the public to use the property and instructs her gatekeeper to enforce rules providing "No vehicles are allowed in the park" and "People of good character only." These words have a semantic or literal meaning, although there can be cases where they are vague or ambiguous, in which case new originalists would resort to construction. But the meaning can also derive from shared suppositions arising out of context. For example, Fallon argues that if the words were uttered in the Jim Crow South, the formulation "People of good character only" would be "widely understood, in context, to indicate that only Caucasians could enter."

Fallon claims, though, that an African American of good character who insists on his right to be admitted has not made a linguistic mistake, because the words may also have a "real conceptual meaning." Whatever most people understand in a given context, there might be a truth about whether the person is "of good character."

The gatekeeper might also think of himself as bound by the intended meaning. If the gatekeeper knows that the owner does not want bicycles in the park, he might interpret the word "vehicles" accordingly.

Next, Fallon imagines, someone inside the park is badly injured. The gatekeeper might allow an ambulance to enter on the ground that ordinary linguistic conventions ascribe a reasonable meaning to an utterance.

Finally, suppose that despite the "no vehicles" directive, the gatekeeper routinely admits an ice cream truck into the park without incurring an objection from the park owner. Should a new gatekeeper admit the ice cream truck? Fallon argues that "whatever 'No vehicles in the park' meant in the first instance, it is at least plausible and possibly correct to say that it has now acquired an interpreted meaning" different from its original meaning.

Which, if any of Fallon's variations of "meaning" are ruled out by new originalism? If Fallon is correct that "meaning" can have these different meanings, how should an interpreter of constitutional text choose between the various possibilities?

Compare Lawrence B. Solum, *The Fixation Thesis: The Role of Historical Fact in Original Meaning,* 91 Notre Dame L. Rev. 1, 21, 22, 25 (2015), in which the author defends the proposition that the communicative content of constitutional text is fixed at the time of its origination – a proposition that he calls the "fixation thesis."

Solum derives the thesis from observations about how language works in general:

> [If] you were reading a book of recipes written in the eighteenth century and [you] learned that "kale" was the eighteenth-century word for what we now call "radishes," you would be very unlikely to insist that the recipe actually referred to the acephala group of barassica oleracea, the green or purple leafed vegetable, which is quite unlike what we call a "radish." Of course, you might be inspired to try the recipe with some leaves from a plant in the acephala group of barassica oleracea, but that would be an experimental deviation from the recipe and *not* a case of following the recipe.

Solum is careful to explain that the fixation thesis is a "claim about meaning in the communicative sense: what is fixed is communicative content." It is not "a claim about the correct applications of the constitutional text to particular fact patterns or to general types of fact patterns – although the fixed communicative content may be given legal effect that determines or partially determines such applications." Is it possible to separate abstract communicative content from correct applications? For example, can one provide an abstract definition the word "arms" as used in the second amendment without thinking about possible applications of the abstract definition to particular cases?

Does the fixation thesis resolve Fallon's complaint about the ambiguous mean-ing of "meaning"?

Even if Solum is correct that the fixation thesis explains how language works in general, does it follow that constitutional interpretation should adhere to the thesis? Solum argues as follows:

> Constitutional communication is simply a form of [communication]. If the Fixation Thesis holds for communication generally [then] it would be somewhat mysterious if it did not hold for constitutional communication. Conventional semantic meanings and regularities of syntax and grammar, when combined with context, provide an account of how communication is possible. We can convey meaning because words and phrases are used in regular ways and can be combined using regular patters of syntax and gram-mar. We can deliver more content still by relying on our readers' knowledge of the communicative context. But once we understand these mechanisms, they imply fixation. Anyone who accepts the Generalized Fixation Thesis, but denies that the communicative content of the constitutional text is fixed owes us an explanation.

Might such an explanation rest on the different social purposes served by inter-pretation in different settings? Suppose, for example, that one's object is to gain the greatest possible aesthetic or intellectual satisfaction from reading novel. It is not obvious that one would want to treat its meaning as fixed at the time it was written. What social purpose is served by constitutional interpretation?

Page 726. Before subsection e of the Note, add the following:

For a detailed defense of common law constitutionalism, see Strauss, Fore-word: Does the Constitution Mean What It Says, 129 Harv. L. Rev. 1 (2015). The author argues that "[if] we read the text of the Constitution in a straightforward way, American constitutional law 'contradicts' the text of the Constitution more often than one might think. Adhering to the text would require us to relinquish many of the most important and well-established principles of constitutional law." He provides many examples, including the following:

- According to the text, the President and the federal courts could abridge the freedom of speech and prohibit the free exercise of religion, because the First Amendment, by its terms, applies only to "Congress."
- The text would permit States to disfranchise, for example, poor people or gay people, because the Equal Protection Clause of the Fourteenth Amend-ment does not protect the right to vote.

- The text would permit the federal government to engage in discrimination on the basis of race or sex, because the Equal Protection Clause applies only to the states.

From these and other examples, Strauss concludes that constitutional text functions in the same way that precedent does in a common law system.

> [There] are times when established principles are simply inconsistent with the text. Beyond that, constitutional "interpretation" usually has little to do, in practice, with the words of the text. There are times when the text is decisive, and it is never acceptable to announce that you are ignoring the text. But routinely the text, although not flatly inconsistent with the outcome of a case, has very little to do with the way the case is argued or decided. In most litigated cases, constitutional law resembles the common law much more closely than it resembles a text-based system.

How do judges decide cases within such a system? Strauss suggests that they mediate between interests in sovereignty, adaptation, and settlement. Sovereignty refers to "the interest in having some institution that can intervene and change things." Constitutional text can sometimes be important because it reflects this interest. However, sovereignty must be balanced against the need for adaptation when circumstances change and require gradual adjustments of legal norms. Finally, there is an interest in settlement in cases where it is more important to resolve an issue one way or the other than to resolve it optimally.

Is Strauss's description of our constitutional practice accurate? Consider again Fallon's discussion of the various meanings of "meaning." See this Supplement, *supra*, at material associated with Page 724 of the Main Text. Might some or all of Strauss' textual anomalies be resolved by resorting to a more capacious view of interpretation?

Assuming Strauss is right as a descriptive matter, does his description carry normative implications? Is there a "principled" way for judges to balance the three needs that he identifies? Notice that judge-made constitutional law, unlike standard common law, is not subject to easy correction by the political branches. Does common law constitutionalism give judges too much discretion?

D.   Substantive Due Process

Page 763.   Before section 7 of the Note, add the following:

6a. *Are the reports of Lochner's death premature?* Consider Colby & Smith, The Return of Lochner, 100 Corn. L. Rv. 527 (2015):

[The] orthodoxy in modern conservative legal thought is on the verge of changing. There are increasing signs that the movement is ready, once again, to embrace *Lochner*—although perhaps not in name—by recommitting to some form of robust judicial protection for economic rights . . .

[Although] there are likely many factors contributing to this change, it has been greatly facilitated by important modifications to the theory of [originalism]. . . .

[Originalism] has slowly changed from a theory of judging, concerned principally with judicial restraint [to] an interpretive methodology that seeks objective semantic textual meaning. [Unlike] its forerunner, this "new originalism" can readily accommodate claims that the Fourteenth Amendment (and perhaps other provisions of the Constitution as well) protects an unenumerated right to freedom of contract.

As you read the material that follows, consider the extent to which *Lochner*-like ideas lie behind aspects of free speech, due process, takings clause, and state action doctrine. Notice also how the Court's contemporary dormant commerce clause jurisprudence, discussed in Chapter IID of the Main Volume, arguably sometimes treat market allocations as constitutionally mandatory. Can these constitutional provisions be given meaning without reference to a presumptive baseline formed by market transactions?

E. Fundamental Interests and the Equal Protection Clause

Page 795. At the end of the Note, add the following:

Harris v. Arizona Ind. Redistricting Commn., 136 S. Ct. 1301 (2016) upheld a state redistricting scheme with a maximum population deviation of under 10 percent. Writing for a unanimous Court, Justice Breyer stated that

those attacking a state-approved plan must show that it is more probable than not that a deviation of less than 10% reflects the predominance of illegitimate reapportionment factors rather than the "legitimate considerations" to which we have referred in *Reynolds* and other cases. Given the inherent difficulty of measuring and comparing factors that may legitimately account for small deviations from strict mathematical equality, we believe that attacks on deviations under 10% will succeed only rarely, in unusual cases.

In *Harris*, itself, the Court found that the challengers failed to prove their claim because the deviations predominately reflected efforts to comply with the Voting Rights Act rather than to secure political advantage for one party.

7. *The Unit of Measurement.* The cases discussed above address the extent to which jurisdictions may depart from the ideal of equality. But how should equality be measured? Must districts be equal with respect to the number of inhabitants? The number of eligible or registered voters? The number of actual voters? How often (and with what degree of accuracy) must the measurement be taken?

Both Article I, §2, cl.2 and §2 of the Fourteenth Amendment provide that members of Congress shall be apportioned among the states "according to their respective numbers." However, the Constitution is silent about how members of Congress should be apportioned *within* states and about how state legislators should be apportioned.

In practice, all states now utilize a total population measure as determined by the decennial census, but surprisingly, for more than a half century after its decisions in *Reynolds* and *Wesberry,* the Court said virtually nothing about the legality of this practice. It finally addressed the question in Evenwel v. Abbott, 136 S. Ct. 1120 (2016). Districting for the state senate of Texas yielded a maximum total-population deviation of 8.04 percent, well within the Supreme Court's guidelines, but if equality was measured by the total number of eligible or registered voters, the maximum population deviation exceeded 40 percent. Appellants, residents of a district with a large number of voters, claimed that their votes were unconstitutionally diluted under *Reynolds'* one-person-one vote standard. A three-judge district court rejected their claim.

When the case reached the Supreme Court, appellants argued that the Constitution *required* the state to adopt a voter-based standard. The state responded that the constitution *permitted* this standard, but that it also permitted a total-population approach. In an *amicus* brief, the United States argued that the Constitution *prohibited* a voter based standard and required the total-population approach. In an opinion written by Justice Ginsburg, the Court rejected appellants' claim that the Constitution required a voter-based standard, but held that "we need not and do not resolve whether [States] may draw districts to equalize voter-eligible population."

The Court began its analysis by noting that the original framers chose to allocate seats among the states based upon total population. The framers of the fourteenth amendment considered, but rejected, a proposal to alter this allocation so as to reflect voter population. The Court acknowledged that neither of these decisions directly governed the case before it (which involved intrastate redistricting for the state legislature rather than interstate allocations for Congress), but it emphasized that the theory of representation underlying appellants' claim was inconsistent with the Article I and fourteenth amendment approach. "It cannot be that the Fourteenth Amendment calls for the apportionment of congressional districts based on total population, but simultaneously prohibits States from apportioning their own legislative districts on the same basis."

The Court recognized that it "has typically refused to analogize to features of the federal electoral system – here, the constitutional scheme governing congressional apportionment – when considering challenges to state and local election laws." For example, "in *Reynolds,* the Court rejected Alabama's argument that it had permissibly modeled its State Senate apportionment scheme – one Senator for each county – on the United States Senate." But *Reynolds*

> involved features of the federal electoral system that contravene the principles of both voter *and* representational equality in favor of interests that have no relevance outside the federal context. Senate seats were allocated to the States on an equal basis to respect state sovereignty and increase the odds that smaller States would ratify the Constitution. . . .
>
> By contrast [the] constitutional scheme for congressional apportionment rests in part on the same representational concerns that exist regarding state and local legislative districting. The Framers' answer to the apportionment question in the congressional context therefore undermines appellants' contention that districts must be based on voter population.

The Court also noted that its own past decisions had

> consistently looked to total population figures when evaluating whether districting maps violate the Equal protection Clause by deviating impermissibly from perfect population equality. [It] would hardly make sense for the Court to have mandated voter equality *sub silentio* and then used a total-population baseline to evaluate compliance with that rule.

Finally, the Court argued that "[adopting] voter-eligible apportionment as constitutional command would upset a well-functioning approach to districting that all 50 States and countless local jurisdictions have followed for decades, even centuries," and that "[as] the Framers of the Constitution and the Fourteenth Amendment comprehended, representatives serve all residents, not just those eligible or registered to vote."

In an opinion concurring in the judgment, Justice Thomas argued that there was no sound basis for the one person one vote rule in any form. "[The Constitution] leaves States significant leeway in apportioning their own districts to equalize total population, to equalize eligible voters, or to promote any other principle consistent with a republican form of government."

In another opinion concurring in the judgment, Justice Alito (joined in relevant part by Justice Thomas) agreed with the majority that "[both] practical considerations and precedent support the conclusion that the use of total population is consistent with the one-person, one-vote rule." Justice Alito also agreed with the majority that the Court had no need in this case to consider whether a state might use a measure other than total population. Justice Alito nonetheless expressed his disagreement with the majority's reliance on the Constitution's allocation of House seats among the states as a basis for its decision.

According to the Court, a state is permitted (and perhaps required) to assume that a representative serves residents of her district even if they are not permitted to vote. Is this assumption plausible? If it is correct, why can't a state assume that a representative serves residents of the entire state, including people who cannot vote in her district because they live somewhere else?

Page 803.   Before section c, add the following:

In Arizona State Legislature v. Arizona Independent Redistricting Comm., 135 S. Ct. 2652 (2015), the Court, in an opinion by Justice Ginsburg, upheld Arizona's decision to vest redistricting decisions in an independent redistricting commission. Petitioners argued that the commission violated Article I, § 4, cl. 1 of the Constitution which provides that "[the] Times, Places and Manner of holding Elections for Senators and Representatives, shall be prescribed in each state by the Legislature [thereof]." The Court rejected this argument, noting that "[the] history and purpose of the Clause weigh heavily against such a preclusion, as does the animating principle of our Constitution that the people themselves are the originating source of all powers of government." Chief Justice Roberts, joined by Justices Scalia, Thomas, and Alito; Justice Scalia, joined by Justice Thomas; and Justice Thomas, joined by Justice Scalia filed dissenting opinions.

F.   Modern Substantive Due Process: Privacy, Personhood, and Family

Page 900.   At the end of the last full paragraph on the page, add the following:

As respondents have noted, and the District Courts recognized, some recitations in the Act are factually incorrect. Whether or not accurate at the time, some of the important findings have been superseded. Two examples suffice. Congress determined no medical schools provide instruction on the prohibited procedure. The testimony in the District Courts, however, demonstrated intact D & E is taught at medical schools. Congress also found there existed a medical consensus that the prohibited procedure is never medically necessary. The evidence presented in the District Courts contradicts that conclusion. Uncritical deference to Congress's factual findings in these cases is inappropriate.

Page 909.   Before Section 3, add the following:

WHOLE WOMAN'S HEALTH v. HELLERSTEDT

136 S. Ct. 2292 (2016)

JUSTICE BREYER delivered the opinion of the Court.

[Texas House Bill 2 requires physicians performing abortions to "have active admitting privileges at a hospital that . . . is located not further than 30 miles from the location at which the abortion is performed" and to meet "the minimum standards . . . for ambulatory surgical centers." (ASC). These standards include detailed specifications concerning the nursing staff, building dimensions, and other building requirements. For example, the standards included a requirement for "a full surgical suite" with detailed specifications about the operating room and the recovery room, requirements for specific corridor widths and requirements for advanced heating, ventilation, and air conditioning systems.

[Petitioners, a group of abortion providers, filed suit in federal district court, claiming that House Bill 2 imposed an undue burden on the abortion right. After a four-day trial, the district court ruled in their favor and enjoined enforcement of the bill. Among other findings of fact, the district court determined that:

- the number of licensed abortion facilities in Texas dropped almost by half leading up to and in the wake of enforcement of the admitting-privileges requirement;
- if the surgical-center provision were allowed to take effect, the number of abortion facilities would be reduced to seven or eight for the entire state;
- all of these facilities would be in Houston, Austin, San Antonio, and the Dallas/Fort Worth area;
- these providers could not meet the demand of the entire state;
- if the requirements were allowed to go into effect, 2 million women of reproductive age would live more than 50 miles from an abortion provider, 1.3 million would live more than 100 miles from a provider, and 900,000 would live more than 150 miles from a provider, and 750,000 would live more than 200 miles from a provider;
- Abortion is much safer than many common medical procedures, such as colonscopies, vasectomies, and plastic surgery, that are not covered by the regulations;
- Risks are not appreciably lowered for patience undergoing abortions at ambulatory surgical centers.

[The court of appeals reversed the District Court and, with minor exceptions, found that the provisions were constitutional. It found that both the admitting privileges requirement and the surgical-center requirement were rationally related to the state interest in protecting the health and welfare of women seeking abortions and that the district court had erred by substituting its own judgment about these health effects for that of the legislature. Moreover, the court of appeals held, appellants had failed to show that the provisions imposed an undue burden on "a large fraction of women."

[The Supreme Court reversed the Court of Appeals and held that the Texas statute was facially unconstitutional.

[In an omitted section of the Court's opinion, it rejected appellee's argument that its claims were barred by res judicata. It then turned to the merits].

III

Undue Burden—Legal Standard

The Court of Appeals' articulation of the relevant standard is incorrect. The first part of the Court of Appeals' test may be read to imply that a district court should not consider the existence or nonexistence of medical benefits when considering whether a regulation of abortion constitutes an undue burden. The rule announced in *Casey*, however, requires that courts consider the burdens a law imposes on abortion access together with the benefits those laws confer. And the second part of the test is wrong to equate the judicial review applicable to the regulation of a constitutionally protected personal liberty with the less strict review applicable where, for example, economic legislation is at issue. . . .

The statement that legislatures, and not courts, must resolve questions of medical uncertainty is also inconsistent with this Court's case law. Instead, the Court, when determining the constitutionality of laws regulating abortion procedures, has placed considerable weight upon evidence and argument presented in judicial proceedings. . . .

Unlike in *Gonzales*, the relevant statute here does not set forth any legislative findings. Rather, one is left to infer that the legislature sought to further a constitutionally acceptable objective (namely, protecting women's health). For a district court to give significant weight to evidence in the judicial record in these circumstances is consistent with this Court's case law. . . .

IV

Undue Burden—Admitting-Privileges Requirement . . . .

The evidence upon which the [district] court based this conclusion included, among other things:

- A collection of at least five peer-reviewed studies on abortion complications in the first trimester, showing that the highest rate of major complications—including those complications requiring hospital admission—was less than one-quarter of 1%. . . .

- Expert testimony to the effect that complications rarely require hospital admission, much less immediate transfer to a hospital from an outpatient clinic. . . .

We add that, when directly asked at oral argument whether Texas knew of a single instance in which the new requirement would have helped even one woman obtain better treatment, Texas admitted that there was no evidence in the record of such a case. . . .

At the same time, the record evidence indicates that the admitting-privileges requirement places a "substantial obstacle in the path of a woman's choice." . . .

In our view, the record contains sufficient evidence that the admitting-privileges requirement led to the closure of half of Texas' clinics, or thereabouts. . . .

Those closures meant fewer doctors, longer waiting times, and increased crowding. Record evidence also supports the finding that after the admitting-privileges provision went into effect, the "number of women of reproductive age living in a county . . . more than 150 miles from a provider increased from approximately 86,000 to 400,000." . . .

[The] dissent suggests that one benefit of H. B. 2's requirements would be that they might "force unsafe facilities to shut down" 'To support that assertion, the dissent points to the Kermit Gosnell scandal. Gosnell, a physician in Pennsylvania, was convicted of first-degree murder and manslaughter. He "staffed his facility with unlicensed and indifferent workers, and then let them practice medicine unsupervised" and had "[d]irty facilities; unsanitary instruments; an absence of functioning monitoring and resuscitation equipment; the use of cheap, but dangerous, drugs; illegal procedures; and inadequate emergency access for when things inevitably went wrong." Gosnell's behavior was terribly wrong. But there is no reason to believe that an extra layer of regulation would have affected that behavior. Determined wrongdoers, already ignoring existing statutes and safety measures, are unlikely to be convinced to adopt safe practices by a new overlay of regulations. Regardless, Gosnell's deplorable crimes could escape detection only because his facility went uninspected for more than 15 years. Pre-existing Texas law already contained numerous detailed regulations covering abortion facilities, including a requirement that facilities be inspected at least annually. The record contains nothing to suggest that H. B. 2 would be more effective than pre-existing Texas law at deterring wrongdoers like Gosnell from criminal behavior.

V

Undue Burden—Surgical-Center Requirement. . . .

There is considerable evidence in the record supporting the District Court's findings indicating that the statutory provision requiring all abortion facilities to meet all surgical-center standards does not benefit patients and is not necessary. The District Court found that "risks are not appreciably lowered for patients who undergo abortions at ambulatory surgical centers as compared to nonsurgical-center facilities." The court added that women "will not obtain better care or experience more frequent positive outcomes at an ambulatory surgical center as compared to a previously licensed facility." And these findings are well supported.

The record makes clear that the surgical-center requirement provides no benefit when complications arise in the context of an abortion produced through medication. That is because, in such a case, complications would almost always arise only after the patient has left the facility. The record also contains evidence indicating that abortions taking place in an abortion facility are safe — indeed, safer than numerous procedures that take place outside hospitals and to which Texas does not apply its surgical-center requirements. [Nationwide], childbirth is 14 times more likely than abortion to result in death, but Texas law allows a midwife to oversee childbirth in the patient's own home. [Medical] treatment after an incomplete miscarriage often involves a procedure identical to that involved in a nonmedical abortion, but it often takes place outside a hospital or surgical center. And Texas partly or wholly grandfathers (or waives in whole or in part the surgical-center requirement for) about two-thirds of the facilities to which the surgical-center standards apply. But it neither grandfathers nor provides waivers for any of the facilities that perform abortions. . . .

At the same time, the record provides adequate evidentiary support for the District Court's conclusion that the surgical-center requirement places a substantial obstacle in the path of women seeking an abortion. The parties stipulated that the requirement would further reduce the number of abortion facilities available to seven or eight facilities, located in Houston, Austin, San Antonio, and Dallas/Fort Worth. In the District Court's view, the proposition that these "seven or eight providers could meet the demand of the entire State stretches credulity." We take this statement as a finding that these few facilities could not "meet" that "demand." . . .

More fundamentally, in the face of no threat to women's health, Texas seeks to force women to travel long distances to get abortions in crammed-to-capacity superfacilities. Patients seeking these services are less likely to get the kind of individualized attention, serious conversation, and emotional support that doctors at less taxed facilities may have offered. Healthcare facilities and medical professionals are not fungible commodities. Surgical centers attempting to accommodate sudden, vastly increased demand may find that quality of care declines. Another commonsense inference that the District Court made is that these effects would be harmful to, not supportive of, women's health. . . .

Finally, the District Court found that the costs that a currently licensed abortion facility would have to incur to meet the surgical-center requirements were considerable, ranging from $1 million per facility (for facilities with adequate space) to $3 million per facility (where additional land must be purchased). This evidence supports the conclusion that more surgical centers will not soon fill the gap when licensed facilities are forced to close. . . .

VI

We consider three additional arguments that Texas makes and deem none persuasive.

First, Texas argues that facial invalidation of both challenged provisions is precluded by H. B. 2's severability clause. . . .

Severability clauses, it is true, do express the enacting legislature's preference for a narrow judicial remedy. As a general matter, we attempt to honor that preference. But our cases have never required us to proceed application by conceivable application when confronted with a facially unconstitutional statutory provision. . . .

Texas [argues] that instead of finding the entire surgical-center provision unconstitutional, we should invalidate (as applied to abortion clinics) only those specific surgical-center regulations that unduly burden the provision of abortions, while leaving in place other surgical-center regulations [As] we have explained, Texas' attempt to broadly draft a requirement to sever "applications" does not require us to proceed in piecemeal fashion when we have found the statutory provisions at issue facially unconstitutional. . . .

Second, Texas claims that the provisions at issue here do not impose a substantial obstacle because the women affected by those laws are not a "large fraction" of Texan women "of reproductive age," which Texas reads *Casey* to have required. But *Casey* used the language "large fraction" to refer to "a large fraction of cases in which [the provision at issue] is *relevant*," a class narrower than "all women," "pregnant women," or even "the class of *women seeking abortions* identified by the State." (emphasis added). Here, as in *Casey*, the relevant denominator is "those [women] for whom [the provision] is an actual rather than an irrelevant restriction."

Third, Texas looks for support to Simopoulos v. Virginia, 462 U.S. 506 (1983), a case in which this Court upheld a surgical-center requirement as applied to second trimester abortions This case, however, unlike *Simopoulos,* involves restrictions applicable to all abortions, not simply to those that take place during the second trimester. Most abortions in Texas occur in the first trimester, not the second. More importantly, in *Casey* we discarded the trimester framework, and we now use "viability" as the relevant point at which a State may begin limiting women's access to abortion for reasons unrelated to maternal health. Because the second trimester includes time that is both previability and postviability, *Simopoulos* cannot provide clear guidance. . . .

JUSTICE GINSBURG, concurring. . . .

When a State severely limits access to safe and legal procedures, women in desperate circumstances may resort to unlicensed rogue practitioners, *faute de mieux*, at great risk to their health and safety. Targeted Regulation of Abortion

Providers laws like H. B. 2 that "do little or nothing for health, but rather strew impediments to abortion," cannot survive judicial inspection.

JUSTICE THOMAS, dissenting. . . .

I

[In this section of his opinion, Justice Thomas criticizes the Court for granting third-party standing to abortion providers whose own constitutional rights are not invaded by the statute.]

II. . . .

I remain fundamentally opposed to the Court's abortion jurisprudence. Even taking *Casey* as the baseline, however, the majority radically rewrites the undue-burden test in three ways. First, today's decision requires courts to "consider the burdens a law imposes on abortion access together with the benefits those laws confer." Second, today's opinion tells the courts that, when the law's justifications are medically uncertain, they need not defer to the legislature, and must instead assess medical justifications for abortion restrictions by scrutinizing the record themselves. Finally, even if a law imposes no "substantial obstacle" to women's access to abortions, the law now must have more than a "reasonabl[e] relat[ion] to . . . a legitimate state interest." (internal quotation marks omitted). These precepts are nowhere to be found in *Casey* or its successors, and transform the undue-burden test to something much more akin to strict scrutiny. . . .

III

The majority's furtive reconfiguration of the standard of scrutiny applicable to abortion restrictions also points to a deeper problem. The undue-burden standard is just one variant of the Court's tiers-of-scrutiny approach to constitutional adjudication. And the label the Court affixes to its level of scrutiny in assessing whether the government can restrict a given right—be it "rational basis," intermediate, strict, or something else—is increasingly a meaningless formalism. As the Court applies whatever standard it likes to any given case, nothing but empty words separates our constitutional decisions from judicial fiat. . . .

Though the tiers of scrutiny have become a ubiquitous feature of constitutional law, they are of recent vintage. . . .

The illegitimacy of using "made-up tests" to "displace longstanding national traditions as the primary determinant of what the Constitution means" has long been apparent. The Constitution does not prescribe tiers of scrutiny. The three basic tiers[are] no more scientific than their names suggest, and a further element

112

of randomness is added by the fact that it is largely up to us which test will be applied in each case.

But the problem now goes beyond that. If our recent cases illustrate anything, it is how easily the Court tinkers with levels of scrutiny to achieve its desired result. This Term, it is easier for a State to survive strict scrutiny despite discriminating on the basis of race in college admissions than it is for the same State to regulate how abortion doctors and clinics operate under the putatively less stringent undue-burden test. All the State apparently needs to show to survive strict scrutiny is a list of aspirational educational goals (such as the 'cultivat[ion of] a set of leaders with legitimacy in the eyes of the citizenry') and a 'reasoned, principled explanation' for why it is pursuing them—then this Court defers. *Fisher v. University of Tex. at Austin* [discussed in this Supplement in materials associated with page 598 of the main text]. Yet the same State gets no deference under the undue-burden test, despite producing evidence that abortion safety, one rationale for Texas' law, is medically debated. Likewise, it is now easier for the government to restrict judicial candidates' campaign speech than for the Government to define marriage — even though the former is subject to strict scrutiny and the latter was supposedly subject to some form of rational-basis review. Compare *Williams-Yulee v. Florida Bar*, 575 U. S. ___, ___-___ (2015) (slip op., at 8-9), with *United States v. Windsor*, 570 U. S. ___, ___ (2013) (slip op., at 20).

These more recent decisions reflect the Court's tendency to relax purportedly higher standards of review for less-preferred rights. . . .

The Court should abandon the pretense that anything other than policy preferences underlies its balancing of constitutional rights and interests in any given case.

IV

It is tempting to identify the Court's invention of a constitutional right to abortion in Roe v. Wade as the tipping point that transformed third-party standing doctrine and the tiers of scrutiny into an unworkable morass of special exceptions and arbitrary applications. But those roots run deeper, to the very notion that some constitutional rights demand preferential treatment. During the *Lochner* era, the Court considered the right to contract and other economic liberties to be fundamental requirements of due process of law. The Court in 1937 repudiated *Lochner*'s foundations. But the Court then created a new taxonomy of preferred rights.

In 1938, seven Justices heard a constitutional challenge to a federal ban on shipping adulterated milk in interstate commerce. Without economic substantive due process, the ban clearly invaded no constitutional right. See United States v. Carolene Products Co., 304 U.S. 144, 152-153 (1938). Within Justice Stone's opinion for the Court, however, was a footnote that just three other Justices joined—the famous *Carolene Products* Footnote 4. . . .

Though the footnote was pure dicta, the Court seized upon it to justify its special treatment of certain personal liberties like the First Amendment and the right against discrimination on the basis of race—but also rights not enumerated in the Constitution. As the Court identified which rights deserved special protection, it developed the tiers of scrutiny as part of its equal protection (and, later, due process) jurisprudence as a way to demand extra justifications for encroachments on these rights. And, having created a new category of fundamental rights, the Court loosened the reins to recognize even putative rights like abortion, which hardly implicate "discrete and insular minorities." . . .

Eighty years on, the Court has come full circle. The Court has simultaneously transformed judicially created rights like the right to abortion into preferred constitutional rights, while disfavoring many of the rights actually enumerated in the Constitution. But our Constitution renounces the notion that some constitutional rights are more equal than others. A plaintiff either possesses the constitutional right he is asserting, or not—and if not, the judiciary has no business creating ad hoc exceptions so that others can assert rights that seem especially important to vindicate. A law either infringes a constitutional right, or not; there is no room for the judiciary to invent tolerable degrees of encroachment. Unless the Court abides by one set of rules to adjudicate constitutional rights, it will continue reducing constitutional law to policy-driven value judgments until the last shreds of its legitimacy disappear.

* * *

Today's decision will prompt some to claim victory, just as it will stiffen opponents' will to object. But the entire Nation has lost something essential. The majority's embrace of a jurisprudence of rights-specific exceptions and balancing tests is "a regrettable concession of defeat—an acknowledgement that we have passed the point where 'law,' properly speaking, has any further application." Scalia, The Rule of Law as a Law of Rules, 56 U.Chi. L. Rev. 1175, 1189 (1989). I respectfully dissent.

JUSTICE ALITO, with whom [CHIEF JUSTICE ROBERTS] and JUSTICE THOMAS join, dissenting.

I.

[In this section, and in section II of his opinion, Justice Alito argues that res judicata bars petitioners' claim]

III. . . .

Under our cases, petitioners must show that the admitting privileges and ASC requirements impose an "undue burden" on women seeking abortions. And in order to obtain the sweeping relief they seek— facial invalidation of those provisions—they must show, at a minimum, that these provisions have an unconstitutional impact on at least a "large fraction" of Texas women of reproductive age. Such a situation could result if the clinics able to comply with the new requirements either lacked the requisite overall capacity or were located too far away to serve a "large fraction" of the women in question.

Petitioners did not make that showing. Instead of offering direct evidence, they relied on two crude inferences. First, they pointed to the number of abortion clinics that closed after the enactment of H. B. 2, and asked that it be inferred that all these closures resulted from the two challenged provisions. They made little effort to show why particular clinics closed. Second, they pointed to the number of abortions performed annually at ASCs before H. B. 2 took effect and, because this figure is well below the total number of abortions performed each year in the State, they asked that it be inferred that ASC-compliant clinics could not meet the demands of women in the State. See App. 237-238. Petitioners failed to provide any evidence of the actual capacity of the facilities that would be available to perform abortions in compliance with the new law . . .

A

I do not dispute the fact that H. B. 2 caused the closure of some clinics. Indeed, it seems clear that H. B. 2 was intended to force unsafe facilities to shut down. The law was one of many enacted by States in the wake of the Kermit Gosnell scandal, in which a physician who ran an abortion clinic in Philadelphia was convicted for the first-degree murder of three infants who were born alive and for the manslaughter of a patient. Gosnell had not been actively supervised by state or local authorities or by his peers, and the Philadelphia grand jury that investigated the case recommended that the Commonwealth adopt a law requiring abortion clinics to comply with the same regulations as ASCs. If Pennsylvania had had such a requirement in force, the Gosnell facility may have been shut down before his crimes. And if there were any similarly unsafe facilities in Texas, H. B. 2 was clearly intended to put them out of business.

While there can be no doubt that H. B. 2 caused some clinics to cease operation, the absence of proof regarding the reasons for particular closures is a problem because some clinics have or may have closed for at least four reasons other than the two H. B. 2 requirements at issue here. These are:

> 1. *H. B. 2's restriction on medication abortion.* In [an earlier] case, petitioners challenged the provision of H. B. 2 that regulates medication abortion, but that part of the statute was upheld by the Fifth Circuit and not relitigated in this case. The record in this case indicates that in the first six months after this restriction took effect, the number of medication abortions dropped by 6,957 (compared to the same period the previous year).

115

2. *Withdrawal of Texas family planning funds.* In 2011, Texas passed a law preventing family planning grants to providers that perform abortions and their affiliates. In the first case, petitioners' expert admitted that some clinics closed 'as a result of the defunding,' and as discussed below, this withdrawal appears specifically to have caused multiple clinic closures in West Texas.

3. *The nationwide decline in abortion demand.* Petitioners' expert testimony relies on a study from the Guttmacher Institute which concludes that "[t]he national abortion rate has resumed its decline, and *no evidence was found that the overall drop in abortion incidence was related to the decrease in providers or to restrictions implemented between 2008 and 2011.*" . . . .

4. *Physician retirement (or other localized factors).* Like everyone else, most physicians eventually retire, and the retirement of a physician who performs abortions can cause the closing of a clinic or a reduction in the number of abortions that a clinic can perform. When this happens, the closure of the clinic or the reduction in capacity cannot be attributed to H. B. 2 unless it is shown that the retirement was caused by the admitting privileges or surgical center requirements as opposed to age or some other factor. . . .

B

Even if the District Court had properly filtered out immaterial closures, its analysis would have been incomplete for a second reason. Petitioners offered scant evidence on the capacity of the clinics that are able to comply with the admitting privileges and ASC requirements, or on those clinics' geographic distribution. Reviewing the evidence in the record, it is far from clear that there has been a material impact on access to abortion. . . .

Faced with increased demand, ASCs could potentially increase the number of abortions performed without prohibitively expensive changes. Among other things, they might hire more physicians who perform abortions, utilize their facilities more intensively or efficiently, or shift the mix of services provided. Second, what matters for present purposes is not the capacity of just those ASCs that performed abortions prior to the enactment of H. B. 2 but the capacity of those that would be available to perform abortions after the statute took effect. And since the enactment of H. B. 2, the number of ASCs performing abortions has increased by 50%—from six in 2012 to nine today. . . .

So much for capacity. The other potential obstacle to abortion access is the distribution of facilities throughout the State. This might occur if the two challenged H. B. 2 requirements, by causing the closure of clinics in some rural areas, led to a situation in which a "large fraction" of women of reproductive age live too far away from any open clinic. Based on the Court's holding in [Casey] it appears that the need to travel up to 150 miles is not an undue burden, and the evidence in this case shows that if the only clinics in the State were those that would have remained open if the judgment of the Fifth Circuit had not been enjoined, roughly 95% of the women of reproductive age in the State would live within 150 miles of an open facility (or lived outside that range before H. B. 2). Because the record does not show why particular facilities closed, the real figure may be even higher than 95%.

We should decline to hold that these statistics justify the facial invalidation of the H. B. 2 requirements. The possibility that the admitting privileges requirement *might* have caused a closure in Lubbock is no reason to issue a facial injunction exempting Houston clinics from that requirement. I do not dismiss the situation of those women who would no longer live within 150 miles of a clinic as a result of H. B. 2. But under current doctrine such localized problems can be addressed by narrow as-applied challenges.

IV

Even if the Court were right to hold that res judicata does not bar this suit and that H. B. 2 imposes an undue burden on abortion access—it is, in fact, wrong on both counts—it is still wrong to conclude that the admitting privileges and surgical center provisions must be enjoined in their entirety. H. B. 2 has an extraordinarily broad severability clause that must be considered before enjoining any portion or application of the law. Both challenged provisions should survive in substantial part if the Court faithfully applies that clause. Regrettably, it enjoins both in full, heedless of the (controlling) intent of the state legislature. . . .

B

Applying severability to the surgical center requirement calls for the identification of the particular provisions of the ASC regulations that result in the imposition of an undue burden. These regulations are lengthy and detailed, and while compliance with some might be expensive, compliance with many others would not. And many serve important health and safety purposes. Thus, the surgical center requirements cannot be judged as a package. . . .

Under the Supremacy Clause, federal courts may strike down state laws that violate the Constitution or conflict with federal statutes, Art. VI, cl. 2, but in exercising this power, federal courts must take great care. The power to invalidate a state law implicates sensitive federal-state relations. Federal courts have no authority to carpet-bomb state laws, knocking out provisions that are perfectly consistent with federal law, just because it would be too much bother to separate them from unconstitutional provisions. . . .

By forgoing severability, the Court strikes down numerous provisions that could not plausibly impose an undue burden. For example, surgical center patients must "be treated with respect, consideration, and dignity." That's now enjoined. [Justice Alito provides several other examples of uncontroversial provisions]. . . .

At a minimum, both of the requirements challenged here should be held constitutional as applied to clinics in any Texas city that will have a surgical center providing abortions (*i.e.*, those areas in which there cannot possibly have been an undue burden on abortion access). Moreover, as even the District Court found, the surgical center requirement is clearly constitutional as to new abortion facilities and facilities already licensed as surgical centers. And we should uphold every application of every surgical center regulation that does not pose an undue burden—at the very least, all of the regulations as to which petitioners have never made a specific complaint supported by specific evidence. . . .

Page 937.   At the end of the Note, add the following:

UNITED STATES v. WINDSOR

133 S. Ct. 2675 (2013)

Justice Kennedy delivered the opinion of the Court.

I

[Section 3 of the Defense of Marriage Act, 1 U.S.C. § 7 (DOMA) provides:

> In determining the meaning of any Act of Congress, or of any ruling, regulation, or interpretation of the various administrative bureaus and agencies of the United States, the word "marriage" means only a legal union between one man and one woman as husband and wife, and the word "spouse" refers only to a person of the opposite sex who is a husband or a wife.

This provision controls over 1,000 federal laws whose coverage turns on marital status.

Respondent Edith Windsor married Thea Spyer in Canada in 2007. The couple lived in New York, which recognized their marriage, until Spyer died in 2009. Spyer left her estate to Windsor but, because DOMA denied federal recognition to same-sex spouses, Windsor did not qualify for the marital exemption from the federal estate tax. Windsor was therefore compelled to pay $363,053, which she would not have owed if she had been married to a man.]

the opinion, the Court holds that the case is properly before it. scussed in Chapter 1 F 2 of this Supplement.]

III

[It] seems fair to conclude that, until recent years, many citizens had not even considered the possibility that two persons of the same sex might aspire to occupy the same status and dignity as that of a man and woman in lawful marriage. For marriage between a man and a woman no doubt had been thought of by most people as essential to the very definition of that term and to its role and function throughout the history of civilization. That belief, for many who long have held it, became even more urgent, more cherished when challenged. For others, however, came the beginnings of a new perspective, a new insight. Accordingly some States concluded that same-sex marriage ought to be given recognition and validity in the law for those same-sex couples who wish to define themselves by their commitment to each other. The limitation of lawful marriage to heterosexual couples, which for centuries had been deemed both necessary and fundamental, came to be seen in New York and certain other States as an unjust exclusion. . . .

Against this background of lawful same-sex marriage in some States, the design, purpose, and effect of DOMA should be considered as the beginning point in deciding whether it is valid under the Constitution. By history and tradition the definition and regulation of marriage [has] been treated as being within the authority and realm of the separate States. Yet it is further established that Congress, in enacting discrete statutes, can make determinations that bear on marital rights and privileges. . . .

Though these discrete examples establish the constitutionality of limited federal laws that regulate the meaning of marriage in order to further federal policy, DOMA has a far greater reach; for it enacts a directive applicable to over 1,000 federal statutes and the whole realm of federal regulations. And its operation is directed to a class of persons that the laws of New York, and of 11 other States, have sought to protect. . . .

In order to assess the validity of that intervention it is necessary to discuss the extent of the state power and authority over marriage as a matter of history and tradition. State laws defining and regulating marriage, of course, must respect the constitutional rights of persons, see, *e.g.,* [*Loving v. Virginia*]; but, subject to those guarantees, "regulation of domestic relations" is "an area that has long been regarded as a virtually exclusive province of the States." . . .

Against this background DOMA rejects the long-established precept that the incidents, benefits, and obligations of marriage are uniform for all married couples within each State, though they may vary, subject to constitutional guarantees, from one State to the next. Despite these considerations, it is unnecessary to decide whether this federal intrusion on state power is a violation of the Constitution because it disrupts the federal balance. The State's power in defining the marital relation is of central relevance in this case quite apart from principles of federalism. Here the State's decision to give this class of persons the right to marry conferred upon them a dignity and status of immense import. When the State used its historic and essential authority to define the marital relation in this way, its role and its power in making the decision enhanced the recognition, dignity, and protection of the class in their own community. DOMA, because of its reach and extent, departs from this history and tradition of reliance on state law to define marriage. " '[D]iscriminations of an unusual character especially suggest careful consideration to determine whether they are obnoxious to the constitutional provision.' " [*Romer v. Evans.*]

The Federal Government uses this state-defined class for the opposite purpose — to impose restrictions and disabilities. That result requires this Court now to address whether the resulting injury and indignity is a deprivation of an essential part of the liberty protected by the Fifth Amendment. What the State of New York treats as alike the federal law deems unlike by a law designed to injure the same class the State seeks to protect. . . .

The States' interest in defining and regulating the marital relation, subject to constitutional guarantees, stems from the understanding that marriage is more than a routine classification for purposes of certain statutory benefits. Private, consensual sexual intimacy between two adult persons of the same sex may not be punished by the State, and it can form "but one element in a personal bond that is more enduring." [*Lawrence v. Texas.*] By its recognition of the validity of same-sex marriages performed in other jurisdictions and then by authorizing same-sex unions and same-sex marriages, New York sought to give further protection and dignity to that bond. For same-sex couples who wished to be married, the State acted to give their lawful conduct a lawful status. This status is a far-reaching legal acknowledgment of the intimate relationship between two people, a relationship deemed by the State worthy of dignity in the community equal with all other marriages. It reflects both the community's considered perspective on the historical roots of the institution of marriage and its evolving understanding of the meaning of equality.

IV

DOMA seeks to injure the very class New York seeks to protect. By doing so it violates basic due process and equal protection principles applicable to the Federal Government. See U.S. Const., Amdt. 5; Bolling v. Sharpe, 347 U.S. 497 (1954). The Constitution's guarantee of equality "must at the very least mean that a bare congressional desire to harm a politically unpopular group cannot" justify disparate treatment of that group. [*Department of Agriculture v. Marino.*] In determining whether a law is motived by an improper animus or purpose, " '[d]iscriminations of an unusual character' " especially require careful consideration. DOMA cannot survive under these principles. The responsibility of the States for the regulation of domestic relations is an important indicator of the substantial societal impact the State's classifications have in the daily lives and customs of its people. DOMA's unusual deviation from the usual tradition of recognizing and accepting state definitions of marriage here operates to deprive same-sex couples of the benefits and responsibilities that come with the federal recognition of their marriages. This is strong evidence of a law having the purpose and effect of disapproval of that class. The avowed purpose and practical effect of the law here in question are to impose a disadvantage, a separate status, and so a stigma upon all who enter into same-sex marriages made lawful by the unquestioned authority of the States.

The history of DOMA's enactment and its own text demonstrate that interference with the equal dignity of same-sex marriages, a dignity conferred by the States in the exercise of their sovereign power, was more than an incidental effect of the federal statute. It was its essence. The House Report announced its conclusion that "it is both appropriate and necessary for Congress to do what it can to defend the institution of traditional heterosexual marriage. . . . H.R. 3396 is appropriately entitled the 'Defense of Marriage Act.' The effort to redefine 'marriage' to extend to homosexual couples is a truly radical proposal that would fundamentally alter the institution of marriage." The House concluded that DOMA expresses "both moral disapproval of homosexuality, and a moral conviction that heterosexuality better comports with traditional (especially Judeo-Christian) morality." The stated purpose of the law was to promote an "interest in protecting the traditional moral teachings reflected in heterosexual-only marriage laws." Were there any doubt of this far-reaching purpose, the title of the Act confirms it: The Defense of Marriage. . . .

The Act's demonstrated purpose is to ensure that if any State decides to recognize same-sex marriages, those unions will be treated as second-class marriages for purposes of federal law. This raises a most serious question under the Constitution's Fifth Amendment.

DOMA's operation in practice confirms this purpose. When New York adopted a law to permit same-sex marriage, it sought to eliminate inequality; but DOMA frustrates that objective through a system-wide enactment with no identified connection to any particular area of federal law. DOMA writes inequality into the entire United States Code. The particular case at hand concerns the estate tax, but DOMA is more than a simple determination of what should or should not be allowed as an estate tax refund. Among the over 1,000 statutes and numerous federal regulations that DOMA controls are laws pertaining to Social Security, housing, taxes, criminal sanctions, copyright, and veterans' benefits.

DOMA's principal effect is to identify a subset of state-sanctioned marriages and make them unequal. The principal purpose is to impose inequality, not for other reasons like governmental efficiency. Responsibilities, as well as rights, enhance the dignity and integrity of the person. And DOMA contrives to deprive some couples married under the laws of their State, but not other couples, of both rights and responsibilities. By creating two contradictory marriage regimes within the same State, DOMA forces same-sex couples to live as married for the purpose of state law but unmarried for the purpose of federal law, thus diminishing the stability and predictability of basic personal relations the State has found it proper to acknowledge and protect. By this dynamic DOMA undermines both the public and private significance of state-sanctioned same-sex marriages; for it tells those couples, and all the world, that their otherwise valid marriages are unworthy of federal recognition. This places same-sex couples in an unstable position of being in a second-tier marriage. The differentiation demeans the couple, whose moral and sexual choices the Constitution protects, see Lawrence v. Texas, and whose relationship the State has sought to dignify. And it humiliates tens of thousands of children now being raised by same-sex couples. The law in question makes it even more difficult for the children to understand the integrity and closeness of their own family and its concord with other families in their community and in their daily lives.

Under DOMA, same-sex married couples have their lives burdened, by reason of government decree, in visible and public ways. By its great reach, DOMA touches many aspects of married and family life, from the mundane to the profound. It prevents same-sex married couples from obtaining government healthcare benefits they would otherwise receive. It deprives them of the Bankruptcy Code's special protections for domestic-support obligations. It forces them to follow a complicated procedure to file their state and federal taxes jointly.

For certain married couples, DOMA's unequal effects are even more serious. The federal penal code makes it a crime to "assaul[t], kidna[p], or murde[r] . . . a member of the immediate family" of "a United States official, a United States judge, [or] a Federal law enforcement officer," with the intent to influence or retaliate against that official. Although a "spouse" qualifies as a member of the officer's "immediate family," DOMA makes this protection inapplicable to same-sex spouses.

DOMA also brings financial harm to children of same-sex couples. It raises the cost of health care for families by taxing health benefits provided by employers to their workers' same-sex spouses. And it denies or reduces benefits allowed to families upon the loss of a spouse and parent, benefits that are an integral part of family security. DOMA divests married same-sex couples of the duties and responsibilities that are an essential part of married life and that they in most cases would be honored to accept were DOMA not in force. For instance, because it is expected that spouses will support each other as they pursue educational opportunities, federal law takes into consideration a spouse's income in calculating a student's federal financial aid eligibility. Same-sex married couples are exempt from this requirement. The same is true with respect to federal ethics rules. Federal executive and agency officials are prohibited from "participat[ing] personally and substantially" in matters as to which they or their spouses have a financial interest. [Under] DOMA, however, these Government-integrity rules do not apply to same-sex spouses. . . .

The liberty protected by the Fifth Amendment's Due Process Clause contains within it the prohibition against denying to any person the equal protection of the laws. While the Fifth Amendment itself withdraws from Government the power to degrade or demean in the way this law does, the equal protection guarantee of the Fourteenth Amendment makes that Fifth Amendment right all the more specific and all the better understood and preserved.

The class to which DOMA directs its restrictions and restraints are those persons who are joined in same-sex marriages made lawful by the State. DOMA singles out a class of persons deemed by a State entitled to recognition and protection to enhance their own liberty. It imposes a disability on the class by refusing to acknowledge a status the State finds to be dignified and proper. DOMA instructs all federal officials, and indeed all persons with whom same-sex couples interact, including their own children, that their marriage is less worthy than the marriages of others. The federal statute is invalid, for no legitimate purpose overcomes the purpose and effect to disparage and to injure those whom the State, by its marriage laws, sought to protect in personhood and dignity. By seeking to displace this protection and treating those persons as living in marriages less respected than others, the federal statute is in violation of the Fifth Amendment. This opinion and its holding are confined to those lawful marriages.

The judgment of the Court of Appeals for the Second Circuit is affirmed.

It is so ordered.

CHIEF JUSTICE ROBERTS, dissenting.

[While] I disagree with the result to which the majority's analysis leads it in this case, I think it more important to point out that its analysis leads no further. The Court does not have before it, and the logic of its opinion does not decide, the distinct question whether the States, in the exercise of their "historic and essential authority to define the marital relation," may continue to utilize the traditional definition of marriage.

The majority goes out of its way to make this explicit in the penultimate sentence of its opinion. It states that "[t]his opinion and its holding are confined to those lawful marriages"—referring to same-sex marriages that a State has already recognized as a result of the local "community's considered perspective on the historical roots of the institution of marriage and its evolving understanding of the meaning of equality." Justice Scalia believes this is a " 'bald, unreasoned disclaime[r].' " In my view, though, the disclaimer is a logical and necessary consequence of the argument the majority has chosen to adopt. The dominant theme of the majority opinion is that the Federal Government's intrusion into an area "central to state domestic relations law applicable to its residents and citizens" is sufficiently "unusual" to set off alarm bells. I think the majority goes off course, as I have said, but it is undeniable that its judgment is based on federalism. . . .

JUSTICE SCALIA, with whom JUSTICE THOMAS joins, and with whom [CHIEF JUS-TICE ROBERTS] joins as to Part I, dissenting.

I

[In this portion of his dissent, Justice Scalia argues that the Court lacks jurisdiction over the case. This aspect of the dissent is discussed in Chapter 1 F 2 of this Supplement.]

II . . .

B

As I have observed before, the Constitution does not forbid the government to enforce traditional moral and sexual norms. See Lawrence v. Texas (Scalia, J., dissenting). I will not swell the U.S. Reports with restatements of that point. It is enough to say that the Constitution neither requires nor forbids our society to approve of same-sex marriage, much as it neither requires nor forbids us to approve of no-fault divorce, polygamy, or the consumption of alcohol.

However, even setting aside traditional moral disapproval of same-sex marriage (or indeed same-sex sex), there are many perfectly valid—indeed, downright boring—justifying rationales for this legislation. Their existence ought to be the end of this case. For they give the lie to the Court's conclusion that only those with hateful hearts could have voted "aye" on this Act. And more importantly, they serve to make the contents of the legislators' hearts quite irrelevant: "It is a familiar principle of constitutional law that this Court will not strike down an otherwise constitutional statute on the basis of an alleged illicit legislative motive." [United States v. O'Brien, 391 U.S. 524 (1974)]. Or at least it *was* a familiar principle. By holding to the contrary, the majority has declared open season on any law that (in the opinion of the law's opponents and any panel of like-minded federal judges) can be characterized as mean-spirited.

The majority concludes that the only motive for this Act was the "bare . . . desire to harm a politically unpopular group." Bear in mind that the object of this condemnation is not the legislature of some once-Confederate Southern state (familiar objects of the Court's scorn), but our respected coordinate branches, the Congress and Presidency of the United States. Laying such a charge against them should require the most extraordinary evidence, and I would have thought that every attempt would be made to indulge a more anodyne explanation for the statute. . . .

To choose just one of these defenders' arguments, DOMA avoids difficult choice-of-law issues that will now arise absent a uniform federal definition of marriage. . . .

[The] majority says that the supporters of this Act acted with *malice*—with *the "purpose"* "to disparage and to injure" same-sex couples. It says that the motivation for DOMA was to "demean," to "impose inequality," to "impose . . . a stigma," to deny people "equal dignity," to brand gay people as "unworthy and to "*humiliat[e]*" their children (emphasis added).

I am sure these accusations are quite untrue. To be sure (as the majority points out), the legislation is called the Defense of Marriage Act. But to defend traditional marriage is not to condemn, demean, or humiliate those who would prefer other arrangements, any more than to defend the Constitution of the United States is to condemn, demean, or humiliate other constitutions. To hurl such accusations so casually demeans *this institution.* In the majority's judgment, any resistance to its holding is beyond the pale of reasoned disagreement. To question its high-handed invalidation of a presumptively valid statute is to act (the majority is sure) with *the purpose* to "disparage," "injure," "degrade," "demean," and "humiliate" our fellow human beings, our fellow citizens, who are homosexual. All that, simply for supporting an Act that did no more than codify an aspect of marriage that had been unquestioned in our society for most of its existence—indeed, had been unquestioned in virtually all societies for virtually all of human history. It is one thing for a society to elect change; it is another for a court of law to impose change by adjudging those who oppose it *hostes humani generis,* enemies of the human race.

* * *

The penultimate sentence of the majority's opinion is a naked declaration that "[t]his opinion and its holding are confined" to those couples "joined in same-sex marriages made lawful by the State." I have heard such "bald, unreasoned disclaimer[s]" before. [*Lawrence.*] When the Court declared a constitutional right to homosexual sodomy, we were assured that the case had nothing, nothing at all to do with "whether the government must give formal recognition to any relationship that homosexual persons seek to enter." Now we are told that DOMA is invalid because it "demeans the couple, whose moral and sexual choices the Constitution protects,"—with an accompanying citation of *Lawrence.* It takes real cheek for today's majority to assure us, as it is going out the door, that a constitutional requirement to give formal recognition to same-sex marriage is not at issue here—when what has preceded that assurance is a lecture on how superior the majority's moral judgment in favor of same-sex marriage is to the Congress's hateful moral judgment against it. I promise you this: The only thing that will "confine" the Court's holding is its sense of what it can get away with.

I do not mean to suggest disagreement with The Chief Justice's view, that lower federal courts and state courts can distinguish today's case when the issue before them is state denial of marital status to same-sex couples—or even that this Court could *theoretically* do so. Lord, an opinion with such scatter-shot rationales as this one (federalism noises among them) can be distinguished in many ways. And

125

deserves to be. State and lower federal courts should take the Court at its word and distinguish away.

In my opinion, however, the view that *this* Court will take of state prohibition of same-sex marriage is indicated beyond mistaking by today's opinion. As I have said, the real rationale of today's opinion, whatever disappearing trail of its legalistic argle-bargle one chooses to follow, is that DOMA is motivated by "'bare . . . desire to harm'" couples in same-sex marriages. How easy it is, indeed how inevitable, to reach the same conclusion with regard to state laws denying same-sex couples marital status. Consider how easy (inevitable) it is to make the following substitutions in a passage from today's opinion:

> ~~DOMA's~~ *This state law's* principal effect is to identify a subset of ~~state-sanctioned marriages~~ *constitutionally protected sexual relationships*, see *Lawrence,* and make them unequal. The principal purpose is to impose inequality, not for other reasons like governmental efficiency. Responsibilities, as well as rights, enhance the dignity and integrity of the person. And ~~DOMA~~ *this state law* contrives to deprive some couples ~~married under the laws of their State~~ *enjoying constitutionally protected sexual relationships,* but not other couples, of both rights and responsibilities. . . .

Similarly transposable passages—deliberately transposable, I think—abound. In sum, that Court which finds it so horrific that Congress irrationally and hatefully robbed same-sex couples of the "personhood and dignity" which state legislatures conferred upon them, will of a certitude be similarly appalled by state legislatures' irrational and hateful failure to acknowledge that "personhood and dignity" in the first place. As far as this Court is concerned, no one should be fooled; it is just a matter of listening and waiting for the other shoe. . . .

[Few] public controversies touch an institution so central to the lives of so many, and few inspire such attendant passion by good people on all sides. Few public controversies will ever demonstrate so vividly the beauty of what our Framers gave us, a gift the Court pawns today to buy its stolen moment in the spotlight: a system of government that permits us to rule *ourselves*. Since DOMA's passage, citizens on all sides of the question have seen victories and they have seen defeats. There have been plebiscites, legislation, persuasion, and loud voices—in other words, democracy. Victories in one place for some, see North Carolina Const., Amdt. 1 (providing that "[m]arriage between one man and one woman is the only domestic legal union that shall be valid or recognized in this State") (approved by a popular vote, 61% to 39% on May 8, 2012), are offset by victories in other places for others, see Maryland Question 6 (establishing "that Maryland's civil marriage laws allow gay and lesbian couples to obtain a civil marriage license") (approved by a popular vote, 52% to 48%, on November 6, 2012). Even in a *single State,* the question has come out differently on different occasions. Compare Maine Question 1 (permitting "the State of Maine to issue marriage licenses to same-sex couples") (approved by a popular vote, 53% to 47%, on November 6, 2012) with Maine Question 1 (rejecting "the new law that lets same-sex couples marry") (approved by a popular vote, 53% to 47%, on November 3, 2009).

In the majority's telling, this story is black-and-white: Hate your neighbor or come along with us. The truth is more complicated. It is hard to admit that one's political opponents are not monsters, especially in a struggle like this one, and the challenge in the end proves more than today's Court can handle. Too bad. A reminder that disagreement over something so fundamental as marriage can still be politically legitimate would have been a fit task for what in earlier times was called the judicial temperament. We might have covered ourselves with honor today, by promising all sides of this debate that it was theirs to settle and that we would respect their resolution. We might have let the People decide.

But that the majority will not do. Some will rejoice in today's decision, and some will despair at it; that is the nature of a controversy that matters so much to so many. But the Court has cheated both sides, robbing the winners of an honest victory, and the losers of the peace that comes from a fair defeat. We owed both of them better. I dissent.

Justice Alito, with whom Justice Thomas joins as to Parts II and III, dissenting. . . .

I

[In this section of his opinion, Justice Alito argues that the case is properly before the Court. This part of the opinion is discussed in Chapter 1 F 2 of this Supplement.]

II . . .

Same-sex marriage presents a highly emotional and important question of public policy — but not a difficult question of constitutional law. The Constitution does not guarantee the right to enter into a same-sex marriage. Indeed, no provision of the Constitution speaks to the issue.

The Court has sometimes found the Due Process Clauses to have a substantive component that guarantees liberties beyond the absence of physical restraint. And the Court's holding that "DOMA is unconstitutional as a deprivation of the liberty of the person protected by the Fifth Amendment of the Constitution," suggests that substantive due process may partially underlie the Court's decision today. But it is well established that any "substantive" component to the Due Process Clause protects only "those fundamental rights and liberties which are, objectively, 'deeply rooted in this Nation's history and tradition,'" Washington v. Glucksberg, as well as " 'implicit in the concept of ordered liberty,' such that 'neither liberty nor justice would exist if they were sacrificed.'" *Glucksberg* (quoting Palko v. Connecticut).

It is beyond dispute that the right to same-sex marriage is not deeply rooted in this Nation's history and tradition. In this country, no State permitted same-sex marriage until the Massachusetts Supreme Judicial Court held in 2003 that limiting marriage to opposite-sex couples violated the State Constitution. Nor is the right to same-sex marriage deeply rooted in the traditions of other nations. No country allowed same-sex couples to marry until the Netherlands did so in 2000.

What Windsor and the United States seek, therefore, is not the protection of a deeply rooted right but the recognition of a very new right, and they seek this innovation not from a legislative body elected by the people, but from unelected judges. Faced with such a request, judges have cause for both caution and humility.

The family is an ancient and universal human institution. Family structure reflects the characteristics of a civilization, and changes in family structure and in the popular understanding of marriage and the family can have profound effects. Past changes in the understanding of marriage—for example, the gradual ascendance of the idea that romantic love is a prerequisite to marriage—have had far-reaching consequences. But the process by which such consequences come about is complex, involving the interaction of numerous factors, and tends to occur over an extended period of time.

We can expect something similar to take place if same-sex marriage becomes widely accepted. The long-term consequences of this change are not now known and are unlikely to be ascertainable for some time to come. There are those who think that allowing same-sex marriage will seriously undermine the institution of marriage. Others think that recognition of same-sex marriage will fortify a now-shaky institution.

At present, no one—including social scientists, philosophers, and historians—can predict with any certainty what the long-term ramifications of widespread acceptance of same-sex marriage will be. And judges are certainly not equipped to make such an assessment. The Members of this Court have the authority and the responsibility to interpret and apply the Constitution. Thus, if the Constitution contained a provision guaranteeing the right to marry a person of the same sex, it would be our duty to enforce that right. But the Constitution simply does not speak to the issue of same-sex marriage. In our system of government, ultimate sovereignty rests with the people, and the people have the right to control their own destiny. Any change on a question so fundamental should be made by the people through their elected officials.

III

Perhaps because they cannot show that same-sex marriage is a fundamental right under our Constitution, Windsor and the United States couch their arguments in equal protection terms. They argue that § 3 of DOMA discriminates on the basis of sexual orientation, that classifications based on sexual orientation should trigger a form of "heightened" scrutiny, and that § 3 cannot survive such scrutiny. They further maintain that the governmental interests that § 3 purports to serve are not sufficiently important and that it has not been adequately shown that § 3 serves those interests very well. The Court's holding, too, seems to rest on "the equal protection guarantee of the Fourteenth Amendment," — although the Court is careful not to adopt most of Windsor's and the United States' argument.

In my view, the approach that Windsor and the United States advocate is misguided. Our equal protection framework, upon which Windsor and the United States rely, is a judicial construct that provides a useful mechanism for analyzing a certain universe of equal protection cases. But that framework is ill suited for use in evaluating the constitutionality of laws based on the traditional understanding of marriage, which fundamentally turn on what marriage is. . . .

In asking the Court to determine that § 3 of DOMA is subject to and violates heightened scrutiny, Windsor and the United States thus ask us to rule that the presence of two members of the opposite sex is as rationally related to marriage as white skin is to voting or a Y-chromosome is to the ability to administer an estate. That is a striking request and one that unelected judges should pause before granting. Acceptance of the argument would cast all those who cling to traditional beliefs about the nature of marriage in the role of bigots or superstitious fools.

By asking the Court to strike down DOMA as not satisfying some form of heightened scrutiny, Windsor and the United States are really seeking to have the Court resolve a debate between two competing views of marriage.

The first and older view, which I will call the "traditional" or "conjugal" view, sees marriage as an intrinsically opposite-sex institution. BLAG notes that virtually every culture, including many not influenced by the Abrahamic religions, has limited marriage to people of the opposite sex. And BLAG attempts to explain this phenomenon by arguing that the institution of marriage was created for the purpose of channeling heterosexual intercourse into a structure that supports child rearing. Others explain the basis for the institution in more philosophical terms. They argue that marriage is essentially the solemnizing of a comprehensive, exclusive, permanent union that is intrinsically ordered to producing new life, even if it does not always do so. While modern cultural changes have weakened the link between marriage and procreation in the popular mind, there is no doubt that, throughout human history and across many cultures, marriage has been viewed as an exclusively opposite-sex institution and as one inextricably linked to procreation and biological kinship.

The other, newer view is what I will call the "consent-based" vision of marriage, a vision that primarily defines marriage as the solemnization of mutual commitment — marked by strong emotional attachment and sexual attraction — between two persons. At least as it applies to heterosexual couples, this view of marriage now plays a very prominent role in the popular understanding of the institution. Indeed, our popular culture is infused with this understanding of marriage. Proponents of same-sex marriage argue that because gender differentiation is not relevant to this vision, the exclusion of same-sex couples from the institution of marriage is rank discrimination.

The Constitution does not codify either of these views of marriage (although I suspect it would have been hard at the time of the adoption of the Constitution or the Fifth Amendment to find Americans who did not take the traditional view for granted). The silence of the Constitution on this question should be enough to end the matter as far as the judiciary is concerned. Yet, Windsor and the United States implicitly ask us to endorse the consent-based view of marriage and to reject the traditional view, thereby arrogating to ourselves the power to decide a question that philosophers, historians, social scientists, and theologians are better qualified to explore. Because our constitutional order assigns the resolution of questions of this nature to the people, I would not presume to enshrine either vision of marriage in our constitutional jurisprudence. . . .

To the extent that the Court takes the position that the question of same-sex marriage should be resolved primarily at the state level, I wholeheartedly agree. I hope that the Court will ultimately permit the people of each State to decide this question for themselves. Unless the Court is willing to allow this to occur, the whiffs of federalism in the today's opinion of the Court will soon be scattered to the wind.

In any event, § 3 of DOMA, in my view, does not encroach on the prerogatives of the States, assuming of course that the many federal statutes affected by DOMA have not already done so. Section 3 does not prevent any State from recognizing same-sex marriage or from extending to same-sex couples any right, privilege, benefit, or obligation stemming from state law. All that § 3 does is to define a class of persons to whom federal law extends certain special benefits and upon whom federal law imposes certain special burdens. In these provisions, Congress used marital status as a way of defining this class — in part, I assume, because it viewed marriage as a valuable institution to be fostered and in part because it viewed married couples as comprising a unique type of economic unit that merits special regulatory treatment. Assuming that Congress has the power under the Constitution to enact the laws affected by § 3, Congress has the power to define the category of persons to whom those laws apply. . . .

OBERGEFELL v. HODGES

135 S. Ct. 2584 (2015)

JUSTICE KENNEDY delivered the opinion of the Court.

The Constitution promises liberty to all within its reach, a liberty that includes certain specific rights that allow persons, within a lawful realm, to define and express their identity. The petitioners in these cases seek to find that liberty by marrying someone of the same sex and having their marriages deemed lawful on the same terms and conditions as marriages between persons of the opposite sex. . . .

II

Before addressing the principles and precedents that govern these cases, it is appropriate to note the history of the subject now before the Court.

A

From their beginning to their most recent page, the annals of human history reveal the transcendent importance of marriage. The lifelong union of a man and a woman always has promised nobility and dignity to all persons, without regard to their station in life. Marriage is sacred to those who live by their religions and offers unique fulfillment to those who find meaning in the secular realm. Its dynamic allows two people to find a life that could not be found alone, for a marriage becomes greater than just the two persons. Rising from the most basic human needs, marriage is essential to our most profound hopes and aspirations.

The centrality of marriage to the human condition makes it unsurprising that the institution has existed for millennia and across civilizations. . . .

That history is the beginning of these cases. The respondents say it should be the end as well. To them, it would demean a timeless institution if the concept and lawful status of marriage were extended to two persons of the same sex. Marriage, in their view, is by its nature a gender-differentiated union of man and woman. This view long has been held—and continues to be held— in good faith by reasonable and sincere people here and throughout the world.

The petitioners acknowledge this history but contend that these cases cannot end there. Were their intent to demean the revered idea and reality of marriage, the petitioners' claims would be of a different order. But that is neither their purpose nor their submission. To the contrary, it is the enduring importance of marriage that underlies the petitioners' contentions. This, they say, is their whole point. Far from seeking to devalue marriage, the petitioners seek it for themselves because of their respect—and need—for its privileges and responsibilities. And their immutable nature dictates that same-sex marriage is their only real path to this profound commitment.

Recounting the circumstances of three of these cases illustrates the urgency of the petitioners' cause from their perspective. Petitioner James Obergefell, [met] John Arthur over two decades ago. They fell in love and started a life together, establishing a lasting, committed relation. In 2011, however, Arthur was diagnosed with amyotrophic lateral sclerosi, or ALS. This debilitating disease is progressive, with no known cure. Two years ago, Obergefell and Arthur decided to commit to one another, resolving to marry before Arthur died. To fulfill their mutual promise, they traveled from Ohio to Maryland, where same-sex marriage was legal. It was difficult for Arthur to move, and so the couple were wed inside a medical transport plane as it remained on the tarmac in Baltimore. Three months later, Arthur died. Ohio law does not permit Obergefell to be listed as the surviving spouse on Arthur's death certificate. By statute, they must remain strangers even in death, a state-imposed separation Obergefell deems "hurtful for the rest of time." He brought suit to be shown as the surviving spouse on Arthur's death certificate.

April DeBoer and Jayne Rowse are co-plaintiffs in the case from Michigan. They celebrated a commitment ceremony to honor their permanent relation in 2007. They both work as nurses, DeBoer in a neonatal unit and Rowse in an emergency unit. In 2009, DeBoer and Rowse fostered and then adopted a baby boy. Later that same year, they welcomed another son into their family. The new baby, born prematurely and abandoned by his biological mother, required around-the-clock care. The next year, a baby girl with special needs joined their family. Michigan, however, permits only opposite-sex married couples or single individuals to adopt, so each child can have only one woman as his or her legal parent. If an emergency were to arise, schools and hospitals may treat the three children as if they had only one parent. And, were tragedy to befall either DeBoer or Rowse, the other would have no legal rights over the children she had not been permitted to adopt. This couple seeks relief from the continuing uncertainty their unmarried status creates in their lives.

Army Reserve Sergeant First Class Ijpe DeKoe and his partner Thomas Kostura, co-plaintiffs in the Tennessee case, fell in love. In 2011, DeKoe received orders to deploy to Afghanistan. Before leaving, he and Kostura married in New York. A week later, DeKoe began his deployment, which lasted for almost a year. When he returned, the two settled in Tennessee, where DeKoe works full-time for the Army Reserve. Their lawful marriage is stripped from them whenever they reside in Tennessee, returning and disappearing as they travel across state lines. DeKoe, who served this Nation to preserve the freedom the Constitution protects, must endure a substantial burden.

The cases now before the Court involve other petitioners as well, each with their own experiences. Their stories reveal that they seek not to denigrate marriage but rather to live their lives, or honor their spouses' memory, joined by its bond.

B

The ancient origins of marriage confirm its centrality, but it has not stood in isolation from developments in law and society. The history of marriage is one of both continuity and change. That institution—even as confined to opposite-sex relations—has evolved over time.

For example, marriage was once viewed as an arrangement by the couple's parents based on political, religious, and financial concerns; but by the time of the Nation's founding it was understood to be a voluntary contract between a man and a woman. As the role and status of women changed, the institution further evolved. Under the centuries-old doctrine of coverture, a married man and woman were treated by the State as a single, male-dominated legal entity. See 1 W. Blackstone, Commentaries on the Laws of England 430 (1765). As women gained legal, political, and property rights, and as society began to understand that women have their own equal dignity, the law of coverture was abandoned. These and other developments in the institution of marriage over the past centuries were not mere superficial changes. Rather, they worked deep transformations in its structure, affecting aspects of marriage long viewed by many as essential.

These new insights have strengthened, not weakened, the institution of marriage. Indeed, changed understandings of marriage are characteristic of a Nation where new dimensions of freedom become apparent to new generations, often through perspectives that begin in pleas or protests and then are considered in the political sphere and the judicial process.

This dynamic can be seen in the Nation's experiences with the rights of gays and lesbians. Until the mid–20th century, same-sex intimacy long had been condemned as immoral by the state itself in most Western nations, a belief often embodied in the criminal law. For this reason, among others, many persons did not deem homosexuals to have dignity in their own distinct identity. A truthful declaration by same-sex couples of what was in their hearts had to remain unspoken. Even when a greater awareness of the humanity and integrity of homosexual persons came in the period after World War II, the argument that gays and lesbians had a just claim to dignity was in conflict with both law and widespread social conventions. Same-sex intimacy remained a crime in many States. Gays and lesbians were prohibited from most government employment, barred from military service, excluded under immigration laws, targeted by police, and burdened in their rights to associate. . . .

[The Court recounts the history of judicial involvement with issues of homosexuality and same-sex marriage.]

Numerous cases about same-sex marriage have reached the United States Courts of Appeals in recent years. In accordance with the judicial duty to base their decisions on principled reasons and neutral discussions, without scornful or disparaging commentary, courts have written a substantial body of law considering all sides of these issues. That case law helps to explain and formulate the underlying principles this Court now must consider. With the exception of the opinion here under review and one other Courts of Appeals have held that excluding same-sex couples from marriage violates the Constitution. There also have been many thoughtful District Court decisions addressing same-sex marriage—and most of them, too, have concluded same-sex couples must be allowed to marry. In addition the highest courts of many States have contributed to this ongoing dialogue in decisions interpreting their own State Constitutions. . . .

After years of litigation, legislation, referenda, and the discussions that attended these public acts, the States are now divided on the issue of same-sex marriage.

III

Under the Due Process Clause of the Fourteenth Amendment, no State shall "deprive any person of life, liberty, or property, without due process of law." The fundamental liberties protected by this Clause include most of the rights enumerated in the Bill of Rights. In addition these liberties extend to certain personal choices central to individual dignity and autonomy, including intimate choices that define personal identity and beliefs.

The identification and protection of fundamental rights is an enduring part of the judicial duty to interpret the Constitution. That responsibility, however, "has not been reduced to any formula." Rather, it requires courts to exercise reasoned judgment in identifying interests of the person so fundamental that the State must accord them its respect. That process is guided by many of the same considerations relevant to analysis of other constitutional provisions that set forth broad principles rather than specific requirements. History and tradition guide and discipline this inquiry but do not set its outer boundaries. That method respects our history and learns from it without allowing the past alone to rule the present.

The nature of injustice is that we may not always see it in our own times. The generations that wrote and ratified the Bill of Rights and the Fourteenth Amendment did not presume to know the extent of freedom in all of its dimensions, and so they entrusted to future generations a charter protecting the right of all persons to enjoy liberty as we learn its meaning. When new insight reveals discord between the Constitution's central protections and a received legal stricture, a claim to liberty must be addressed.

Applying these established tenets, the Court has long held the right to marry is protected by the Constitution. . . .

It cannot be denied that this Court's cases describing the right to marry presumed a relationship involving opposite-sex partners. The Court, like many institutions, has made assumptions defined by the world and time of which it is a part. This was evident in *Baker v. Nelson,* a one-line summary decision issued in 1972, holding the exclusion of same-sex couples from marriage did not present a substantial federal question.

Still, there are other, more instructive precedents. This Court's cases have expressed constitutional principles of broader reach. In defining the right to marry these cases have identified essential attributes of that right based in history, tradition, and other constitutional liberties inherent in this intimate bond. And in assessing whether the force and rationale of its cases apply to same-sex couples, the Court must respect the basic reasons why the right to marry has been long protected.

This analysis compels the conclusion that same-sex couples may exercise the right to marry. The four principles and traditions to be discussed demonstrate that the reasons marriage is fundamental under the Constitution apply with equal force to same-sex couples.

A first premise of the Court's relevant precedents is that the right to personal choice regarding marriage is inherent in the concept of individual autonomy. . . .

Choices about marriage shape an individual's destiny. . . .

The nature of marriage is that, through its enduring bond, two persons together can find other freedoms, such as expression, intimacy, and spirituality. This is true for all persons, whatever their sexual orientation. There is dignity in the bond between two men or two women who seek to marry and in their autonomy to make such profound choices.

A second principle in this Court's jurisprudence is that the right to marry is fundamental because it supports a two-person union unlike any other in its importance to the committed individuals. . . .

The right to marry thus dignifies couples who "wish to define themselves by their commitment to each other." [*Windsor*] Marriage responds to the universal fear that a lonely person might call out only to find no one there. It offers the hope of companionship and understanding and assurance that while both still live there will be someone to care for the other. . . .

A third basis for protecting the right to marry is that it safeguards children and families and thus draws meaning from related rights of childrearing, procreation, and education. [By] giving recognition and legal structure to their parents' relationship, marriage allows children "to understand the integrity and closeness of their own family and its concord with other families in their community and in their daily lives." [*Windsor*]. Marriage also affords the permanency and stability important to children's best interests.

As all parties agree, many same-sex couples provide loving and nurturing homes to their children, whether biological or adopted. And hundreds of thousands of children are presently being raised by such couples. . . .

Excluding same-sex couples from marriage thus conflicts with a central premise of the right to marry. Without the recognition, stability, and predictability marriage offers, their children suffer the stigma of knowing their families are somehow lesser. They also suffer the significant material costs of being raised by unmarried parents, relegated through no fault of their own to a more difficult and

135

uncertain family life. The marriage laws at issue here thus harm and humiliate the children of same-sex couples.

That is not to say the right to marry is less meaningful for those who do not or cannot have children. An ability, desire, or promise to procreate is not and has not been a prerequisite for a valid marriage in any State. In light of precedent protecting the right of a married couple not to procreate, it cannot be said the Court or the States have conditioned the right to marry on the capacity or commitment to procreate. The constitutional marriage right has many aspects, of which childbearing is only one.

Fourth and finally, this Court's cases and the Nation's traditions make clear that marriage is a keystone of our social order.

In Maynard v. Hill, 125 U.S. 190, 211 (1888), the Court [explained] that marriage is "the foundation of the family and of society, without which there would be neither civilization nor progress." Marriage, the *Maynard* Court said, has long been " 'a great public institution, giving character to our whole civil polity.' " *Id.*, at 213. This idea has been reiterated even as the institution has evolved in substantial ways over time, superseding rules related to parental consent, gender, and race once thought by many to be essential.

For that reason, just as a couple vows to support each other, so does society pledge to support the couple, offering symbolic recognition and material benefits to protect and nourish the union. Indeed, while the States are in general free to vary the benefits they confer on all married couples, they have throughout our history made marriage the basis for an expanding list of governmental rights, benefits, and responsibilities. These aspects of marital status include: taxation; inheritance and property rights; rules of intestate succession; spousal privilege in the law of evidence; hospital access; medical decisionmaking authority; adoption rights; the rights and benefits of survivors; birth and death certificates; professional ethics rules; campaign finance restrictions; workers' compensation benefits; health insurance; and child custody, support, and visitation rules. Valid marriage under state law is also a significant status for over a thousand provisions of federal law. The States have contributed to the fundamental character of the marriage right by placing that institution at the center of so many facets of the legal and social order.

There is no difference between same- and opposite-sex couples with respect to this principle. Yet by virtue of their exclusion from that institution, same-sex couples are denied the constellation of benefits that the States have linked to marriage. This harm results in more than just material burdens. Same-sex couples are consigned to an instability many opposite-sex couples would deem intolerable in their own lives. As the State itself makes marriage all the more precious by the significance it attaches to it, exclusion from that status has the effect of teaching that gays and lesbians are unequal in important respects. It demeans gays and lesbians for the State to lock them out of a central institution of the Nation's society.

Same-sex couples, too, may aspire to the transcendent purposes of marriage and seek fulfillment in its highest meaning.

The limitation of marriage to opposite-sex couples may long have seemed natural and just, but its inconsistency with the central meaning of the fundamental right to marry is now manifest. With that knowledge must come the recognition that laws excluding same-sex couples from the marriage right impose stigma and injury of the kind prohibited by our basic charter.

Objecting that this does not reflect an appropriate framing of the issue, the respondents refer to which called for a " 'careful description' " of fundamental rights. They assert the petitioners do not seek to exercise the right to marry but rather a new and nonexistent "right to same-sex marriage." *Glucksberg* did insist that liberty under the Due Process Clause must be defined in a most circumscribed manner, with central reference to specific historical practices. Yet while that approach may have been appropriate for the asserted right there involved (physician-assisted suicide), it is inconsistent with the approach this Court has used in discussing other fundamental rights, including marriage and intimacy. *Loving* did not ask about a "right to interracial marriage"; *Turner* did not ask about a "right of inmates to marry"; and *Zablocki* did not ask about a "right of fathers with unpaid child support duties to marry." Rather, each case inquired about the right to marry in its comprehensive sense, asking if there was a sufficient justification for excluding the relevant class from the right.

That principle applies here. If rights were defined by who exercised them in the past, then received practices could serve as their own continued justification and new groups could not invoke rights once denied. This Court has rejected that approach, both with respect to the right to marry and the rights of gays and lesbians.

The right to marry is fundamental as a matter of history and tradition, but rights come not from ancient sources alone. They rise, too, from a better informed understanding of how constitutional imperatives define a liberty that remains urgent in our own era. Many who deem same-sex marriage to be wrong reach that conclusion based on decent and honorable religious or philosophical premises, and neither they nor their beliefs are disparaged here. But when that sincere, personal opposition becomes enacted law and public policy, the necessary consequence is to put the imprimatur of the State itself on an exclusion that soon demeans or stigmatizes those whose own liberty is then denied. Under the Constitution, same-sex couples seek in marriage the same legal treatment as opposite-sex couples, and it would disparage their choices and diminish their personhood to deny them this right.

The right of same-sex couples to marry that is part of the liberty promised by the Fourteenth Amendment is derived, too, from that Amendment's guarantee of the equal protection of the laws. The Due Process Clause and the Equal Protection

Clause are connected in a profound way, though they set forth independent principles. Rights implicit in liberty and rights secured by equal protection may rest on different precepts and are not always co-extensive, yet in some instances each may be instructive as to the meaning and reach of the other. In any particular case one Clause may be thought to capture the essence of the right in a more accurate and comprehensive way, even as the two Clauses may converge in the identification and definition of the right. . . .

In *Lawrence* the Court acknowledged the interlocking nature of these constitutional safeguards in the context of the legal treatment of gays and lesbians. Although *Lawrence* elaborated its holding under the Due Process Clause, it acknowledged, and sought to remedy, the continuing inequality that resulted from laws making intimacy in the lives of gays and lesbians a crime against the State. *Lawrence* therefore drew upon principles of liberty and equality to define and protect the rights of gays and lesbians, holding the State "cannot demean their existence or control their destiny by making their private sexual conduct a crime."

This dynamic also applies to same-sex marriage. It is now clear that the challenged laws burden the liberty of same-sex couples, and it must be further acknowledged that they abridge central precepts of equality. Here the marriage laws enforced by the respondents are in essence unequal: same-sex couples are denied all the benefits afforded to opposite-sex couples and are barred from exercising a fundamental right. Especially against a long history of disapproval of their relationships, this denial to same-sex couples of the right to marry works a grave and continuing harm. The imposition of this disability on gays and lesbians serves to disrespect and subordinate them. And the Equal Protection Clause, like the Due Process Clause, prohibits this unjustified infringement of the fundamental right to marry.

[The] Court now holds that same-sex couples may exercise the fundamental right to marry. No longer may this liberty be denied to them. *Baker v. Nelson* must be and now is overruled, and the State laws challenged by Petitioners in these cases are now held invalid to the extent they exclude same-sex couples from civil marriage on the same terms and conditions as opposite-sex couples.

There may be an initial inclination in these cases to proceed with caution—to await further legislation, litigation, and debate. The respondents warn there has been insufficient democratic discourse before deciding an issue so basic as the definition of marriage . . .

Yet there has been far more deliberation than this argument acknowledges. There have been referenda, legislative debates, and grassroots campaigns, as well as countless studies, papers, books, and other popular and scholarly writings. There has been extensive litigation in state and federal courts. Judicial opinions addressing the issue have been informed by the contentions of parties and counsel, which, in turn, reflect the more general, societal discussion of same-sex marriage and its meaning that has occurred over the past decades. As more than 100 *amici* make clear in their filings, many of the central institutions in American life—state and local governments, the military, large and small businesses, labor unions, religious organizations, law enforcement, civic groups, professional organizations, and universities—have devoted substantial attention to the question. This has led to an enhanced understanding of the issue—an understanding reflected in the arguments now presented for resolution as a matter of constitutional law.

Of course, the Constitution contemplates that democracy is the appropriate process for change, so long as that process does not abridge fundamental rights. [But] when the rights of persons are violated, "the Constitution requires redress by the courts," notwithstanding the more general value of democratic decision-making. This holds true even when protecting individual rights affects issues of the utmost importance and sensitivity.

The dynamic of our constitutional system is that individuals need not await legislative action before asserting a fundamental right. The Nation's courts are open to injured individuals who come to them to vindicate their own direct, personal stake in our basic charter. An individual can invoke a right to constitutional protection when he or she is harmed, even if the broader public disagrees and even if the legislature refuses to act. [The] issue before the Court here is the legal question whether the Constitution protects the right of same-sex couples to marry.

This is not the first time the Court has been asked to adopt a cautious approach to recognizing and protecting fundamental rights. In *Bowers*, a bare majority upheld a law criminalizing same-sex intimacy. That approach might have been viewed as a cautious endorsement of the democratic process, which had only just begun to consider the rights of gays and lesbians. Yet, in effect, *Bowers* upheld state action that denied gays and lesbians a fundamental right and caused them pain and humiliation. As evidenced by the dissents in that case, the facts and principles necessary to a correct holding were known to the *Bowers* Court. That is why *Lawrence* held *Bowers* was "not correct when it was decided." Although *Bowers* was eventually repudiated in *Lawrence*, men and women were harmed in the interim, and the substantial effects of these injuries no doubt lingered long after *Bowers* was overruled. Dignitary wounds cannot always be healed with the stroke of a pen.

A ruling against same-sex couples would have the same effect—and, like *Bowers*, would be unjustified under the Fourteenth Amendment. The petitioners' stories make clear the urgency of the issue they present to the Court. [Properly] presented with the petitioners' cases, the Court has a duty to address these claims and answer these questions. . . .

Were the Court to uphold the challenged laws as constitutional, it would teach the Nation that these laws are in accord with our society's most basic compact.

Were the Court to stay its hand to allow slower, case-by-case determination of the required availability of specific public benefits to same-sex couples, it still would deny gays and lesbians many rights and responsibilities intertwined with marriage.

The respondents also argue allowing same-sex couples to wed will harm marriage as an institution by leading to fewer opposite-sex marriages. This may occur, the respondents contend, because licensing same-sex marriage severs the connection between natural procreation and marriage. That argument, however, rests on a counterintuitive view of opposite-sex couple's decisionmaking processes regarding marriage and parenthood. Decisions about whether to marry and raise children are based on many personal, romantic, and practical considerations; and it is unrealistic to conclude that an opposite-sex couple would choose not to marry simply because same-sex couples may do so. The respondents have not shown a foundation for the conclusion that allowing same-sex marriage will cause the harmful outcomes they describe. Indeed, with respect to this asserted basis for excluding same-sex couples from the right to marry, it is appropriate to observe these cases involve only the rights of two consenting adults whose marriages would pose no risk of harm to themselves or third parties.

Finally, it must be emphasized that religions, and those who adhere to religious doctrines, may continue to advocate with utmost, sincere conviction that, by divine precepts, same-sex marriage should not be condoned. The First Amendment ensures that religious organizations and persons are given proper protection as they seek to teach the principles that are so fulfilling and so central to their lives and faiths, and to their own deep aspirations to continue the family structure they have long revered. The same is true of those who oppose same-sex marriage for other reasons. In turn, those who believe allowing same-sex marriage is proper or indeed essential, whether as a matter of religious conviction or secular belief, may engage those who disagree with their view in an open and searching debate. The Constitution, however, does not permit the State to bar same-sex couples from marriage on the same terms as accorded to couples of the opposite sex. . . .

* * *

No union is more profound than marriage, for it embodies the highest ideals of love, fidelity, devotion, sacrifice, and family. In forming a marital union, two people become something greater than once they were. As some of the petitioners in these cases demonstrate, marriage embodies a love that may endure even past death. It would misunderstand these men and women to say they disrespect the idea of marriage. Their plea is that they do respect it, respect it so deeply that they seek to find its fulfillment for themselves. Their hope is not to be condemned to live in loneliness, excluded from one of civilization's oldest institutions. They ask for equal dignity in the eyes of the law. The Constitution grants them that right. . . .

Chief Justice ROBERTS, with whom Justice SCALIA and Justice THOMAS join, dissenting.

Petitioners make strong arguments rooted in social policy and considerations of fairness. They contend that same-sex couples should be allowed to affirm their love and commitment through marriage, just like opposite-sex couples. That position has undeniable appeal; over the past six years, voters and legislators in eleven States and the District of Columbia have revised their laws to allow marriage between two people of the same sex.

But this Court is not a legislature. Whether same-sex marriage is a good idea should be of no concern to us. Under the Constitution, judges have power to say what the law is, not what it should be. . . .

Although the policy arguments for extending marriage to same-sex couples may be compelling, the legal arguments for requiring such an extension are not. The fundamental right to marry does not include a right to make a State change its definition of marriage. And a State's decision to maintain the meaning of marriage that has persisted in every culture throughout human history can hardly be called irrational. In short, our Constitution does not enact any one theory of marriage. The people of a State are free to expand marriage to include same-sex couples, or to retain the historic definition.

Today, however, the Court takes the extraordinary step of ordering every State to license and recognize same-sex marriage. Many people will rejoice at this decision, and I begrudge none their celebration. But for those who believe in a government of laws, not of men, the majority's approach is deeply disheartening. Supporters of same-sex marriage have achieved considerable success persuading their fellow citizens — through the democratic process — to adopt their view. That ends today. Five lawyers have closed the debate and enacted their own vision of marriage as a matter of constitutional law. Stealing this issue from the people will for many cast a cloud over same-sex marriage, making a dramatic social change that much more difficult to accept.

The majority's decision is an act of will, not legal judgment. The right it announces has no basis in the Constitution or this Court's precedent. The majority expressly disclaims judicial "caution" and omits even a pretense of humility, openly relying on its desire to remake society according to its own "new insight" into the "nature of injustice." As a result, the Court invalidates the marriage laws of more than half the States and orders the transformation of a social institution that has formed the basis of human society for millennia, for the Kalahari Bushmen and the Han Chinese, the Carthaginians and the Aztecs. Just who do we think we are? . . .

Understand well what this dissent is about: It is not about whether, in my judgment, the institution of marriage should be changed to include same-sex couples.
It is instead about whether, in our democratic republic, that decision should rest
with the people acting through their elected representatives, or with five lawyers who happen to hold commissions authorizing them to resolve legal disputes
according to law. The Constitution leaves no doubt about the answer.

I . . .

A . . .

[The] universal definition of marriage as the union of a man and a woman is
no historical coincidence. Marriage did not come about as a result of a political
movement, discovery, disease, war, religious doctrine, or any other moving force
of world history — and certainly not as a result of a prehistoric decision to exclude
gays and lesbians. It arose in the nature of things to meet a vital need: ensuring
that children are conceived by a mother and father committed to raising them in
the stable conditions of a lifelong relationship.

The premises supporting this concept of marriage are so fundamental that they
rarely require articulation. The human race must procreate to survive. Procreation
occurs through sexual relations between a man and a woman. When sexual relations result in the conception of a child, that child's prospects are generally better if the mother and father stay together rather than going their separate ways.
Therefore, for the good of children and society, sexual relations that can lead to
procreation should occur only between a man and a woman committed to a lasting bond.

Society has recognized that bond as marriage. And by bestowing a respected
status and material benefits on married couples, society encourages men and
women to conduct sexual relations within marriage rather than without. . . .

This singular understanding of marriage has prevailed in the United States
throughout our history. . . .

The Constitution itself says nothing about marriage, and the Framers thereby
entrusted the States with "[t]he whole subject of the domestic relations of husband
and wife." *Windsor.* There is no dispute that every State at the founding — and
every State throughout our history until a dozen years ago — defined marriage in
the traditional, biologically rooted way. . . .

As the majority notes, some aspects of marriage have changed over time. . . .

[The changes] did not, however, work any transformation in the core structure
of marriage as the union between a man and a woman. If you had asked a person
on the street how marriage was defined, no one would ever have said, "Marriage
is the union of a man and a woman, where the woman is subject to coverture." The
majority may be right that the "history of marriage is one of both continuity and
change," but the core meaning of marriage has endured. . . .

142

II

Petitioners first contend that the marriage laws of their States violate the Due Process Clause. . . .

The majority purports to identify four "principles and traditions" in this Court's due process precedents that support a fundamental right for same-sex couples to marry. In reality, however, the majority's approach has no basis in principle or tradition, except for the unprincipled tradition of judicial policymaking that characterized discredited decisions such as Lochner v. New York. Stripped of its shiny rhetorical gloss, the majority's argument is that the Due Process Clause gives same-sex couples a fundamental right to marry because it will be good for them and for society. If I were a legislator, I would certainly consider that view as a matter of social policy. But as a judge, I find the majority's position indefensible as a matter of constitutional law. . . .

A

Allowing unelected federal judges to select which unenumerated rights rank as "fundamental"—and to strike down state laws on the basis of that determination—raises obvious concerns about the judicial role. Our precedents have accordingly insisted that judges "exercise the utmost care" in identifying implied fundamental rights, "lest the liberty protected by the Due Process Clause be subtly transformed into the policy preferences of the Members of this Court." . . .

The need for restraint in administering the strong medicine of substantive due process is a lesson this Court has learned the hard way. The Court first applied substantive due process to strike down a statute in Dred Scott v. Sandford. There the Court invalidated the Missouri Compromise on the ground that legislation restricting the institution of slavery violated the implied rights of slaveholders. . . .

Dred Scott's holding was overruled on the battlefields of the Civil War and by constitutional amendment after Appomattox, but its approach to the Due Process Clause reappeared. In a series of early 20th-century cases, most prominently *Lochner v. New York,* this Court invalidated state statutes that presented "meddlesome interferences with the rights of the individual," and "undue interference with liberty of person and freedom of contract." . . .

Eventually, the Court recognized its error and vowed not to repeat it. . . .

Rejecting *Lochner* does not require disavowing the doctrine of implied fundamental rights, and this Court has not done so. But to avoid repeating *Lochner*'s error of converting personal preferences into constitutional mandates, our modern substantive due process cases have stressed the need for "judicial self-restraint." Our precedents have required that implied fundamental rights be "objectively, deeply rooted in this Nation's history and tradition," and "implicit in the concept of ordered liberty, such that neither liberty nor justice would exist if they were sacrificed." *Glucksberg.*

B

The majority acknowledges none of this doctrinal background, and it is easy to see why: Its aggressive application of substantive due process breaks sharply with decades of precedent and returns the Court to the unprincipled approach of *Lochner*.

1

The majority's driving themes are that marriage is desirable and petitioners desire it. [The] "right to marry" cases stand for the important but limited proposition that particular restrictions on access to marriage *as traditionally defined* violate due process. These precedents say nothing at all about a right to make a State change its definition of marriage, which is the right petitioners actually seek here. Neither petitioners nor the majority cites a single case or other legal source providing any basis for such a constitutional right. None exists, and that is enough to foreclose their claim.

2

Neither *Lawrence* nor any other precedent in the privacy line of cases supports the right that petitioners assert here. Unlike criminal laws banning contraceptives and sodomy, the marriage laws at issue here involve no government intrusion. They create no crime and impose no punishment. Same-sex couples remain free to live together, to engage in intimate conduct, and to raise their families as they see fit. No one is "condemned to live in loneliness" by the laws challenged in these cases—no one. At the same time, the laws in no way interfere with the "right to be let alone." . . .

[The] privacy cases provide no support for the majority's position, because petitioners do not seek privacy. Quite the opposite, they seek public recognition of their relationships, along with corresponding government benefits. Our cases have consistently refused to allow litigants to convert the shield provided by constitutional liberties into a sword to demand positive entitlements from the State. . . .

3

To be fair, the majority does not suggest that its individual autonomy right is entirely unconstrained. The constraints it sets are precisely those that accord with its own "reasoned judgment," informed by its "new insight" into the "nature of injustice," which was invisible to all who came before but has become clear "as we learn [the] meaning" of liberty. . . .

One immediate question invited by the majority's position is whether States may retain the definition of marriage as a union of two people. Although the majority randomly inserts the adjective "two" in various places, it offers no reason at all why the two-person element of the core definition of marriage may be preserved while the man-woman element may not. Indeed, from the standpoint of history and tradition, a leap from opposite-sex marriage to same-sex marriage is much greater than one from a two-person union to plural unions, which have deep roots in some cultures around the world. If the majority is willing to take the big leap, it is hard to see how it can say no to the shorter one. . . .

I do not mean to equate marriage between same-sex couples with plural marriages in all respects. There may well be relevant differences that compel different legal analysis. But if there are, petitioners have not pointed to any. . . . .

4

Near the end of its opinion, the majority offers perhaps the clearest insight into its decision. Expanding marriage to include same-sex couples, the majority insists, would "pose no risk of harm to themselves or third parties." This argument again echoes *Lochner,* which relied on its assessment that "we think that a law like the one before us involves neither the safety, the morals nor the welfare of the public, and that the interest of the public is not in the slightest degree affected by such an act."

Then and now, this assertion of the "harm principle" sounds more in philosophy than law. The elevation of the fullest individual self-realization over the constraints that society has expressed in law may or may not be attractive moral philosophy. But a Justice's commission does not confer any special moral, philosophical, or social insight sufficient to justify imposing those perceptions on fellow citizens under the pretense of "due process." . . .

III

In addition to their due process argument, petitioners contend that the Equal Protection Clause requires their States to license and recognize same-sex marriages. The majority does not seriously engage with this claim. Its discussion is, quite frankly, difficult to follow. The central point seems to be that there is a "synergy between" the Equal Protection Clause and the Due Process Clause, and that some precedents relying on one Clause have also relied on the other. . . .

[The majority] fails to provide even a single sentence explaining how the Equal Protection Clause supplies independent weight for its position, nor does it attempt to justify its gratuitous violation of the canon against unnecessarily resolving constitutional questions. In any event, the marriage laws at issue here do not violate the Equal Protection Clause, because distinguishing between opposite-sex and same-sex couples is rationally related to the States' "legitimate state interest" in "preserving the traditional institution of marriage."

It is important to note with precision which laws petitioners have challenged. Although they discuss some of the ancillary legal benefits that accompany marriage, such as hospital visitation rights and recognition of spousal status on official documents, petitioners' lawsuits target the laws defining marriage generally rather than those allocating benefits specifically. The equal protection analysis might be different, in my view, if we were confronted with a more focused challenge to the denial of certain tangible benefits. Of course, those more selective claims will not arise now that the Court has taken the drastic step of requiring every State to license and recognize marriages between same-sex couples.

IV

The legitimacy of this Court ultimately rests "upon the respect accorded to its judgments." That respect flows from the perception—and reality—that we exercise humility and restraint in deciding cases according to the Constitution and law. The role of the Court envisioned by the majority today, however, is anything but humble or restrained. Over and over, the majority exalts the role of the judiciary in delivering social change. . . .

Those who founded our country would not recognize the majority's conception of the judicial role. They after all risked their lives and fortunes for the precious right to govern themselves. They would never have imagined yielding that right on a question of social policy to unaccountable and unelected judges. And they certainly would not have been satisfied by a system empowering judges to override policy judgments so long as they do so after "a quite extensive discussion." In our democracy, debate about the content of the law is not an exhaustion requirement to be checked off before courts can impose their will. . . .

When decisions are reached through democratic means, some people will inevitably be disappointed with the results. But those whose views do not prevail at least know that they have had their say, and accordingly are—in the tradition of our political culture—reconciled to the result of a fair and honest debate. In addition, they can gear up to raise the issue later, hoping to persuade enough on the winning side to think again.

But today the Court puts a stop to all that. By deciding this question under the Constitution, the Court removes it from the realm of democratic decision. There will be consequences to shutting down the political process on an issue of such profound public significance. Closing debate tends to close minds. People denied a voice are less likely to accept the ruling of a court on an issue that does not seem to be the sort of thing courts usually decide. As a thoughtful commentator observed about another issue, "The political process was moving . . . , not swiftly enough for advocates of quick, complete change, but majoritarian institutions were listening and acting. Heavy-handed judicial intervention was difficult to justify and appears to have provoked, not resolved, conflict." Ginsburg, Some Thoughts on Autonomy and Equality in Relation to *Roe* v. *Wade,* 63 N.C.L.Rev. 375, 385–386 (1985) (footnote omitted). Indeed, however heartened the proponents of same-sex marriage might be on this day, it is worth acknowledging what they have lost, and lost forever: the opportunity to win the true acceptance that comes from persuading their fellow citizens of the justice of their cause. And they lose this just when the winds of change were freshening at their backs. . . .

Respect for sincere religious conviction has led voters and legislators in every State that has adopted same-sex marriage democratically to include accommodations for religious practice. The majority's decision imposing same-sex marriage cannot, of course, create any such accommodations. The majority graciously suggests that religious believers may continue to "advocate" and "teach" their views of marriage. The First Amendment guarantees, however, the freedom to "*exercise*" religion. Ominously, that is not a word the majority uses.

Hard questions arise when people of faith exercise religion in ways that may be seen to conflict with the new right to same-sex marriage — when, for example, a religious college provides married student housing only to opposite-sex married couples, or a religious adoption agency declines to place children with same-sex married couples. Indeed, the Solicitor General candidly acknowledged that the tax exemptions of some religious institutions would be in question if they opposed same-sex marriage. There is little doubt that these and similar questions will soon be before this Court. Unfortunately, people of faith can take no comfort in the treatment they receive from the majority today.

Perhaps the most discouraging aspect of today's decision is the extent to which the majority feels compelled to sully those on the other side of the debate. The majority offers a cursory assurance that it does not intend to disparage people who, as a matter of conscience, cannot accept same-sex marriage. That disclaimer is hard to square with the very next sentence, in which the majority explains that "the necessary consequence" of laws codifying the traditional definition of marriage is to "demea[n] or stigmatiz[e]" same-sex couples. . . .

* * *

If you are among the many Americans — of whatever sexual orientation — who favor expanding same-sex marriage, by all means celebrate today's decision. Celebrate the achievement of a desired goal. Celebrate the opportunity for a new expression of commitment to a partner. Celebrate the availability of new benefits. But do not celebrate the Constitution. It had nothing to do with it.

I respectfully dissent.

Justice SCALIA, with whom Justice THOMAS joins, dissenting. . . .

[It] is not of special importance to me what the law says about marriage. It is of overwhelming importance, however, who it is that rules me. Today's decree says that my Ruler, and the Ruler of 320 million Americans coast-to-coast, is a majority of the nine lawyers on the Supreme Court. The opinion in these cases is the furthest extension in fact — and the furthest extension one can even imagine — of the Court's claimed power to create "liberties" that the Constitution and its Amendments neglect to mention. This practice of constitutional revision by an unelected committee of nine, always accompanied (as it is today) by extravagant praise of liberty, robs the People of the most important liberty they asserted in the Declaration of Independence and won in the Revolution of 1776: the freedom to govern themselves.

I

Until the courts put a stop to it, public debate over same-sex marriage displayed American democracy at its best. Individuals on both sides of the issue passionately, but respectfully, attempted to persuade their fellow citizens to accept their views. . . .

The Constitution places some constraints on self-rule—constraints adopted *by the People themselves* when they ratified the Constitution and its Amendments. [These]cases ask us to decide whether the Fourteenth Amendment contains a limitation that requires the States to license and recognize marriages between two people of the same sex. Does it remove *that* issue from the political process? Of course not. . . .

[When] the Fourteenth Amendment was ratified in 1868, every State limited marriage to one man and one woman, and no one doubted the constitutionality of doing so. That resolves these cases. . . .

But the Court ends this debate, in an opinion lacking even a thin veneer of law. Buried beneath the mummeries and straining-to-be-memorable passages of the opinion is a candid and startling assertion: No matter *what* it was the People ratified, the Fourteenth Amendment protects those rights that the Judiciary, in its "reasoned judgment," thinks the Fourteenth Amendment ought to protect. . . .

This is a naked judicial claim to legislative—indeed, *super*-legislative—power; a claim fundamentally at odds with our system of government. Except as limited by a constitutional prohibition agreed to by the People, the States are free to adopt whatever laws they like, even those that offend the esteemed Justices' "reasoned judgment." A system of government that makes the People subordinate to a committee of nine unelected lawyers does not deserve to be called a democracy.

Judges are selected precisely for their skill as lawyers; whether they reflect the policy views of a particular constituency is not (or should not be) relevant. Not surprisingly then, the Federal Judiciary is hardly a cross-section of America. Take, for example, this Court, which consists of only nine men and women, all of them successful lawyers who studied at Harvard or Yale Law School. Four of the nine are natives of New York City. Eight of them grew up in east- and west-coast States. Only one hails from the vast expanse in-between. Not a single Southwesterner or even, to tell the truth, a genuine Westerner (California does not count). Not a single evangelical Christian (a group that comprises about one quarter of Americans), or even a Protestant of any denomination. The strikingly unrepresentative character of the body voting on today's social upheaval would be irrelevant if they were functioning as *judges,* answering the legal question whether the American people had ever ratified a constitutional provision that was understood to proscribe the traditional definition of marriage. But of course the Justices in today's majority are not voting on that basis; *they say they are not.* And to allow the policy question of same-sex marriage to be considered and resolved by a select, patrician, highly unrepresentative panel of nine is to violate a principle even more fundamental than no taxation without representation: no social transformation without representation.

II

But what really astounds is the hubris reflected in today's judicial Putsch. The five Justices who compose today's majority are entirely comfortable concluding that every State violated the Constitution for all of the 135 years between the Fourteenth Amendment's ratification and Massachusetts' permitting of same-sex marriages in 2003. They have discovered in the Fourteenth Amendment a "fundamental right" overlooked by every person alive at the time of ratification, and almost everyone else in the time since. They see what lesser legal minds — minds like Thomas Cooley, John Marshall Harlan, Oliver Wendell Holmes, Jr., Learned Hand, Louis Brandeis, William Howard Taft, Benjamin Cardozo, Hugo Black, Felix Frankfurter, Robert Jackson, and Henry Friendly — could not. They are certain that the People ratified the Fourteenth Amendment to bestow on them the power to remove questions from the democratic process when that is called for by their "reasoned judgment." These Justices *know* that limiting marriage to one man and one woman is contrary to reason; they *know* that an institution as old as government itself, and accepted by every nation in history until 15 years ago, cannot possibly be supported by anything other than ignorance or bigotry. And they are willing to say that any citizen who does not agree with that, who adheres to what was, until 15 years ago, the unanimous judgment of all generations and all societies, stands against the Constitution.

The opinion is couched in a style that is as pretentious as its content is egotistic. It is one thing for separate concurring or dissenting opinions to contain extravagances, even silly extravagances, of thought and expression; it is something else for the official opinion of the Court to do so.[22] Of course the opinion's showy profundities are often profoundly incoherent. "The nature of marriage is that,

---

22. If, even as the price to be paid for a fifth vote, I ever joined an opinion for the Court that began: "The Constitution promises liberty to all within its reach, a liberty that includes certain specific rights that allow persons, within a lawful realm, to define and express their identity," I would hide my head in a bag. The Supreme Court of the United States has descended from the disciplined legal reasoning of John Marshall and Joseph Story to the mystical aphorisms of the fortune cookie.

through its enduring bond, two persons together can find other freedoms, such as expression, intimacy, and spirituality." (Really? Who ever thought that intimacy and spirituality [whatever that means] were freedoms? And if intimacy is, one would think Freedom of Intimacy is abridged rather than expanded by marriage. Ask the nearest hippie. Expression, sure enough, *is* a freedom, but anyone in a long-lasting marriage will attest that that happy state constricts, rather than expands, what one can prudently say.) Rights, we are told, can "rise . . . from a better informed understanding of how constitutional imperatives define a liberty that remains urgent in our own era." (Huh? How can a better informed understanding of how constitutional imperatives [whatever that means] define [whatever that means] an urgent liberty [never mind], give birth to a right?) And we are told that, "[i]n any particular case," either the Equal Protection or Due Process Clause "may be thought to capture the essence of [a] right in a more accurate and comprehensive way," than the other, "even as the two Clauses may converge in the identification and definition of the right." (What say? What possible "essence" does substantive due process "capture" in an "accurate and comprehensive way"? It stands for nothing whatever, except those freedoms and entitlements that this Court *really* likes. And the Equal Protection Clause, as employed today, identifies nothing except a difference in treatment that this Court *really* dislikes. Hardly a distillation of essence. If the opinion is correct that the two clauses "converge in the identification and definition of [a] right," that is only because the majority's likes and dislikes are predictably compatible.) I could go on. The world does not expect logic and precision in poetry or inspirational pop-philosophy; it demands them in the law. The stuff contained in today's opinion has to diminish this Court's reputation for clear thinking and sober analysis.

* * *

Hubris is sometimes defined as o'erweening pride; and pride, we know, goeth before a fall. The Judiciary is the "least dangerous" of the federal branches because it has "neither Force nor Will, but merely judgment; and must ultimately depend upon the aid of the executive arm" and the States, "even for the efficacy of its judgments." With each decision of ours that takes from the People a question properly left to them — with each decision that is unabashedly based not on law, but on the "reasoned judgment" of a bare majority of this Court — we move one step closer to being reminded of our impotence.

Justice THOMAS, with whom Justice SCALIA joins, dissenting.

The Court's decision today is at odds not only with the Constitution, but with the principles upon which our Nation was built. Since well before 1787, liberty has been understood as freedom from government action, not entitlement to government benefits. The Framers created our Constitution to preserve that understanding of liberty. Yet the majority invokes our Constitution in the name of a "liberty" that the Framers would not have recognized, to the detriment of the liberty they sought to protect. Along the way, it rejects the idea—captured in our Declaration of Independence—that human dignity is innate and suggests instead that it comes from the Government. This distortion of our Constitution not only ignores the text, it inverts the relationship between the individual and the state in our Republic. I cannot agree with it. . . .

II

Even if the doctrine of substantive due process were somehow defensible—it is not—petitioners still would not have a claim. To invoke the protection of the Due Process Clause at all—whether under a theory of "substantive" or "procedural" due process—a party must first identify a deprivation of "life, liberty, or property." The majority claims these state laws deprive petitioners of "liberty," but the concept of "liberty" it conjures up bears no resemblance to any plausible meaning of that word as it is used in the Due Process Clauses. . . .

Even assuming that the "liberty" in those Clauses encompasses something more than freedom from physical restraint, it would not include the types of rights claimed by the majority. In the American legal tradition, liberty has long been understood as individual freedom *from* governmental action, not as a right *to* a particular governmental entitlement. . . .

B . . .

Petitioners cannot claim, under the most plausible definition of "liberty," that they have been imprisoned or physically restrained by the States for participating in same-sex relationships. To the contrary, they have been able to cohabitate and raise their children in peace. They have been able to hold civil marriage ceremonies in States that recognize same-sex marriages and private religious ceremonies in all States. They have been able to travel freely around the country, making their homes where they please. Far from being incarcerated or physically restrained, petitioners have been left alone to order their lives as they see fit. . . .

III . . .

B

Aside from undermining the political processes that protect our liberty, the majority's decision threatens the religious liberty our Nation has long sought to protect. . . .

In our society, marriage is not simply a governmental institution; it is a religious institution as well. Today's decision might change the former, but it cannot change the latter. It appears all but inevitable that the two will come into conflict, particularly as individuals and churches are confronted with demands to participate in and endorse civil marriages between same-sex couples. . . .

Justice ALITO, with whom Justice SCALIA and Justice THOMAS join, dissenting. . . .

II

Attempting to circumvent the problem presented by the newness of the right found in these cases, the majority claims that the issue is the right to equal treatment. Noting that marriage is a fundamental right, the majority argues that a State has no valid reason for denying that right to same-sex couples. This reasoning is dependent upon a particular understanding of the purpose of civil marriage. Although the Court expresses the point in loftier terms, its argument is that the fundamental purpose of marriage is to promote the well-being of those who choose to marry. Marriage provides emotional fulfillment and the promise of support in times of need. And by benefiting persons who choose to wed, marriage indirectly benefits society because persons who live in stable, fulfilling, and supportive relationships make better citizens. It is for these reasons, the argument goes, that States encourage and formalize marriage, confer special benefits on married persons, and also impose some special obligations. This understanding of the States' reasons for recognizing marriage enables the majority to argue that same-sex marriage serves the States' objectives in the same way as opposite-sex marriage.

This understanding of marriage, which focuses almost entirely on the happiness of persons who choose to marry, is shared by many people today, but it is not the traditional one. For millennia, marriage was inextricably linked to the one thing that only an opposite-sex couple can do: procreate. . . .

If this traditional understanding of the purpose of marriage does not ring true to all ears today, that is probably because the tie between marriage and procreation has frayed. Today, for instance, more than 40% of all children in this country are born to unmarried women. This development undoubtedly is both a cause and a result of changes in our society's understanding of marriage.

While, for many, the attributes of marriage in 21st-century America have changed, those States that do not want to recognize same-sex marriage have not yet given up on the traditional understanding. They worry that by officially abandoning the older understanding, they may contribute to marriage's further decay. It is far beyond the outer reaches of this Court's authority to say that a State may not adhere to the understanding of marriage that has long prevailed, not just in this country and others with similar cultural roots, but also in a great variety of countries and cultures all around the globe. . . .

III . . .

[Today's decision] will be used to vilify Americans who are unwilling to assent to the new orthodoxy. In the course of its opinion, the majority compares traditional marriage laws to laws that denied equal treatment for African–Americans and women. The implications of this analogy will be exploited by those who are determined to stamp out every vestige of dissent.

Perhaps recognizing how its reasoning may be used, the majority attempts, toward the end of its opinion, to reassure those who oppose same-sex marriage that their rights of conscience will be protected. We will soon see whether this proves to be true. I assume that those who cling to old beliefs will be able to whisper their thoughts in the recesses of their homes, but if they repeat those views in public, they will risk being labeled as bigots and treated as such by governments, employers, and schools.

The system of federalism established by our Constitution provides a way for people with different beliefs to live together in a single nation. If the issue of same-sex marriage had been left to the people of the States, it is likely that some States would recognize same-sex marriage and others would not. It is also possible that some States would tie recognition to protection for conscience rights. The majority today makes that impossible. By imposing its own views on the entire country, the majority facilitates the marginalization of the many Americans who have traditional ideas. Recalling the harsh treatment of gays and lesbians in the past, some may think that turnabout is fair play. But if that sentiment prevails, the Nation will experience bitter and lasting wounds.

Today's decision will also have a fundamental effect on this Court and its ability to uphold the rule of law. If a bare majority of Justices can invent a new right and impose that right on the rest of the country, the only real limit on what future majorities will be able to do is their own sense of what those with political power and cultural influence are willing to tolerate. Even enthusiastic supporters of same-sex marriage should worry about the scope of the power that today's majority claims.

Today's decision shows that decades of attempts to restrain this Court's abuse of its authority have failed. A lesson that some will take from today's decision is that preaching about the proper method of interpreting the Constitution or the virtues of judicial self-restraint and humility cannot compete with the temptation to achieve what is viewed as a noble end by any practicable means. I do not doubt that my colleagues in the majority sincerely see in the Constitution a vision of liberty that happens to coincide with their own. But this sincerity is cause for concern, not comfort. What it evidences is the deep and perhaps irremediable corruption of our legal culture's conception of constitutional interpretation.

Most Americans—understandably—will cheer or lament today's decision because of their views on the issue of same-sex marriage. But all Americans, whatever their thinking on that issue, should worry about what the majority's claim of power portends.

G.   Procedural Due Process

Page 961.   Before section 2 of the Note, add the following:

   e. *Marital cohabitation.* In Kerry v. Din, 135 S. Ct. 2128 (2015), petitioner,
a United States citizen, challenged the refusal of the United States to grant an
immigrant visa to her husband, a resident of Afghanistan. Under the applicable
statute, a citizen may seek to have a noncitizen classified as an immediate relative.
If the noncitizen is so classified, he may apply for a visa, but the visa cannot be
granted if the statute makes him ineligible. The government classified petitioner's
husband as an immediate relative, but then found him ineligible under a section of
the statute that prohibited the granting of visas to individuals who had engaged in
"terrorist activities." Petitioner then filed suit, claiming that she had been deprived
of liberty without due process of law. She claimed a liberty interest in living
with her husband in the United States, and asserted that due process was denied
with respect to that interest because the government failed to provide her with a
further explanation of the denial. The Court of Appeals ruled in her favor, but the
Supreme Court, in a 5-to-4 decision, reversed.
   No single opinion gained majority support. Announcing the judgment of the
Court, but writing only for himself, Chief Justice Roberts, and Justice Alito,
Justice Scalia found that petitioner had failed to identify a constitutionally protected liberty interest. He began his analysis by noting that the due process
clause "had its origin in Magna Carta," and that Edward Coke, writing at the
close of the eighteenth century, had interpreted Magna Carta liberty protections
to include guarantees like the right not to be subject to imprisonment, exile,
or torture except under the law of the land. "[Petitioner] of course, could not
conceivably claim that the denial of [her husband's] visa application deprived
her—or for that matter even [her husband] – of life or property; and under the
above described historical understanding, a claim that it deprived her of liberty
is equally absurd."
   Justice Scalia acknowledged that "the Court has seen fit on several occasions to
expand the meaning of 'liberty' under the Due Process Clause to include certain
implied 'fundamental rights.' (The reasoning presumably goes like this: If you
have a right to do something, you are free to do it, and deprivation of freedom is
a deprivation of 'liberty'—never mind the original meaning of that word in the
Due Process Clause.)" These rights, Justice Scalia explained, were protected by
substantive due process and could not be denied at all even if procedural protections were provided. But even if one were to accept "the textually unsupportable
doctrine of implied fundamental rights," petitioner's argument would fail.

[Before] conferring constitutional status upon previously unrecognized "liberty," we have required "a careful description of the asserted fundamental liberty interest," as well as a demonstration that the interest is "objectively, deeply rooted in this Nation's history and tradition, and implicit in the concept of ordered liberty." [citing Washington v. Glucksberg, Page 944 of the Main Volume].

Petitioner relied upon her liberty interest in marriage or in being free from arbitrary restrictions on the right to live with a spouse.

To be sure, this Court has at times indulged a propensity for grandiloquence when reviewing the sweep of implied rights, describing them so broadly that they would include not only the interests [petitioner] asserts but many others as well. [Citing Meyer v. Nebraska, P. 841 of the Main Volume]. But this Court is not bound by dicta, especially dicta that have been repudiated by the holdings of our subsequent cases. And the actual holdings of the cases [petitioner] relies upon hardly establish the capacious right she now asserts. . . .

Nothing in the cases [petitioner] cites establishes a free-floating and categorical liberty interest in marriage (or any other formulation [petitioner] offers) sufficient to trigger constitutional protection whenever a regulation in any way touches an aspect of the marital relationship. Even if our cases could be construed so broadly, the relevant question is not whether the asserted interest "is consistent with this Court's substantive-due-process line of cases," but whether it is supported by "this Nation's history and practice."

Justice Scalia also rejected the assertion that there were procedural due process rights that attached to nonfundamental liberty interests. He characterized this notion as a "dangerous doctrine" that "vastly expands the scope of our implied-rights jurisprudence by setting it free from the requirement that the liberty interest be 'objectively, deeply rooted in this Nation's history and tradition, and implicit in the concept of ordered liberty.'"

Because Justice Scalia found no liberty interest, he thought that it was unnecessary to decide whether the process afforded petitioner would have been adequate if there had been a liberty interest.

Justice Kennedy, in an opinion joined by Justice Alito, concurred in the judgment. He would have found that even if petitioner had identified a protected liberty interest, the process afforded her was sufficient to satisfy the due process clause. (This aspect of the case is discussed at the supplement to Page 968 of the Main Volume).

Justice Breyer, joined by Justices Ginsburg, Sotomayor, and Kagan, wrote a dissenting opinion:

> Our cases make clear that the Due Process Clause entitles [petitioner] to [procedural] rights as long as (1) she seeks protection for a liberty interest sufficiently important for procedural protection to flow "implicit[ly]" from the design, object, and nature of the Due Process Clause, or (2) nonconstitutional law (a statute, for example) creates "an expectation" that a person will not be deprived of that kind of liberty without fair procedures.
>
> The liberty for which [petitioner] seeks protection easily satisfies both standards. As this Court has long recognized, the institution of marriage, which encompasses the right of spouses to live together and to raise a family, is central to human life, requires and enjoys community support, and plays a central role in most individuals' "orderly pursuit of happiness." . . .
>
> At the same time, the law, including visa law, surrounds marriage with a host of legal protections to the point that it creates a strong expectation that government will not deprive married individuals of their freedom to live together without strong reasons and (in individual cases) without fair procedure.

Page 968. Before section 2 of the Note, add the following:

Compare Turner to Kerry v. Din, 135 S. Ct. 2128 (2015). Petitioner was a resident United States citizen. Her husband, a noncitizen, was denied a visa to enter the United States on the ground that he had engaged in "terrorist activities." The government refused to provide any additional information to support the denial. The Supreme Court rejected Petitioner's claim that this refusal denied her right to procedural due process, but no opinion gained majority support. Justice Scalia, in an opinion announcing the judgment of the Court and joined by Chief Justice Roberts and Justice Thomas, asserted that petitioner had failed to allege that a constitutionally protected liberty interest had been infringed. (This portion of the opinion is discussed at the supplement to Page 961 of the Main Volume). Justice Kennedy, in an opinion joined by Justice Alito, assumed arguendo that a liberty interest was implicated, but asserted that petitioner had received all the process that was due. He based this conclusion on "due consideration of the congressional power to make rules for the exclusion of aliens, and the ensuing power to delegate authority to the Attorney General to exercise substantial discretion in that field."

> Absent an affirmative showing of bad faith on the part of the consular officer who denied [petitioner's husband] a visa—which [petitioner] has

not plausibly alleged with sufficient particularity—[we should not] "look behind" the government's exclusion of [petitioner's husband] for additional factual details beyond what its express reliance on [the statute excluding those engaged in terrorist activity] encompasses. . . .

The government, furthermore, was not required [to] point to a more specific provision within [the statute even though] the statutory provision the consular officer cited covers a broad range of conduct. . . .

Congress evaluated the benefits and burdens of notice in this sensitive area and assigned discretion to the Executive to decide when more detailed disclosure is appropriate. This considered judgment gives additional support to the independent conclusion that the notice given was constitutionally adequate, particularly in light of the national security concerns that the terrorism bar addresses.

Justice Breyer, in an opinion joined by Justices Ginsburg, Sotomayor, and Kagan, dissented. He concluded that, at a minimum, the petitioner was entitled to "a statement of reasons, some kind of explanation, as to why the State Department denied her husband a visa."

[A] statement of reasons, even one provided after a visa denial, serves much the same function as a "notice" of a proposed action. It allows [petitioner], who suffered a "serious loss," a fair "opportunity to meet" "the case" that has produced separation from her husband. . . .

I recognize that our due process cases often determine the constitutional insistence upon a particular procedure by balancing, with respect to that procedure, the "private interest" at stake, "the risk of an erroneous deprivation" absent the sought-after protection, and the Government's interest in not providing additional procedure. Here "balancing" would not change the result. The "private interest" is important, the risk of an "erroneous deprivation" is significant, and the Government's interest in not providing a reason is normally small, at least administratively speaking.

H.   The Contracts and Takings Clauses

Page 1003.   At the end of section 3 of the Note, add the following:

Compare Arkansas Game & Fish Commission v. United States, 133 S. Ct. 511 (2012). The Commission owned a wildlife management area along the banks of the Black River, and regularly harvested timber in the reserve as part of its forest management efforts. One hundred fifteen miles upstream from the management area is the Clearwater Dam (the Dam), constructed by the United States Corps of Engineers in 1948. Shortly after constructing the Dam, the Corps adopted a Water Control Manual, which determined the rates at which water would be released from the Dam. In 1993, the Corps approved a planned deviation from the release rate in response to requests from farmers to provide for a longer harvest period. To reduce accumulation of water in the lake behind the Dam, the Corps extended the period in which a high amount of water would be released, resulting in flooding in the management area above historical norms. The flooding resulted in the destruction of timber in the management area and necessitated costly reclamation measures. Had the Corps released the water at a lower rate, the farmers would have had a shorter harvest season, but the timber would not have been damaged. The Court, in a unanimous decision written by Justice Ginsburg, held that government-induced flooding can amount to a taking even if it is temporary in duration.

If the Corps had not released the water, the farmers would have had a shorter harvest season. Why wouldn't this have been a taking? Suppose that the management area would have been flooded if the Dam had not been built in the first place. Would release of the extra water still be a taking? Would the result be different if the Corps built the Dam but then tore it down? If the initial Water Control Manual had provided for release of water at the higher rate?

For an argument that the takings clause might make the government liable for regulatory inaction and that therefore "property owners could be constitutionally entitled either to governmental intervention on their behalf or to compensation if the government fails to act," see Serkin, Passive Takings: The State's Affirmative Duty to Protect Property, 113 Mich. L. Rev. 345 (2014). For a more general discussion of constitutional problems posed by government nonfeasance, see Chapter 9 of the Main Volume.

Page 1007.   Before section f of the Note, add the following:

The Court relied on *Loretto* in Horne v. Dept. of Agriculture, 135 S. Ct. 1039 (2015) to invalidate a marketing order issued by the Department of Agriculture that required raisin growers to physically set aside a certain percentage of their crops for the government to dispose of in a way best suited to maintaining an orderly market. The order, issued under the Agricultural Marketing Agreement Act of 1937, gave the Raisin Administrative Committee, a government entity composed largely of growers appointed by the Secretary of Agriculture, the authority to determine the allocation. The Committee then disposed of the raisins, with raisin growers retaining an interest in any net proceeds from sales after deductions for export subsidies and the Committee's administrative expenses.

Petitioners refused to set aside raisins for the government, whereupon the government assessed a fine against them. Petitioners claimed that the assessment constituted a per se taking under *Loretto*. In an 8-to-1 decision, the Court, per Chief Justice Roberts, agreed. The Court began its analysis by holding that the per se rule applied to the taking of personal, as well as real property. Although the Court had previously noted that *regulation* of personal property might make the property economically useless without constituting a taking, the same rule did not apply to the sort of direct appropriation that occurred in this case. Here, the actual raisins were transferred from the growers to the government and the growers lost "the entire 'bundle' of property rights in the appropriated raisins."

> The Government thinks it "strange" and the dissent "baffling" that the Hornes object to the reserve requirement, when they nonetheless concede that "the government may prohibit sale of raisins without effecting a per se taking." But that distinction flows naturally from the settled difference in our takings jurisprudene between appropriation and regulation. A physical taking of raisins and a regulatory limit on production may have the same economic impact on a grower. The Constitution, however, is concerned with means as well as ends.

This conclusion was not affected by the fact that the Government reserved to the growers a contingent interest in a portion of the value of the property. "[Once] there is a taking, as in the case of a physical appropriation, any payment from the Government in connection with that action goes, at most, to the question of just compensation."

The Court also concluded that the requirement that growers relinquish some of the raisins could not be justified as a condition on permission to sell the remaining raisins in interstate commerce. (This portion of the opinion is discussed in the supplement to Page 1011 of the Main Volume.)

Finally, the Court rejected the government's contention that the amount of compensation due should be reduced by the increased value of the raisins petitioner was able to sell due to the price support and other benefits from the regulatory program. (This portion of the opinion is discussed in the Supplement to Page 1013 of the Main Volume)

Justice Thomas wrote a brief concurring opinion.

Justice Breyer, joined by Justices Ginsburg and Kagan, wrote an opinion concurring in part and dissenting in part, arguing that the case should be remanded for a determination of whether any compensation was due given the benefits Petitioner received because of the regulatory program. (This portion of the opinion is discussed in the Supplement to Page 1013 of the Main Volume).

Justice Sotomayor wrote a dissenting opinion. She argued that the per se *Loretto* rule applied "if and only if each of the [petitioners] property rights in the portion of raisins that the Order designated as reserve has been destroyed." Here, petitioners "retain at least one meaningful property interest in the reserve raisins; the right to receive some money for their disposition." Moreover, according to Justice Sotomayor,

> The Court's focus on the physical nature of the intrusion [suggests] that merely arranging for the sale of the reserve raisins would not be a *per se* taking. The rub for the Court must therefore be not that the Government is doing these things, but that it is accomplishing them by the altogether understandable requirement that the reserve raisins be physically set aside. I know of no principle, however, providing that if the Government achieves a permissible regulatory end by asking regulated individuals or entities to physically move the property subject to the regulation, it has committed a *per se* taking rather than a potentially regulatory taking. . . .
>
> [What] makes the Court's twisting of the doctrine even more baffling is that it ultimately instructs the Government that it can permissibly achieve its market control goals by imposing a quota without offering raisin producers a way of reaping any return whatsoever on the raisins they cannot sell. I have trouble understanding why anyone would prefer that.

Page 1011. At the end of section 1 of the Note, add the following:

Compare Koontz v. St. Johns River Water Management District, 133 S. Ct. 2586 (2013). Petitioner owned a parcel of land that required state permits in order to develop. Petitioner suggested certain limitations on the development to mitigate the environmental damage, but the state Water Management District found these insufficient. Instead, the District proposed that petitioner either take further measures to mitigate the damage on his own property or that he hire contractors to make improvements on other property owned by the District. Petitioner refused to take these measures, and the District denied petitioner's application. Relying upon *Nollan,* Petitioner then filed suit in state court, but the Florida Supreme Court held that *Nollan* was distinguishable because there the state had approved an application on the condition that the land owner acceded to the state's demands, whereas here, the state had denied the application because he refused to make the concessions.

The United States Supreme Court, in a five-to-four decision, rejected this distinction and reversed the judgment below. Writing for the Court, Justice Alito stated that the principles undergirding *Nollan* "do not change depending on whether the government *approves* a permit on the condition that the applicant turn over property or *denies* a permit because the applicant refuses to do so. We have often concluded that denials of governmental benefits were impermissible under the unconstitutional conditions doctrine."

Neither party disputed the proposition that the District could have simply refused to grant the permit. How was petitioner made worse off by the District's suggestion of actions petitioner could take that would lead it to grant the permit? Consider in this regard Justice Alito's observation that "land-use permit applicants are especially vulnerable to the type of coercion that the unconstitutional conditions doctrine prohibits because the government often has broad discretion to deny a permit that is worth far more than property it would like to take." Compare the following observations in Justice Kagan's dissenting opinion:

> Consider the matter from the standpoint of the District's lawyer. The District, she learns, has found that [petitioner's] permit applications do not satisfy legal requirements. It can deny the permits on that basis; or it can suggest ways for [petitioner] to bring his application into compliance. If every suggestion could become the subject of a lawsuit under *Nollan,* [the] lawyer can give but one recommendation: Deny the permits without giving [petitioner] any advice — even if he asks for guidance. [Nothing] in the Takings Clause requires that folly.

In Horne v. Department of Agriculture, 135 S. Ct. 1039 (2015), the Court rejected the argument that the government's taking of raisins from private producers as part of a program designed to regulate the raisin market could be justified as a condition on permission granted to the raisin owners to sell their product in interstate markets. The government relied on *Monsanto* (discussed at pp 1009-10 of the Main Volume), where the Court held that the Environmental Protection Agency could require companies manufacturing pesticides to disclose health and safety information as a condition to receiving a permit to sell their products. The *Monsanto* Court held that the even though the manufacturers had a property interest in these trade secrets, the disclosure was not a taking because the manufacturers received a "valuable Government benefit" in exchange — viz., permission to sell the chemicals. The *Horne* Court rejected this analogy:

> Selling produce in interstate commerce, although certainly subject to reasonable government regulation, is [not] a special governmental benefit that the Government may hold hostage, to be ransomed by the waiver of constitutional protection. Raisins are not dangerous pesticides; they are a healthy snack.

Justice Sotomayor wrote an opinion dissenting on this and other points. (*Horne* is discussed in greater detail in the supplement to Page 1007 of the Main Volume.)

Page 1011.   At the end of section 2 of the Note, add the following:

Suppose instead of demanding a property interest to which it was otherwise not entitled, the state simply demands cash in return for a permit application. As noted above, in Koontz v. St. Johns River Water Management District, 133 S. Ct. 2586 (2013), the District offered to allow petitioner to proceed with development if petitioner paid for improvements on a different parcel owned by the District. The Florida Supreme Court held that this situation was not governed by *Nollan* and *Dolan* because the requirement of a monetary payment did not constitute a "taking."

In his opinion for a five-to-four majority, Justice Alito rejected this reasoning: "[If] we accepted this argument it would be very easy for land-use permitting officials to evade the limitations of *Nollan* and *Dolan*. Because the government need only provide a permit applicant with one alternative that satisfies the nexus and rough proportionality standards, a permitting authority wishing to exact an easement could simply give the owner a choice of either surrendering an easement or making a payment equal to the easement's value."

The Court recognized that the takings clause does not apply to government-imposed financial obligations that do not operate upon or alter an identified property interest. Here, however, it found that the demand for money did operate upon such an interest "by directing the owner of a particular piece of property to make a monetary payment." The monetary obligation therefore "burdened petitioner's ownership of a specific parcel of land."

The Court acknowledged that neither a requirement that petitioner pay money to the state when not associated with a permit application nor the outright denial of a permit application would constitute a taking. How, then, can putting petitioner to a choice between these two options be a taking? Compare Rumsfeld v. FAIR, 547 U.S. 47 (2006), discussed in the main volume at page 1417. A federal statute provided that if a university denied access to military recruiters, it would lose access to federal funds. The Court, in a unanimous opinion written by Chief Justice Roberts, upheld the amendment on the ground that universities did not have a constitutional right either to the federal funds or to exclude the military. Are *Rumsfeld* and *Koontz* consistent?

Page 1013.   At the end of section 4 of the Note, add the following:

Compare Arkansas Game & Fish Commission v. United States, 133 S. Ct. 511 (2012), where the Court, in a unanimous decision by Justice Ginsburg, held that government action producing temporary flooding of property can constitute a compensable taking. Although the Court held that there was "no automatic exemption from Takings Clause inspection," it also noted that whether there was in fact a taking depended on factors like the length of time that the area was flooded, the degree to which the invasion was intended or foreseeable, the character of the land, and the owner's reasonable investment-backed expectations regarding the land's use.

In Horne v. Department of Agriculture, 135 S. Ct. 1039 (2015), the Court held that the government could not reduce the compensation due to growers whose product the government had taken by the value of the regulatory program to the growers.

> [The] Government cites no support for [its] notion that general regulatory activity [can] constitute just compensation for a specific physical taking. Instead, our cases have set forth a clear and administrable rule for just compensation: "The Court has repeatedly held that just compensation normally is to be measured by 'the market value of the property at the time of the taking.'"

The Court distinguished cases "where the condemning authority may deduct special benefits — such as new access to a waterway or highway, or filling if of swampland — for the amount of compensation it seeks to pay a landowner suffering a partial taking. [Cases] of that sort can raise complicated questions involving the exercise of the eminent domain power, but they do not create a generally applicable exception to the usual compensation rule, based on asserted regulatory benefits of the sort at issue here."

In an opinion concurring in part and dissenting in part, Justice Breyer, joined by Justices Ginsburg and Kagan, disagreed:

> When the Government takes [a] percentage of the annual crop, the raisin owners retain the remaining [raisins]. The reserve requirement is intended [to] enhance the price that [the remaining] raisins will fetch on the open market. And any such enhancement matters. The Court's precedents indicate that, when calculating [just compensation] a court should deduct from the value of the taken [raisins] any enhancement caused by the taking to the value of the remaining [raisins].

(*Horne* is discussed in greater detail in the supplement to Page 1007 of the Main Volume).

VII
FREEDOM OF EXPRESSION

A. Introduction

Page 1035.   After section d of the Note, add the following:

e. R. Collins & D. Skover, On Dissent: Its Meaning in America 103, 115-116 (2013):

[The First Amendment] safeguards the speech of those who refute our creeds, reject our values, renounce our government, and even repudiate our very way of life. This uniquely American principle of free speech provides a haven for irritating ranters and irksome rogues who feel the need to spoil our parade. In short, it protects the voice of the other. [In] one way or the other, the idea of dissent finds followers in every ideological camp. [As] Benjamin Franklin observed, "[i]t is the first responsibility of every citizen to question authority." [The] First Amendment sometimes converts illegal action into lawful action; it transforms what was seen as anarchy into what may be viewed as democratic engagement; and it reconfigures the relationship between society and its critics.

f. Post, *Participatory Democracy and Free Speech*, 97 Va. L. Rev. 477, 482-483, 486 (2011):

[T]he best possible explanation of the shape of First Amendment doctrine is the value of democratic governance. [Democracy] refers to a certain relationship between persons and their government. Democracy is achieved when those who are subject to law believe that they are also potential authors of law. [The] value of democratic legitimation occurs [through] processes of communication in the public sphere. [The] function of public discourse is to enable persons to experience the value of self-government. [Public] discourse includes all communicative processes deemed necessary for the formation of public opinion.

Consider Volokh, *The Trouble with "Public Discourse" as a Limitation on Free Speech Rights*, 97 Va. L. Rev. 567 (2011): "If 'the speech by which public opinion is formed' is especially protected and other speech lacks full protection, then we need to define this category's boundaries with some precision. Yet both the phrase and the label 'public discourse' [are] inadequate to the task." Do the following constitute "public discourse": (1) a conversation between two friends over a beer about politics; (2) an exhibition of 19th century French art; (3) a teacher's out-of-class discussion of contraceptive use with junior high school students; (d) publication of a trade secret?

g. M. Redish, The Adversary First Amendment 1-5 (2013):

> Those free speech theorists who have shaped democratic theories of free expression have almost universally viewed democracy [as] a cooperative pursuit in which individuals collectively "plan for the general welfare" or "forge a common will." [A better understanding of democracy for First Amendment purposes] adopts a notion of representative governance built on the concept of adversary democracy. [Based] on the premise that democracy at its core involves a competition among adverse interests, [the deeper purpose of democracy should be understood] to guarantee individuals the opportunity to seek to affect the outcomes of collective decision making according to their own values and interests as they understand them. [A] valid democratic theory of the First Amendment must [therefore] be construed to reach all speech that allows individuals to discover their personal needs, interests, and goals – in government and in society at large – and to advocate and vote accordingly.

Contrast this understanding of the First Amendment with those of Mieklejohn and Post in terms of the following question: Does the First Amendment protect commercial advertisements for toothpaste?

Page 1037.   Before section 5 of the Note, add the following:

d. *Free speech and conservative libertarianism.* For an argument that much of modern free speech doctrine grows out of libertarian conceptions that also support expansion of property and gun rights and opposition to redistributive legislation, see Heyman, The Conservative-Libertarian Turn in First Amendment Jurisprudence, 117 W. Va. L. Rev. 231 (2014). *See also* Seidman, The Dale Problem: Property and Speech under the Regulatory State, 75 U. Chi. L. Rev. 1541 (2008).

B.   Content-Based Restrictions: Dangerous Ideas and Information

Page 1052.   At the end of section 2 of the Note, add the following:

T. Healy, The Great Dissent: How Oliver Wendell Holmes Changed His Mind—and Changed the History of Free Speech in America 201, 343 (2013), provides a full account of Holmes's transformation. It began with a chance encounter with Learned Hand on a train in the summer of 1919. In the following months, Holmes came "under considerable pressure to rethink" his position. His opinions in *Schenck, Frohwerk,* and *Debs* were "attacked in the pages of the New Republic" by University of Chicago law professor Ernst Freund and in "the Harvard Law Review, challenged in correspondence with Learned Hand, confronted over tea by [Harvard law professor] Zechariah Chafee." The political theorist Harold Laski "fed him one book after another espousing a liberal view of free speech," and a young Felix Frankfurter "tried to arrange for him to write a piece on tolerance in the Atlantic Monthly." Although initially resistant to the criticism, Holmes came around. In 1922, Holmes confessed in a letter to Chafee that before the summer of 1919, when it came to issues of free speech and tolerance, "I was simply ignorant."

Page 1053.   After section 5 of the Note, add the following:

5a. *"Sentences of twenty years imprisonment."* Holmes is clearly appalled that the defendants in *Abrams* were sentenced to terms "of twenty years imprisonment." He implies that the only plausible explanation for such severe punishment is that the defendants were being "made to suffer" not for any actual harm they might have caused to the nation (which he regards as trivial), but because of the government's hostility to their ideas (which he regards as impermissible). Suppose, then, that the defendants had been sentenced to a fine of $100 instead of to twenty years in prison. Should that have changed Holmes's analysis or the result? Should the nature or severity of the penalty be relevant to the constitutionality of a restriction of speech? See Coenen, Of Speech and Sanctions: Toward a Penalty-Sensitive Approach to the First Amendment, 112 Colum. L. Rev. 991 (2012).

Page 1061.   In section 2 of the Note, after the quote from Strauss, add the following:

For the proposition that in some circumstances more speech does not help to correct falsehoods, but only adds to polarization, see Glaeser & Sunstein, Does More Speech Correct Falsehoods?, 43 J. Leg. Stud. 65 (2014).

Page 1070.   After the long quotation from the opinion in *Yates*, add the following:

Harlan's opinion in *Yates* was greeted with puzzlement. One newspaper at the time characterized it as "a masterpiece of hair-splitting" and scholars characterized it as "complex, scholarly, and painfully dull" and as "a sort of *Finnegan's Wake* of impossibly nice distinctions." Nonetheless, "the Justice Department, faced with *Yates*'s insistence upon proof of advocacy to '*do* something, now or in the future, rather than merely to *believe* in something,' soon admitted that 'we cannot satisfy the evidentiary requirements laid down by the Supreme Court' and dismissed" all remaining Smith Act conspiracy cases then pending. R. Lichtman, The Supreme Court and McCarthy Era Repression: One Hundred Decisions 95-96 (2012).

Page 1078.   Before the Note, add the following:

Consider Tarkington, A First Amendment Theory for Protecting Attorney Speech, 45 U.C. Davis L. Rev. 27, 79 (2011):

> The "material support" statute in *Humanitarian Law Project* not only *frustrates* the attorney-client relationship [but] in fact *criminalizes* [it] and imputes culpability for the client's unlawful conduct onto the advising attorney. As with Red Scare statutes aimed at eradicating communism, the "material support" statute, as applied to the plaintiffs, can be said to "quite literally establish[ ] guilt by association alone" because it criminalizes association even if the associating attorney "disagree[s] with th[e] unlawful aims of the [organization]."

Consider also L. Tribe & J. Matz, Uncertain Justice: The Roberts Court and the Constitution 131 (2014): "As the landmark Roberts Court case about free speech in wartime, HLP sends a clear signal: judges must defer, and then defer again, to government when it seeks to justify bans on speech. So long as the 'informed judgment' of the government, some fact-finding on the general subject, and abstract reasoning all support the censorship as a tool against terrorism, it may well survive review. [As] as result, HLP will likely marginalize the Judiciary in protecting free speech in the national security field for many years to come."

Page 1083.   After section 9 of the Note, add the following:

10. *The first amendment rights of government licensees.* To what extent can the government constitutionally regulate the speech of doctors, lawyers, psychologists, and other licensed professionals? In what circumstances, for example, can the government discipline a doctor for recommending sexual-orientation conversion therapy to gay patients? In what circumstances can the government compel a doctor to counsel her patients against abortion? For discussion of these issues, see Haupt, Professional Speech, 125 Yale L. J. 1238 (2016); Zick, Professional Rights Speech, 47 Ariz. St. L.J. 1289 (2015).

Page 1100.   At the end of *Snyder v. Phelps,* add the following:

Suppose a gay teenager dies in a car accident and the members of the Westboro Baptist Church picket his funeral. Suppose further that their speech is directed specifically at the parents of the boy, rather than at the general public. Their signs charge that the son died because he was gay, condemn the parents for failing to "correct" their son's homosexuality, and blame them for his death. Would the case be any different? See Heyman, To Drink the Cup of Fury: Funeral Picketing, Public Discourse, and the First Amendment, 45 Conn. L. Rev. 101 (2012). In the years since *Snyder,* many states have enacted "buffer-zone" laws that prohibit any picketing within a certain distance of a funeral within a certain time before and after the funeral. Are such laws constitutional? See Heyman, supra, at 164-172.

Page 1112.   At the end of section 7 of the Note, add the following:

7a. *Snowden.* If Edward Snowden returns to the United States, could he be prosecuted and convicted, consistent with the First Amendment, for disclosing to journalists and thus to the world massive amounts of classified information about previously secret NSA surveillance programs? Consider the following positions:

a. Snowden accepted a position of trust in his relation to the government. He did not have to accept his job, but he did. A clear condition of that job was his voluntary agreement not to disclose any *classified* information. That agreement is binding. Period.

b. An individual government employee should never have the authority, on his own say, to override the judgments of the elected representatives of the American people and to decide for the nation that classified information should be disclosed to friends and foes alike. The question is *who* gets to decide when classified information should be made public. It should not be any Tom, Dick and Harry government employee or private contractor with a security clearance who thinks he knows better than the President, the Congress, and the courts about how best to protect the nation's security.

c. Suppose the disclosure of the previously secret programs renders them ineffective in the future, thus seriously damaging the nation's ability to ferret out possible terrorist plots. Should Snowden nonetheless have a First Amendment defense if, upon learning about the previously secret programs, the public opposes them as a matter of policy? If the programs are found to have been illegal? If some of the programs he disclosed were illegal and others were legal?

d. Does your view on any of these positions change if the prosecution is directed against the newspaper publishing Snowden's revelations rather than against Snowden himself?

e. Should Snowden's intent matter? Suppose he intended to aid the enemy? He intended to promote democratic review of secret decisions? He thought the disclosures wouldn't be harmful, but they were? For an analysis of the intent question, see Papandrea, National Security Information Disclosures and the Role of Intent, 56 Wm. & M. L. Rev. 1381 (2015).

In Posen, The Leaky Leviathan: Why the Government Condemns and Condones Unlawful Disclosures of Information, 127 Harv. L. Rev. 512, 515 (2013) the author argues that

[most] components of the executive branch have never prioritized criminal, civil, or administrative enforcement against leakers; that a nuanced set of informal social controls has come to supplement, and nearly supplant, the formal disciplinary scheme; that much of what we call leaking occurs in a gray area between full authorization and no [authorization]; that the executive's toleration of these disclosures is a rational, power-enhancing strategy and not simply a product of prosecutorial limitations, a feature, not a bug, of the system; and that to untangle these dynamics is to illuminate important facets of presidential power, bureaucratic governance, and the national security state in America today.

If this analysis is correct, does the occasional criminal prosecution of selected leakers pose a constitutional problem?

For an historical analysis of government secrecy and an argument that "by seeking to keep secret so much for so long, the secrecy system cheapens and undermines our vital secrets," see F. Schwarz, Jr., Democracy in the Dark: The Seduction of Government Secrecy (2015). *See also* H. Kitrosser, Reclaiming Accountability: Transparency, Executive Power, and the U.S. Constitution (2015) (tying excessive secrecy to constitutional theories that defend broad executive power).

Page 1112.   After section 8 of the Note, add the following:

9. *Facts and the First Amendment.* Note that in many cases the government is attempting to restrict the dissemination of facts rather than opinions. The seminal conception of the First Amendment was about the "marketplace of ideas." How do facts fit into this marketplace? Should government efforts to restrict the dissemination of facts be treated the same way as government efforts to restrict the dissemination of ideas? In addition to the cases in this section, consider also the following: (a) an anti-abortion group publishes on its website the names and addresses of abortion providers; (b) a newspaper publishes the name of a rape victim; (c) a reporter discloses the names of covert American agents in Iran. See Bhagwat, Details: Specific Facts and the First Amendment, 86 S. Cal. L. Rev. 1 (2012).

D.   Content-Based Restrictions: "Low" Value

Page 1135.   Before the first full paragraph on the page, add the following:

Consider Lakier, The Invention of Low-Value Speech, 128 Harv. L. Rev. 2166 (2015):

> [The] doctrine of low-value speech allows the government to do what it is not supposed to be able to do: That is, it allows the government to remove ideas it dislikes from public [circulation]. . . .
>
> By emphasizing the historical basis of the low-value categories, the Court has attempted to depict the distinction between high and law-value speech as the product of something other than the perhaps idiosyncratic value judgments and preferences of its individual members. . . .

There is little historical evidence, however, to back up the Court's claim that the categories of low-value speech we recognize [today] constituted, in the eighteenth and nineteenth centuries, well-defined and narrowly limited exceptions to the ordinary constitutional rule. . . .

[Eighteenth] and nineteenth century courts applied the same constitutional principles to the regulation of high-value speech as they applied to the regulation of low-value speech. The general rule [was] that speech—no matter how valuable it might be—could be sanctioned criminally whenever it threatened [to] "disturb the public peace or . . . subvert the government." But almost no speech or writing could be enjoined in advance without violating the constitutional prohibition against prior [restraints]. . . .

By forcing courts to determine the constitutional value of speech by means of a historical test that does not illuminate original understandings of what speech is worth protecting, the [low-value speech doctrine] threatens to create a set of doctrinal distinctions that rest either on hidden value-judgments [or] are the product of factors that are constitutionally irrelevant.

Page 1142.   Before section 5 of the Note, add the following:

e. Kendrick, Speech, Intent, and the Chilling Effect, 54 Wm. & Mary L. Rev. 1633 (2013):

The chilling-effect account holds some appeal. [But] there are reasons to doubt [it]. An argument based on the chilling effect necessarily rests on suppositions about the deterrent effects of law. These suppositions in turn rest upon predictions about the behavior of speakers under counterfactual conditions. Meanwhile, the selection of a remedy, such as an intent requirement, rests on similar predictions about the remedy's speech-protective effects. In short, both the detection of a problem and the imposition of a remedy rest upon intractable empirical suppositions. [In fact], the chilling effect provides at best a weak justification for existing intent requirements in First Amendment law. [Although] at first blush these requirements might seem acceptable as a matter of rough empirical surmise, in reality they often fail to persuade.

Page 1149.   At the end of section c of the Note, add the following:

Ashdown, Distorting Democracy: Campaign Lies in the 21st Century, 20 Wm. & Mary Bill Rts. J. 1085 (2012).

Page 1153.   Before *Hustler*, add the following:

Consider Norton, Lies and the Constitution, 2012 Sup. Ct. Rev. 161, 169, 185-187, 200:

> Unless we are willing to protect all lies or no lies from government regulation, we must make some difficult judgments in determining when the Constitution permits government to punish intentional falsehoods. [Both] the Kennedy and Breyer approaches [in *Alvarez*] defined that core area largely in terms of harm.
>
> [To] this end, we might usefully separate the second- and third-party harms of lies when thinking about whether and when such harms should justify government intervention. [Some lies] harm second parties—that is, the listeners to whom the lie is told. [Examples range from] fraudulent lies that cause monetary harm to cruel lies that cause emotional harm. Lies can also harm individual third parties (i.e., someone other than the listener)—as is the case with defamation, where the harm is generally suffered not by the listeners but by the subject of the lie. Third-party harms can [also] include more generalized harms to government institutions when, for example, lies undermine the public's confidence in important government processes. [Examples would include perjury at a trial, misrepresenting oneself as a police officer, and a candidate's lies about his credentials]. . . .
>
> The great number and variety of lies [undermine] efforts to characterize all—or none—as fully protected by the First Amendment. This requires us to draw some uncomfortable distinctions. [We] can better assess the potential harm of [lies] when we understand them [as threatening either] second-party harms to listeners [or] as third-party harms to the public trust.

Page 1160.   At the bottom of the page, add the following:

5a. *"Revenge porn."* Would a prohibition on "revenge porn" be constitutional? "Revenge porn" refers to the practice of posting nude or sexually suggestive photographs on line without the consent of the person who is photographed. Consider the following proposed statute:

> An actor commits criminal invasion of privacy if the actor harms another person by knowingly disclosing an image of another person whose intimate parts are exposed or who is engaged in a sexual act, when the actor knows that the other person did not consent to the disclosure and when the actor knows that the other person expected that the image would be kept private,

under circumstances where the other person had a reasonable expectation that the image would be kept private. The fact that a person has consented to the possession of an image by another person does not imply consent to disclose that image more broadly.

D.Citron, Hate Crimes in Cyberspace (2014). The proposed statute contains exceptions for "lawful and common practices of law enforcement, criminal reporting, legal proceedings; or medical treatment," for the reporting of unlawful conduct, for voluntary exposures in public or commercial settings, and for disclosures that relate to the public interest.

Is the statute constitutional? If so, how (if at all) is this disclosure different from unconsented disclosure of verbal descriptions of sexual acts or from disclosure of embarrassing information gained through an intimate relationship?

For the argument that laws against revenge porn violate the First Amendment, see Goldberg, Free Speech Consequentialism, 116 Colum. L. Rev. 687, 743-749 (2016):

> [Advocates for the criminalization of revenge porn maintain that such speech is socially harmful and does not] "contribute any benefits to society." Yet this does not separate revenge porn from any number of categories of protected speech that may cause others emotional distress and are considered by some to possess little value. . . . There is not a principled way to create, at the wholesale level, an unprotected category of speech around revenge porn. . . . However, partners can protect their own interests by explicitly asking their partners to agree not to [disclose such images.] The best way to regulate revenge porn is through private (noncriminal) law, as a breach of implied contract. . . .

Page 1165. Before Section 4, add the following:

Can an individual be punished for threatening words if she does not intend for them to be perceived as a threat? In Elonis v. United States, 135 S. Ct. 2001 (2015), the petitioner posted on Facebook a series of threatening statements directed toward his wife and others. He was convicted under a federal statute making it a crime to transmit in interstate commerce "any threat . . . to injure the person of another." The trial court instructed the jury that it could convict if a reasonable person would regard the statements as threats and declined to instruct the jury that the petitioner had to intend to communicate a threat. The Supreme Court, per Chief Justice Roberts, reversed the conviction, but declined to reach the constitutional question. As a matter of statutory construction, the Court held that the government was required to prove more than mere negligence. However, the majority did not specify what mental state was required.

Two separate opinions , written by Justice Alito, concurring in part and dissenting in part, and by Justice Thomas, dissenting, rejected a constitutional requirement of intent to threaten. Justice Alito thought that the statute required no more than recklessness—disregard of a risk of which the perpetrator was aware—and that this requirement was sufficient to satisfy the first amendment.

> True threats inflict great harm and have little if any social value. . . .
>
> [Whether] or not the person making a threat intends to cause harm, the damage is the same. . . .
>
> We have sometimes cautioned that it is necessary to "exten[d] a measure of strategic protection" to otherwise unprotected false statements of fact in order to ensure enough " 'breathing space' " for protected speech. But we have also held that the laws provides adequate breathing space when it requires proof that false statements were made with reckless disregard of their falsity. Requiring proof of recklessness is similarly sufficient here.

Justice Thomas read the statute as requiring neither intent nor recklessness and would have held that neither requirement was constitutionally mandatory. His view was based largely on state statutes and English precedent at the time of the framing that, in his judgment, did not require intent or recklessness with regard to whether words would be perceived as threats.

Page 1173.   At the end of section 1c of the Note, add the following:

Consider also Stone, Ronald Coase's First Amendment, 54 J. Law & Econ. 367, 374 (2011):

> As both logic and history teach, the temptation of public officials to use government power to stifle criticism and distort public debate poses a direct threat to the very existence of a self-governing society. Such behavior not only gives those in power a continuing political advantage over their challengers but also enables them to prevent any criticism or even discussion of their actions. It therefore freezes policies in place. In the sphere of economic regulation, however, that is not the case. As long as free speech is guaranteed, even an inefficient and rent-seeking economic regulation can be publicly criticized and ultimately changed. From a constitutional standpoint, economic freedom simply does not stand on the same footing as freedom of speech.

Page 1173. After section 1e of the Note, add the following:

f. Brudney, The First Amendment and Commercial Advertising, 53 B.C. L. Rev. 1153, 1179, 1168 (2013):

> It has been suggested that because it is speech and serves a communicative function, commercial speech is entitled to the same protection against government regulation as other protected [speech]. As a predicate for First Amendment protection, however, commercial speech's communicative function may not be sufficient to justify such protection. . . .
>
> [This is so because,] in much commercial speech, the speaker's concern is primarily, or only, with the choices to be made by individual consumers for their personal benefit, rather than for the benefit of society as a whole. The question that each consumer is presumed to ask in making his choice is: "What is good, or best, for me?" [But in the case of traditionally protected speech,] the question the addressee or member of the audience is presumed to ask is: "What is good, or best, for the community or society?" Such an inquiry is not of central concern to the speaker-seller or indeed to the listener-buyer [in the context of commercial speech]. . . .

Page 1180. At the end of section 3 of the Note, add the following:

Is the Court's concern with paternalism in these cases warranted? Consider Brudney, The First Amendment and Commercial Speech, 53 B.C. L. Rev. 1153, 1194-1197 (2013):

> Prohibiting or regulating truthful commercial communications about lawful activities that may be of interest to the listener is said to be especially objectionable interference, in that it paternalistically precludes the listener from knowledgeably deciding whether to risk or incur such harm. [In effect, such paternalism interferes with the consumer's ability to make] a possibly harmful choice to satisfy a preference in personal matters [because] the government believes satisfying that preference to be harmful to him or her, as well as to others. . . .
>
> The predicate on which the charge of paternalism rests (the consumers' ability to "perceive their own best interests . . . if they are well enough informed," and to act upon that perception) assumes an apperceptive base of relevant information and knowledge. In the universe of retail mass marketing, the billions of dollars spent by sellers in the aggregate to acculturate

consumers to desire products or services that may (or may not) create unspecified long-term health or safety problems, or other costs, are expenditures that are not offset (and are not likely to be offset without government regulation) by reasonably comparable nongovernmental expenditures for educative "debiasing" efforts.

It is that background, structured by government-created property rules in a market economy, that enables sellers or offerors to shape consumer tastes and preferences so as to affect a consumer's "free" choice in responding to offers. It also raises the question: Which government intervention is, or would be, "paternalistic?" Was the consumer's relevant knowledge for making a choice enhanced by the Court's constitutionally rejecting Virginia's prohibition of price advertisements for prescription drugs? Or was it enhanced by Virginia forbidding such ads? Either way, the government's intervention to enable the consumer "freely" to determine her own best interests is (or is not) "paternalism."

4. *A Corporate Takeover of the First Amendment?* A recent analysis of Supreme Court and lower court decisions finds that in the wake of *Virginia Pharmacy* "corporations have begun to displace individuals" as the primary beneficiaries of the First Amendment. This analysis finds that until *Virginia Pharmacy* only expressive businesses, like media companies, were able to convince the Court to strike down laws regulating their expressive activity, but that since that decision the number of cases in which non-expressive businesses have successfully invoked the protection of the First Amendment has increased dramatically, substantially displacing cases in which individuals are the primary beneficiary of the First Amendment. See Coates, Corporate Speech and the First Amendment: History, Data, and Implications, 30 Const. Comm. 223 (2015).

Page 1192. At the end of section 6 of the Note, add the following:

Even if *Stanley* is limited to the home, might the Court's decision in *Lawrence v. Texas* (page 922 of the main volume) suggest that there is a substantive due process right of sexual privacy that, wholly apart from the First Amendment, guarantees the right to purchase and to view obscene expression? See Kinsley, Sexual Privacy in the Internet Age: How Substantive Due Process Protects Online Obscenity, 16 Vand. J. Ent. & Tech. L. 103 (2013). See also Reliable Consultants, Inc. v. Earle, 517 F.3d 738 (5th Cir. 2008) (invalidating a Texas law prohibiting the sale of sexual devices on substantive due process grounds).

Page 1201.   After section 9 of the Note, add the following:

10. *Obscenity and substantive due process.* Even if obscenity is not protected by the First Amendment, is it protected from prohibition by the doctrine of substantive due process, as articulated in such decisions as *Griswold v. Connecticut, Roe v. Wade, Planned Parenthood v. Casey,* and *Lawrence v. Texas,* supra section VI F? In *Lawrence,* the Court observed that "liberty gives substantial protection to adult persons in deciding how to conduct their private lives in matters pertaining to sex." Does "the right of autonomous decision-making" in private matters include "the protection of both intimate sexual conduct and the commercial transactions that enable and promote sexual intimacy"? Kinsley, Sexual Privacy in the Internet Age: How Substantive Due Process Protects Online Obscenity, 16 Vand. J. Ent. & Tech. L. 103 (2013). See Reliable Consultants, Inc. v. Earle, 517 F.3d 738 (5th Cir. 2008) (invalidating on substantive due process grounds a Texas law prohibiting any person to sell, advertise, give away or lend any device "designed or marketed for sexual stimulation").

Page 1211.   At the end of *United States v. Stevens,* add the following:

Within months of the Supreme Court's decision in *Stevens,* Congress amended § 48. The new provision, titled "Animal crush videos," defines an "animal crush video" as "any photograph, motion-picture film, video or digital recording, or electronic image" that (1) "depicts actual conduct in which one or more living non-human mammals, birds, reptiles, or amphibians is intentionally crushed, burned, drowned, suffocated, impaled or otherwise subjected to serious bodily injury" and (2) "is obscene." The statute exempts any visual depiction of "customary and normal veterinary or agricultural husbandry practices," "the slaughter of animals for food," or "hunting, trapping or fishing." Is this statute constitutional? See United States v. Richards, ___ F. Supp. ___ (S.D. Tex. 2013) (holding that the revised statute violates the First Amendment).

Page 1214.   At the end of *Brown v. Entertainment Merchants Association,* add the following:

Consider Schauer, Harm(s) and the First Amendment, 2011 Sup. Ct. Rev. 81, 108, 110:

Stevens, Snyder, and *Entertainment Merchants* all involved moderately clear harms — to animals, to grieving parents, and [to] potential victims of the aggressiveness of teenagers. [The] First Amendment, as much if not more than the rest of the Constitution, is a mandate to the courts to engage in a common law process of developing the rules, principles, standards, maxims, canons, and precedents that together produce what we call legal doctrine. But in considering the common law nature of that development of First Amendment doctrine, it is important to bear in mind Lord Mansfield's optimistic assessment that the common law "works itself pure." In light of [this] aspiration, it is often appropriate to ask whether the progression of time, the increase in the stock of examples, and the continued testing of provisional rules and principles has produced improvement. . . .

Do you agree with Schauer that "one of the surprising things about *Stevens, Snyder,* and *Entertainment Merchants,* taken as a group, is that they give little cause for optimism about the continuing refinement of First Amendment doctrine"?

E.   Content-Neutral Restrictions

Page 1263.   At the end of the Note, add the following:

How has the Roberts Court interpreted and applied the *Chaplinsky* dictum? In the decades after *Chaplinsky,* defenders of free speech viewed the *Chaplinsky* dictum as an "unfortunate" invitation to the Court to make open-ended value judgments about which speech is and is not to be protected by the First Amendment. Indeed, Harry Kalven criticized it in the early 1970s as a "broad dictum" that "haunted constitutional law." H. Kalven, A Worthy Tradition: Freedom of Speech in America 18 (1988). In light of the Roberts Court's decisions in *Stevens, Snyder, Brown,* and *Alvarez,* however, the *Chaplinsky* dictum seems to have taken on a somewhat different cast. Consider Collins, Exceptional Freedom: The Roberts Court, the First Amendment, and the New Absolutism, 76 Alb. L. Rev. 409, 424 (2013):

[The Roberts Court] has shown no signs of moving away from the jurisprudence of its predecessors in diminishing the domain of *Chaplinsky*'s original exceptions. (For example, pre-Roberts Courts have held that defamation is not entirely unprotected, and lewd and profane speech is sometimes protected.) Moreover, the current Court has generally declined to expressly invoke *Chaplinsky*'s low value [doctrine] as a rationale for enlarging the realm of unprotected expression. In fact, the Court seems to have moved in the opposite direction. [While] some earlier Courts relied on *Chaplinsky's* two-level theory to cabin free speech protection [citing *Roth*], the Roberts Court has sometimes taken an entirely different approach, one that expands the domain of protected speech. In doing so, it has produced an exceptional kind of freedom in which [speech is] categorically protected unless [it is] among the designated kinds of expression definitely exempted from First Amendment protection.

Page 1270.   At the bottom of the page, add the following:

For a detailed defense of content neutrality doctrine, see Kreimer, Good Enough for Government Work: Two Cheers for Content Neutrality, 16 J. Con. L. 1263 (2014).

Page 1274.   At the end of the Note, add the following:

6. *Content or not?* In McCullen v. Coakley, 134 S. Ct. 2518 (2014), the Supreme Court considered the constitutionality of a Massachusetts statute that made it a crime for any person knowingly to stand on a "public way or sidewalk" within 35 feet of an entrance or driveway to any place, other than a hospital, where abortions are performed. The law was designed to eliminate clashes between abortion opponents and advocates of abortion rights that had occurred outside clinics where abortions were performed. The law was challenged by individuals "who approach and talk to women outside such facilities, attempting to dissuade them from having abortions." According to testimony presented at the trial, such individuals have, over time, "persuaded hundreds of women to forgo abortions." The Act exempted persons entering or leaving the facility, employees or agents of the facility, law enforcement and similar personnel, and persons using the sidewalk area solely for the purpose of reaching another destination. The Court, in an opinion by Chief Justice Roberts, invalidated the law as an unconstitutional content-neutral restriction of speech in a traditional public forum. See insert in this Supplement for page 1281 of the main volume.

The challengers also argued, however, that the law was an unconstitutional content-based restriction of speech, because it applied only at facilities that performed abortions and therefore had a disparate impact on those who oppose abortion. Chief Justice Roberts rejected this argument: "To begin, the Act does not draw content based distinctions on its face. The Act would be content based if it required 'enforcement authorities' to 'examine the content of the message that is conveyed to determine whether' a violation has occurred. But it does not. Whether petitioners violate the Act 'depends' not 'on what they say,' but simply on where they say it. Indeed, petitioners can violate the Act merely by standing in a buffer zone, without displaying a sign or uttering a word.

"It is true, of course, that by limiting the buffer zones to abortion clinics, the Act has the 'inevitable effect' of restricting abortion-related speech more than speech on other subjects. But a facially-neutral law does not become content based simply because it may disproportionately affect speech on certain topics. [The] question in such a case is whether the law is 'justified without reference to the content of the regulated speech.' [The] Massachusetts Act is. Its stated purpose is to 'increase public safety at reproductive health care facilities.' [Obstructed] access and congested sidewalks are problems no matter what caused them. A group of individuals can obstruct clinic access and clog sidewalks just as much when they loiter as when they protest abortion or counsel patients. . . . [The challengers argue, however, that] by choosing to pursue these interests only at abortion clinics, [the] Massachusetts Legislature evinced a purpose to 'single[ ] out for regulation speech about one particular topic: abortion.' We cannot infer such a purpose from the Act's limited scope. [The] Massachusetts Legislature [enacted the statute] in response to a problem that was, in its experience, limited to abortion clinics. There was a record of crowding, obstruction, and even violence outside such clinics. There were apparently no similar recurring problems associated with other kinds of healthcare facilities [or other kinds of buildings or activities]. In light of the limited nature of the problem, it was reasonable for the Massachusetts Legislature to enact a limited solution. [We] thus conclude that the Act is neither content nor viewpoint based and therefore need not be analyzed under strict scrutiny."

Justice Scalia, joined by Justices Kennedy and Thomas, filed a concurring opinion in which he maintained that the challenged statute "is content based and fails strict scrutiny": "[It] blinks reality to say [that] a blanket prohibition on the use of streets and sidewalks where speech on only one politically controversial topic is likely to occur— and where that speech can most effectively be communicated—is not content based. Would the Court exempt from strict scrutiny a law banning access to the streets and sidewalks surrounding the site of the Republican National Convention? Or those used annually to commemorate the 1965 Selma-to-Montgomery civil rights marches? Or those outside the Internal Revenue Service? Surely not. . . .

"The structure of the Act also indicates that it rests on content-based concerns. The goals of 'public safety, patient access to healthcare, and the unobstructed use of public sidewalks and roadways,' are already achieved by an earlier-enacted subsection of the statute. [As] the majority recognizes, that provision is easy to enforce. Thus, the speech-free zones carved out [by the challenged statute] add nothing to safety and access; what they achieve, and what they were obviously designed to achieve, is the suppression of speech opposing abortion. . . .

"In concluding that the statute is content based and therefore subject to strict scrutiny, I necessarily conclude that *Hill v. Colorado* should be overruled. [Protecting] people from speech they do not want to hear is not a function that the First Amendment allows the government to undertake in the public streets and sidewalks."

Justice Alito also filed a concurring opinion: "As the Court recognizes, if the Massachusetts law discriminates on the basis of viewpoint, it is unconstitutional, and I believe the law clearly discriminates on this ground. [The] Massachusetts statute generally prohibits any person from entering a buffer zone around an abortion clinic during the clinic's business hours, but the law contains an exemption for 'employees or agents of such facility acting within the scope of their employment.'

"Thus, during business hours, individuals who wish to counsel against abortion or to criticize the particular clinic may not do so within the buffer zone. If they engage in such conduct, they commit a crime. By contrast, employees and agents of the clinic may enter the zone and engage in any conduct that falls within the scope of their employment. A clinic may direct or authorize an employee or agent, while within the zone, to express favorable views about abortion or the clinic, and if the employee exercises that authority, the employee's conduct is perfectly lawful. In short, petitioners and other critics of a clinic are silenced, while the clinic may authorize its employees to express speech in support of the clinic and its work. [It is thus] clear on the face of the Massachusetts law that it discriminates based on viewpoint. Speech in favor of the clinic and its work by employees and agents is permitted; speech criticizing the clinic and its work is a crime. This is blatant viewpoint discrimination."

7. *Content neutrality as a formal rule.* Should the Court insist on strict scrutiny for content-based regulation in circumstances where, on the facts of the particular case, the regulation is unlikely to endanger first amendment values? Conversely, should it insist on only intermediate scrutiny where there is a significant risk that a facially content neutral statute has been gerrymandered because of content? *See* Kendrick, Nonsense on Sidewalks: Content Discrimination in McCullen v. Coakley, 2014 Sup. Ct. Rev. 215, 237:

> Adopting a freewheeling approach, in which intuitions are not channeled into a framework but are imposed directly as law, could have serious ramifications for both the predictability and legitimacy of the Court's jurisprudence. There is something to be said for an approach that, rather than indulging subjective impulses, tries to contain them. When disagreements about a law run so deep, perhaps there are good reasons for approaching the law obliquely, and through predetermined avenues.

Consider in this regard Reed v. Town of Gilbert, 135 S. Ct. 2218 (2015). The Town of Gilbert comprehensively regulated signs in ways that made many distinctions between types of signs. For example, "temporary directional signs relating to a qualifying event" could be no larger than six square feet and could be in place for no longer than twelve hours before the event and one hour afterward. In contrast, "political signs" could be up to thirty-two square feet and could be displayed up to sixty days before a primary election and up to fifteen days following a general election. The Good News Community Church was cited for exceeding the time limits for a sign displaying the time and location of an upcoming service and challenged the regulations as violative of the first amendment. The Court of Appeals treated the signs as content neutral on the ground that the Town's "interests in regulat[ing] temporary signs are unrelated to the content of the sign." The court held that lower level scrutiny therefore applied and upheld the ordinance.

The Supreme Court, in an opinion written by Justice Thomas, reversed. As the Court explained, the court of appeals had "[skipped] the crucial first step in the content-neutrality analysis: determining whether the law is content neutral on its face. A law that is content based on its face is subject to strict scrutiny regardless of the government's benign motive, content-neutral justification, or lack of 'animus toward the ideas contained' in the regulated speech." The Court went on to note that even if a law is facially content neutral, it will still be treated as content based if it cannot be justified without reference to the content of the regulated speech or if it was adopted because of disagreement with the message of the speech. But because the Town's code was "content based on its face," it was subject to heightened scrutiny whether or not it was motivated by opposition to the message conveyed.

> This type of ordinance may seem like a perfectly rational way to regulate signs, but a clear and firm rule governing content neutrality is an essential means of protecting the freedom of speech, even if laws that might seem "entirely reasonable" will sometimes be "struck down because of their content-based nature."

Compare Justice Kagan's opinion, joined by Justices Ginsburg and Breyer, concurring in the judgment:

> Given the Court's analysis, many sign ordinances [are] now in jeopardy. . . .
>
> [Courts will] have to determine that a town has a compelling interest in informing passersby where George Washington slept. And likewise, courts [will] have to find that a town has no way to prevent hidden-driveway mishaps than by specially treating hidden-driveway signs. [The]

consequence – unless courts water down strict scrutiny to something unrecognizable—is that our communities will find themselves in an unenviable bind: They will have to either repeal the exemptions that allow for helpful signs on streets and sidewalks, or else lift their sign restrictions altogether and resign themselves to the resulting clutter.

Although the majority insists that applying strict scrutiny to all such ordinances is "essential" to protecting First Amendment freedoms, I find it challenging to understand why that is so. [Allowing] residents, say, to install a light bulb over "name and address" signs but no others does not distort the marketplace of ideas. Nor does that different treatment give rise to an inference of impermissible government motive.

Justice Kagan would nonetheless have invalidated the ordinance before the Court because "[the] Town of Gilbert's defense of [the ordinance]—most notably, the laws' distinctions between directional signs and others—does not pass strict scrutiny, or intermediate scrutiny, or even the laugh test."

Justice Alito, joined by Justices Kennedy and Sotomayor, joined the majority opinion but filed a separate concurring opinion. Justice Breyer filed a separate opinion concurring only in the judgment.

Page 1281.   Before section 9 of the Note, add the following:

8a. *Demonstrating near an abortion clinic IV.* In McCullen v. Coakley, 134 S. Ct. 2518 (2014), the Supreme Court invalidated a Massachusetts statute that made it a crime for any person knowingly to stand on a "public way or sidewalk" within 35 feet of an entrance or driveway to any place, other than a hospital, where abortions are performed. The law was designed to eliminate clashes between abortion opponents and advocates of abortion rights that had occurred outside clinics where abortions were performed. The law was challenged by individuals "who approach and talk to women outside such facilities, attempting to dissuade them from having abortions." According to testimony presented at the trial, such individuals have, over time, "persuaded hundreds of women to forgo abortions."

Chief Justice Roberts authored the opinion of the Court: "[Public ways and sidewalks] occupy a 'special position in terms of First Amendment protection' because of their historic role as sites for discussion and debate. [Such] traditional public fora are areas that have historically been open to the public for speech activities. [We] have held that the government's ability to restrict speech in such locations is 'very limited.' [Even if such laws are content neutral, they must be] narrowly tailored to serve a significant governmental interest. [For] a content-neutral time, place, or manner regulation to be narrowly tailored, it must not 'burden substantially more speech than is necessary to further the government's legitimate interests.' . . .

"The buffer zones burden substantially more speech than necessary to achieve the Commonwealth's asserted interests. [The] Commonwealth's interests include ensuring public safety outside abortion clinics, preventing harassment and intimidation of patients and clinic staff, and combating deliberate obstruction of clinic entrances. [The Act] itself contains a separate provision [that] prohibits much of this conduct. That provision subjects to criminal punishment '[a]ny person who knowingly obstructs, detains, hinders, impedes or blocks another person's entry to or exit from a reproductive health care facility.' [If] Massachusetts determines that broader prohibitions along the same lines are necessary, it could enact legislation similar to the federal Freedom of Access to Clinic Entrances Act of 1994, which subjects to both criminal and civil penalties anyone who 'by force or threat of force or by physical obstruction, intentionally injures, intimidates or interferes with or attempts to injure, intimidate or interfere with any person because that person is or has been, or in order to intimidate such person or any other person or any class of persons from, obtaining or providing reproductive health services.' [If] the Commonwealth is particularly concerned about harassment, it could also consider an ordinance such as the one adopted in New York City that not only prohibits obstructing access to a clinic, but also makes it a crime 'to follow and harass another person within 15 feet of the premises of a reproductive health care facility.' . . .

"The point is not that Massachusetts must enact all or even any of the proposed measures discussed above. The point is instead that the Commonwealth has available to it a variety of approaches that appear capable of serving its interests without excluding individuals from areas historically open for speech and debate."

Page 1294.   Before the Note, add the following:

Compare the following assessment in Abu El-Haj, All Assemble: Order and Disorder in Law, Politics, and Culture, 16 U. Pa. J. Con. L. 949, 950-52 (2014):

The history of outdoor assembly in the United States is one of continuity and discontinuity. While citizens have periodically taken to the streets in inconvenient and risky ways throughout our history, our contemporary attitudes, as evidenced in law, practice, and public discourse, stand in stark contrast to the attitudes of previous generations of Americans. Contemporary

Americans value individual freedom and various sorts of expression far more than previous generations, but our fears of the disorder associated with outdoor gatherings are undermining the right of peaceable assembly and the critically important form of political participation it safeguards. . . .

The result is that Americans today accept a high level of regulation of outdoor assembly. This is evident in the laws to which assemblies are subject, the responses of local governments to outdoor assemblies, the decisions of courts, and the public's attitudes toward the crowds associated with movements such as Occupy.

Our intolerance of disorder, well short of violence, has implicated our constitutional freedoms. It facilitates a constitutional order that undervalues outdoor assembly and undermines democratic participation.

Page 1309.   Before section 4 of the Note, add the following:

3a. *Specialty license plates.* In Walker v. Texas Div., Sons of Confederate Veterans, Inc., 135 S. Ct. 2239 (2015), the Court, in a 5-to-4 decision written by Justice Breyer, held that Texas had not created a limited or nonpublic forum when it permitted private groups to submit proposals for specialty license plates. It upheld the refusal of the Texas Department of Motor Vehicles to approve a license plate featuring the Confederate battle flag on the ground that the plate constituted government, rather than private, speech. In the Court's view, the license plates were not a nonpublic forum because the state was "not simply managing government property, but instead is engaging in expressive conduct." It based this conclusion on the historical context, observers' reasonable interpretation of the messages conveyed by Texas specialty plates, and the effective control that Texas exerted over the design selection process." Justice Alito, joined by Chief Justice Roberts and Justices Scalia and Kennedy, dissented.

Page 1326.   Before section 4 of the Note, add the following:

Compare Massaro, Tread on Me!, 17 U. Pa. J. Con L. 365, 402-03 (2014):

[Freedom] of speech doctrine [should] include an exception to the "government speech" doctrine for the rare circumstances in which the government exerts *so much* expressive power that its actions are tantamount to direct speech regulation. [One] factor, though not the only one, that should be relevant to determining the contours of this caveat is the extent to which government has monopoly power over the information in question. The lack of options matters. We might think we have a choice of horses, but when Thomas Hobson runs the only stable in town, our horse is always the horse that Hobson selects.

In C. Brettschneider, When the State Speaks, What Should it Say? How Democracies Can Protect Expression and Promote Equality (2012), the author argues that states have an obligation to speak so as to promote "democratic persuasion" but only when it speaks in favor of free and equal citizenship.

Page 1334. At the end of section 3 of the Note, add the following:

Are there circumstances in which the government's own speech might violate the establishment clause? The equal protection clause? See Norton, The Equal Protection Implications of Government's Hateful Speech, 54 Wm. & Mary L. Rev. 159 (2012).

Page 1334. Before section 4 of the Note, add the following:

In Walker v. Texas Div., Sons of Confederate Veterans, Inc., 135 S. Ct. 2239 (2015), the Court upheld the refusal of the Texas Department of Motor Vehicles to approve a specialty license plate design submitted by the Sons of Confederate Veterans and featuring the Confederate battle flag. In a 5-to-4 decision, written by Justice Breyer, the Court relied heavily upon *Summum* to conclude that the plate was government speech and therefore did not have to be viewpoint neutral. In the Court's view, license plates, like monuments in public parks, "long have communicated messages from the States," are " 'often closely identified in the public mind with the [State]' " and are subject to direct government control. The fact that private parties took part in the design and propagation of the message did not extinguish the governmental nature of the message.

Consider Justice Alito's dissent, joined by Chief Justice Roberts and Justices Scalia and Kennedy:

Here is a test. Suppose you sat by the side of a Texas highway and studied the license plates on the vehicles passing by. You would see, in addition to the standard Texas plates, an impressive array of specialty plates. (There are now more than 350 varieties.) . . .

[Would] you really think that the sentiments reflected in these specialty plates are the views of the State of Texas and not those of the owners of the cars? If a car had a plate that says "Rather Be Golfing" passed by at 8:30 am on a Monday morning, would you think: "This is the official policy of the State—better to golf than to work?"

Consider Schauer, Not Just About License Plates: *Walker v. Sons of Confederate Veterans*, Government Speech, and Doctrinal Overlap in the First Amendment, 2015 Sup. Ct. Rev. 265:

The problem of doctrinal [overlap] was especially apparent in [*Walker*]. The precise issues in the case [could] be analyzed in one way if the focus was on what was unquestionably an act of viewpoint discrimination, in another way if the issue was framed in terms of whether Texas's specialty license plates constituted some sort of public forum, in still another way if the state's policy was seen as the imposition of an unconstitutional condition, and, finally, in yet another way if, as the Supreme Court majority saw the case, the Texas policy was analyzed as an example of government speech.

The fundamental problem is that placing the *Walker* facts into any of the just-listed frames or doctrine categories would not be wrong, for each of them was at least plausibly applicable to the controversy in *Walker*. [If] this is so, then we are in a position to speculate about what might have led both the majority and the dissenting Justices to choose the frames that they did. One possibility, of course, is that some or all of the Justices were genuinely wrestling with the ins and outs of each of these four frames, and were trying to decide, from the outset, which frame seemed most suited to the case at hand. [We] might label this the "doctrinal" approach to frame selection. . . .

Once we have concluded, however, that multiple doctrinal frames are plausible, things get trickier. The traditional view, of course, is that the nature of the competing doctrines will be the primary driver in determining which of them should be employed. [But there is] an alternative possibility. This possibility is that doctrine gives the decision makers a set of plausible choices, but that selecting among the plausible choices is largely an extradoctrinal matter. [One] possibility is that the choice among competing plausible doctrinal frames is determined by a judge's [simple] preference for one outcome rather than another in a particular case. [Because] the Confederate flag itself is connected with a [range] of highly salient public controversies about race, about history, about cultural sensitivities, and about so-called political correctness, *Walker* may well be a case in which [factors] other than constitutional doctrine play a significant role in selecting among the relevant frames and thus in determining the outcome.

Page 1337.   At the end of the Note, add the following:

AGENCY FOR INTERNATIONAL DEVELOPMENT v. ALLIANCE FOR OPEN SOCIETY INTERNATIONAL, 133 S. Ct. 2321 (2013). The United States Leadership Against HIV/AIDS, Tuberculosis, and Malaria Act of 2003 (Leadership Act) authorized the appropriation of billions of dollars to fund efforts by nongovernmental organizations to combat HIV/AIDS worldwide. The Act imposed a condition ("The Policy Requirement") on all recipients of funds under the Act: all recipients must explicitly oppose prostitution. This requirement was challenged by recipients of Leadership Act funds who wish to remain neutral on the issue of prostitution. The Court, in a six-to-two decision, held that this requirement violated the First Amendment rights of recipients.

Chief Justice Roberts delivered the opinion of the Court: "The Policy Requirement mandates that recipients of Leadership Act funds explicitly agree with the Government's policy to oppose prostitution. . . . It is, however, a basic First Amendment principle that 'freedom of speech prohibits the government from telling people what they must say.' [Citing *West Virginia Bd. of Educ. v. Barnette*, main volume page 1416; *Wooley v. Maynard*, main volume page 1416]. [Were The Policy Requirement] enacted as a direct regulation of speech, [it] would plainly violate the First Amendment. The question is whether the Government may nonetheless impose that requirement as a condition on the receipt of federal funds. . . .

"[As] a general matter, if a party objects to a condition on the receipt of federal funding, its recourse is to decline the funds. This remains true when the objection is that a condition may affect the recipient's exercise of its First Amendment rights. [Citing *United States v. American Library Ass'n*.] At the same time, however, we have held that the Government 'may not deny a benefit to a person on a basis that infringes his constitutionally protected . . . freedom of speech even if he has no entitlement to that benefit.' In some cases, a funding condition can result in an unconstitutional burden on First Amendment rights. . . .

"The dissent thinks that can only be true when the condition is not relevant to the objectives of the program [or] when the condition is actually coercive, in the sense of an offer that cannot be refused. Our precedents, however, are not so limited. In the present context, the relevant distinction that has emerged from our cases is between conditions that define the limits of the government spending program—those that specify the activities Congress wants to subsidize—and conditions that seek to leverage funding to regulate speech outside the contours of the program itself. The line is hardly clear, in part because the definition of a particular program can always be manipulated to subsume the challenged condition. We have held, however, that 'Congress cannot recast a condition on funding as a mere definition of its program in every case, lest the First Amendment be reduced to a simple semantic exercise.' " [*Velazquez.*]

As an example, Chief Justice Roberts invoked *FCC v. League of Women Voters,* in which "the Court struck down a condition on federal financial assistance to noncommercial broadcast television and radio stations that prohibited all editorializing, including with private funds. Even a station receiving only one percent of its overall budget from the Federal Government, the Court explained, was 'barred absolutely from all editorializing.' [The] law provided no way for a station to limit its use of federal funds to noneditorializing activities, while using private funds 'to make known its views on matters of public importance.' The prohibition thus went beyond ensuring that federal funds not be used to subsidize 'public broadcasting station editorials,' and instead leveraged the federal funding to regulate the stations' speech outside the scope of the program.

"Our decision in *Rust* elaborated on the approach [in] *League of Women Voters.* In *Rust*, [the] organizations received funds from a variety of sources other than the Federal Government for a variety of purposes. The Act, however, prohibited the Title X federal funds from being 'used in programs where abortion is a method of family planning.' To enforce this provision, HHS regulations barred Title X projects from advocating abortion as a method of family planning, and required grantees to ensure that their Title X projects were 'physically and financially separate' from their other projects that engaged in the prohibited activities. . . .

"We explained that Congress can, without offending the Constitution, selectively fund certain programs to address an issue of public concern, without funding alternative ways of addressing the same problem. In Title X, Congress had defined the federal program to encourage only particular family planning methods. The challenged regulations were simply 'designed to ensure that the limits of the federal program are observed,' and 'that public funds [are] spent for the purposes for which they were authorized.' [The] regulations governed only the scope of the grantee's Title X projects, leaving it 'unfettered in its other activities.' [Title X grantees could continue to engage in abortion advocacy as long as they conducted] 'those activities through programs that are separate and independent from the project that receives Title X funds.' Because the regulations did not 'prohibit[ ] the recipient from engaging in the protected conduct outside the scope of the federally funded program,' they did not run afoul of the First Amendment. Here, however, [the] Policy Requirement falls on the unconstitutional side of the line. [By] demanding that funding recipients adopt—as their own—the Government's view on an issue of public concern, the condition by its very nature affects 'protected conduct outside the scope of the federally funded program.' [By] requiring recipients to profess a specific belief, the Policy Requirement goes beyond defining the limits of the federally funded program to defining the recipient. . . .

190

"The Government suggests that the Policy Requirement is necessary because, without it, the grant of federal funds could free a recipient's private funds 'to be used to promote prostitution.' [Citing *Holder v. Humanitarian Law Project.*] That argument assumes that federal funding will simply supplant private funding, rather than pay for new programs or expand existing ones. The Government offers no support for that assumption as a general matter, or any reason to believe it is true here. And if the Government's argument were correct, *League of Women Voters* would have come out differently, and much of the reasoning [of] *Rust* would have been beside the point.

"The Government cites but one case to support that argument, *Holder v. Humanitarian Law Project.* That case concerned the quite different context of a ban on providing material support to terrorist organizations, where the record indicated that support for those organizations' nonviolent operations was funneled to support their violent activities.

"Pressing its argument further, the Government contends that 'if organizations awarded federal funds to implement Leadership Act programs could at the same time promote or affirmatively condone prostitution or sex trafficking, whether using public *or private* funds, it would undermine the government's program and confuse its message opposing prostitution.' But the Policy Requirement goes beyond preventing recipients from using private funds in a way that would undermine the federal program. It requires them to pledge allegiance to the Government's policy of eradicating prostitution. As to that, we cannot improve upon what Justice Jackson wrote for the Court 70 years ago: 'If there is any fixed star in our constitutional constellation, it is that no official, high or petty, can prescribe what shall be orthodox in politics, nationalism, religion, or other matters of opinion or force citizens to confess by word or act their faith therein.' [Quoting *West Virginia Bd. of Educ. v. Barnette.*]

"The Policy Requirement compels as a condition of federal funding the affirmation of a belief that by its nature cannot be confined within the scope of the Government program. In so doing, it violates the First Amendment and cannot be sustained."

Justice Scalia, joined by Justice Thomas, dissented: "The First Amendment does not mandate a viewpoint neutral government. Government must choose between rival ideas and adopt some as its own: competition over cartels, solar energy over coal, weapon development over disarmament, and so forth. Moreover, the government may enlist the assistance of those who believe in its ideas to carry them to fruition; and it need not enlist for that purpose those who oppose or do not support the ideas. That seems to me a matter of the most common common sense. . . .

"The argument is that this commonsense principle will enable the government to discriminate against, and injure, points of view to which it is opposed. Of course the Constitution does not prohibit government spending that discriminates against, and injures, points of view to which the government is opposed; every government program which takes a position on a controversial issue does that. Anti-smoking programs injure cigar aficionados, programs encouraging sexual abstinence injure free-love advocates, etc. The constitutional prohibition at issue here is not a prohibition against discriminating against or injuring opposing points of view, but the First Amendment's prohibition against the coercing of speech. I am frankly dubious that a condition for eligibility to participate in a minor federal program such as this one runs afoul of that prohibition even when the condition is irrelevant to the goals of the program. Not every disadvantage is a coercion.

"But that is not the issue before us here. Here the views that the Government demands an applicant forswear—or that the Government insists an applicant favor—are relevant to the program in question. The program is valid only if the Government is entitled to disfavor the opposing view (here, advocacy of or tolera-tion of prostitution). And if the program can disfavor it, so can the selection of those who are to administer the program. There is no risk that this principle will enable the Government to discriminate arbitrarily against positions it disfavors. It would not, for example, permit the Government to exclude from bidding on defense contracts anyone who refuses to abjure prostitution. But here a central part of the Government's HIV/AIDS strategy is the suppression of prostitution, by which HIV is transmitted. It is entirely reasonable to admit to participation in the program only those who believe in that goal. . . .

"Of course the most obvious manner in which the admission to a program of an ideological opponent can frustrate the purpose of the program is by freeing up the opponent's funds for use in its ideological opposition. [Money] is fungible. The economic reality is that when NGOs can conduct their AIDS work on the Gov-ernment's dime, they can expend greater resources on policies that undercut the Leadership Act. The Government need not establish by record evidence that this will happen. To make it a valid consideration in determining participation in fed-eral programs, it suffices that this is a real and obvious risk. [In] *FCC v. League of Women Voters,* the ban on editorializing [was] disallowed precisely because it did not further a relevant, permissible policy of the Federal Communications Act. . . .

"The majority cannot credibly say that this speech condition is coercive, so it does not. It pussyfoots around the lack of coercion by invalidating the Leadership Act for '*requiring* recipients to profess a specific belief' and '*demanding* that funding recipients adopt—as their own—the Government's view on an issue of public concern.' But like King Cnut's commanding of the tides, here the Govern-ment's 'requiring' and 'demanding' have no coercive effect. In the end, and in the circumstances of this case, [there] is no compulsion at all. It is the reasonable price of admission to a limited government-spending program that each organiza-tion remains free to accept or reject. . . ."

## Page 1398.	At the end of section c of the Note, add the following:

cc. In Brown & Martin, Rhetoric and Reality: Testing the Harm of Campaign Spending, 90 NYU L. Rev. 1066 (2015), the authors note that the Court in *Citizens United* insisted that any perceptions members of the public might have that their elected representatives are ingratiated to large donors "would not undermine the electorate's faith in democracy." The authors argue that "a loss of faith by the electorate implicates a central constitutional value and is a sufficiently compelling interest to justify campaign finance regulation." Moreover, they offer empirical evidence to demonstrate that "the Court should not have been so confident that the electorate's faith in democracy is unaffected either by the appearance of influence or access due to campaign spending or by independent expenditures." If it is true that large campaign expenditures undermine the faith of citizens in democracy, should that be a sufficiently compelling concern to justify otherwise unconstitutional campaign finance restrictions?

## Page 1399.	Before section 2 of the Note, add the following:

e. For a book-length criticism of the conception of corruption that underlies the Court's decision in *Citizens United,* see Z. Teachout, Corruption in America: From Benjamin Franklin's Snuff Box to Citizens United (2014). The author argues that the modern Supreme Court has ignored the way that earlier generations conceived of corruption.

The justices have [likely] been influenced by many political scientists and legal scholars who have adopted the selfish-man theory of human nature in the late twentieth century, an assumption that people will be self-interested in their behavior in all areas. [Such] a theory of human nature is incompatible with the traditional American theory of corruption. . . .

## Page 1400.	Before the Note, add the following:

McCUTCHEON v. FEDERAL ELECTION COMMISSION, 134 S. Ct. 1434 (2014). The federal Bipartisan Campaign Reform Act imposes two types of limits on campaign contributions. The first, called base limits, restricts how much money a donor may contribute to a particular candidate or committee. The second, called aggregate limits, restricts how much money a donor may contribute in total to all candidates or committees. In *Buckley*, the Court upheld the constitutionality of the base contribution limits. This case concerned the constitutionality of the aggregate contribution limits.

For the 2013-2014 election cycle, the aggregate limits permitted an individual to contribute a total of $48,600 to federal candidates and a total of $74,600 to other political committees. In the 2011-2012 election cycle, Shaun McCutcheon contributed a total of $33,088 to sixteen different federal candidates, in compliance with the then-applicable base limits. McCutcheon wanted to contribute $1,776 to each of twelve additional candidates, but was prevented from doing so by the aggregate limit on contributions to candidates. He also wanted to contribute to several additional political committees, including $25,000 to each of the three Republican national party committees, but again was prevented from doing so by the aggregate limit on contributions to political committees. The Republican National Committee wanted to receive the contributions that McCutcheon and other potential contributors wanted to make to it—contributions otherwise permissible under the base limits for national party committees, but foreclosed by the aggregate limit on contributions to political committees.

In June 2012, McCutcheon and the RNC filed a complaint before a three-judge panel of the U.S. District Court for the District of Columbia, maintaining that the aggregate limits on contributions to candidates and to noncandidate political committees were unconstitutional under the First Amendment. The three-judge court dismissed the complaint, holding that the aggregate limits survived First Amendment scrutiny.

The Supreme Court, in a five-to-four decision, held the aggregate contribution limits unconstitutional. Chief Justice Roberts announced the judgment of the Court and delivered an opinion, in which Justices Scalia, Kennedy, and Alito joined:

"The right to participate in democracy through political contributions is protected by the First Amendment, but that right is not absolute. Our cases have held that Congress may regulate campaign contributions to protect against corruption or the appearance of corruption. [Citing *Buckley*.] At the same time, we have made clear that Congress may not regulate contributions simply to reduce the amount of money in politics, or to restrict the political participation of some in order to enhance the relative influence of others. [Citing *Bennett*.] Many people might find those latter objectives attractive. [Money] in politics may at times seem repugnant to some, but so too does much of what the First Amendment vigorously protects. If the First Amendment protects flag burning, funeral protests, and Nazi parades—despite the profound offense such spectacles cause—it surely protects political campaign speech despite popular opposition. . . .

"In a series of cases over the past 40 years, we have spelled out how to draw the constitutional line between the permissible goal of avoiding corruption in the political process and the impermissible desire simply to limit political speech. We have said that government regulation may not target the general gratitude a candidate may feel toward those who support him or his allies, or the political access such support may afford. [Any] regulation must instead target what we have called 'quid pro quo' corruption or its appearance. That Latin phrase captures the notion of a direct exchange of an official act for money. [Campaign] finance restrictions that pursue other objectives . . . impermissibly inject the Government 'into the debate over who should govern.' [Quoting *Bennett*.]

"The statute at issue in this case [restricts] how much money a donor may contribute in total to all candidates or committees. This case does not involve any challenge to the base limits, which we have previously upheld as serving the permissible objective of combatting corruption. The Government contends that the aggregate limits also serve that objective, by preventing circumvention of the base limits. We conclude, however, that the aggregate limits do little, if anything, to address that concern, while seriously restricting participation in the democratic process. The aggregate limits are therefore invalid under the First Amendment. . . .

"The First Amendment 'is designed and intended to remove governmental restraints from the arena of public discussion, putting the decision as to what views shall be voiced largely into the hands of each of us, . . . in the belief that no other approach would comport with the premise of individual dignity and choice upon which our political system rests.' [Quoting *Cohen v. California*.] As relevant here, the First Amendment safeguards an individual's right to participate in the public debate through political expression and political association. When an individual contributes money to a candidate, he exercises both of those rights. [Those] rights are important regardless whether the individual is, on the one hand, a 'lone pamphleteer[ ] or street corner orator' [or] someone who spends 'substantial amounts of money in order to communicate [his] political ideas through sophisticated' means. Either way, he is participating in an electoral debate that we have recognized is 'integral to the operation of the system of government established by our Constitution.' . . .

"To put it in the simplest terms, the aggregate limits prohibit an individual from fully contributing to the campaigns of [all the candidates he wants to support], even if all contributions fall within the base limits Congress views as adequate to protect against corruption. [It] is no answer to say that the individual can simply contribute less money to more people. To require one person to contribute at lower levels than others because he wants to support more candidates or causes is to impose a special burden on broader participation in the democratic process. [The] First Amendment burden is especially great for individuals who do not have ready access to alternative avenues for supporting their preferred politicians and policies. In the context of base contribution limits, *Buckley* observed that a supporter could vindicate his associational interests by personally volunteering his time and energy on behalf of a candidate. Such personal volunteering is not a realistic alternative for those who wish to support a wide variety of candidates or causes. . . .

"With the significant First Amendment costs for individual citizens in mind, we turn to the governmental interests asserted in this case. This Court has identified only one legitimate governmental interest for restricting campaign finances: preventing corruption or the appearance of corruption. We have consistently rejected attempts to suppress campaign speech based on other legislative objectives. No matter how desirable it may seem, it is not an acceptable governmental objective to 'level the playing field,' or to 'level electoral opportunities,' or to 'equaliz[e] the financial resources of candidates.' The First Amendment prohibits such legislative attempts to 'fine-tun[e]' the electoral process, no matter how well intentioned. As we framed the relevant principle in *Buckley*, 'the concept that government may restrict the speech of some elements of our society in order to enhance the relative voice of others is wholly foreign to the First Amendment.' . . .

"Moreover, while preventing corruption or its appearance is a legitimate objective, Congress may target only a specific type of corruption—'quid pro quo' corruption. [Spending] large sums of money in connection with elections, but not in connection with an effort to control the exercise of an officeholder's official duties, does not give rise to such quid pro quo corruption. Nor does the possibility that an individual who spends large sums may garner 'influence over or access to' elected officials or political parties.

"[The] line between quid pro quo corruption and general influence may seem vague at times, but the distinction must be respected in order to safeguard basic First Amendment rights. . . .

" 'When the Government restricts speech, the Government bears the burden of proving the constitutionality of its actions.' Here, the Government seeks to carry that burden by arguing that the aggregate limits further the permissible objective of preventing quid pro quo corruption. The difficulty is that once the aggregate limits kick in, they ban all contributions of any amount. But Congress's selection of a $5,200 base limit indicates its belief that contributions of that amount or less do not create a cognizable risk of corruption. If there is no corruption concern in giving nine candidates up to $5,200 each, it is difficult to understand how a tenth candidate can be regarded as corruptible if given $1,801, and all others corruptible if given a dime. And if there is no risk that additional candidates will be corrupted by donations of up to $5,200, then the Government must defend the aggregate limits by demonstrating that they prevent circumvention of the base limits.

"The problem is that they do not serve that function in any meaningful way. In light of the various statutes and regulations currently in effect, [the] fear that an individual might 'contribute massive amounts of money to a particular candidate through the use of unearmarked contributions' to entities likely to support the candidate, is far too speculative. We 'have never accepted mere conjecture as adequate to carry a First Amendment burden.' [The] primary example of circumvention, in one form or another, envisions an individual donor who contributes the maximum amount under the base limits to a particular candidate, say, Representative Smith. Then the donor also channels 'massive amounts of money' to Smith through a series of contributions to PACs that have stated their intention to support Smith. Various earmarking and antiproliferation rules disarm this example. Importantly, the donor may not contribute to the most obvious PACs: those that support only Smith. Nor may the donor contribute to the slightly less obvious PACs that he knows will route 'a substantial portion' of his contribution to Smith. [Any scheme to funnel huge amounts of money to Smith by indirection, given the restraints already built into the system,] is highly implausible [and] either illegal under current campaign finance laws or divorced from reality. [The] dissent [maintains] that, even with the aggregate limits in place, individuals 'have transferred large sums of money to specific candidates' in excess of the base limits. But the cited sources do not provide any real-world examples of circumvention. . . .

"[Moreover], there are multiple alternatives available to Congress that would serve the Government's anticircumvention interest, while avoiding 'unnecessary abridgment' of First Amendment rights. The most obvious might involve targeted restrictions on transfers among candidates and political committees. There are currently no such limits on transfers among party committees and from candidates to party committees. Perhaps for that reason, a central concern of the District Court [and] the dissent has been the ability of party committees to transfer money freely. If Congress agrees that this is problematic, it might tighten its permissive transfer rules. Doing so would impose a lesser burden on First Amendment rights, as compared to aggregate limits that flatly ban contributions beyond certain levels. [Indeed], Congress has adopted transfer restrictions, and the Court has upheld them, in the context of state party spending. [In addition,] disclosure of contributions minimizes the potential for abuse of the campaign finance system. Disclosure requirements [burden] speech, but—unlike the aggregate limits—they do not impose a ceiling on speech. For that reason, disclosure often represents a less restrictive alternative to flat bans on certain types or quantities of speech. [We] do not mean to opine on the validity of any particular proposal. The point is that there are numerous alternative approaches available to Congress to prevent circumvention of the base limits. . . .

"For the past 40 years, our campaign finance jurisprudence has focused on the need to preserve authority for the Government to combat corruption, without at the same time compromising the political responsiveness at the heart of the democratic process, or allowing the Government to favor some participants in that process over others. [Constituents] have the right to support candidates who share their views and concerns. Representatives are not to follow constituent orders, but can be expected to be cognizant of and responsive to those concerns. Such responsiveness is key to the very concept of self-governance through elected officials. The Government has a strong interest, no less critical to our democratic system, in combatting corruption and its appearance. We have, however, held that this interest must be limited to a specific kind of corruption—quid pro quo corruption—in order to ensure that the Government's efforts do not have the effect of restricting the First Amendment right of citizens to choose who shall govern them. [We] conclude that the aggregate limits on contributions do not further the only governmental interest this Court accepted as legitimate in *Buckley*. They instead intrude without justification on a citizen's ability to exercise 'the most fundamental First Amendment activities.' "

Justice Thomas concurred in the judgment: "I adhere to the view that this Court's decision in *Buckley* denigrates core First Amendment speech and should be overruled.

"[Contributions] to political campaigns, no less than direct expenditures, 'generate essential political speech' by fostering discussion of public issues and candidate qualifications. *Buckley* itself recognized that both contribution and expenditure limits 'operate in an area of the most fundamental First Amendment activities' and 'implicate fundamental First Amendment interests.' But instead of treating political giving and political spending alike, *Buckley* [unjustifiably] distinguished the two, embracing a bifurcated standard of review under which contribution limits receive less rigorous scrutiny. [This] case represents yet another missed opportunity to right the course of our campaign finance jurisprudence by restoring a standard that is faithful to the First Amendment."

Justice Breyer, joined by Justices Ginsburg, Sotomayor, and Kagan, dissented: "Taken together with *Citizens United* [main volume at page 1385], today's decision eviscerates our Nation's campaign finance laws, leaving a remnant incapable of dealing with the grave problems of democratic legitimacy that those laws were intended to resolve. [The] plurality's conclusion rests upon three separate but related claims. Each is fatally flawed. First, the plurality says that given the base limits on contributions to candidates and political committees, aggregate limits do not further any independent governmental objective worthy of protection. And that is because, given the base limits, '[s]pending large sums of money in connection with elections' does not 'give rise to . . . corruption.' In making this argument, the plurality relies heavily upon a narrow definition of 'corruption' that excludes efforts to obtain 'influence over or access to' elected officials or political parties. Second, the plurality assesses the instrumental objective of the aggregate limits, namely, safeguarding the base limits. It finds that they 'do not serve that function in any meaningful way.' That is because, even without the aggregate limits, the possibilities for circumventing the base limits are 'implausible' and 'divorced from reality.' Third, the plurality says the aggregate limits are 'poorly tailored to the Government's interest in preventing circumvention of the base limits.' The plurality imagines several alternative regulations that it says might just as effectively thwart circumvention. Accordingly, it finds, the aggregate caps are out of 'proportion to the [anticorruption] interest served.' . . .

"The plurality's first claim—that large aggregate contributions do not 'give rise' to 'corruption'—is plausible only because the plurality defines 'corruption' too narrowly. [Its] definition of 'corruption' is inconsistent with the Court's prior case law (with the possible exception of *Citizens United*) [and] it misunderstands the constitutional importance of the interests at stake. [The] history of campaign finance reform shows [that] the anticorruption interest that drives Congress to regulate campaign contributions is a far broader, more important interest than the plurality acknowledges. It is an interest in maintaining the integrity of our public governmental institutions. And it is an interest rooted in the Constitution and in the First Amendment itself. [Speech] does not exist in a vacuum. Rather, political communication seeks to secure government action. A politically oriented 'marketplace of ideas' seeks to form a public opinion that can and will influence elected representatives. This is not a new idea. [Citing *Whitney v. California* (Brandeis, J., concurring).] [Accordingly], the First Amendment advances not only the individual's right to engage in political speech, but also the public's interest in preserving a democratic order in which collective speech matters.

"What has this to do with corruption? It has everything to do with corruption. Corruption breaks the constitutionally necessary 'chain of communication' between the people and their representatives. [Where] enough money calls the tune, the general public will not be heard. Insofar as corruption cuts the link between political thought and political action, a free marketplace of political ideas loses its point. [The] 'appearance of corruption' can make matters worse. It can lead the public to believe that its efforts to communicate with its representatives or to help sway public opinion have little purpose. And a cynical public can lose interest in political participation altogether. The upshot is that the interests the Court has long described as preventing 'corruption' or the 'appearance of corruption' are more than ordinary factors to be weighed against the constitutional right to political speech. Rather, they are interests rooted in the First Amendment itself. They are rooted in the constitutional effort to create a democracy responsive to the people—a government where laws reflect the very thoughts, views, ideas, and sentiments, the expression of which the First Amendment protects. Given that end, we can and should understand campaign finance laws as resting upon a broader and more significant constitutional rationale than the plurality's limited definition of 'corruption' suggests. We should see these laws as seeking in significant part to strengthen, rather than weaken, the First Amendment. To say this is not to deny the potential for conflict between (1) the need to permit contributions that pay for the diffusion of ideas, and (2) the need to limit payments in order to help maintain the integrity of the electoral process. But that conflict takes place within, not outside, the First Amendment's boundaries. . . .

"The plurality invalidates the aggregate contribution limits for a second reason. It believes they are no longer needed to prevent contributors from circumventing federal limits on direct contributions to individuals, political parties, and political action committees. [The] plurality is wrong. Here, as in *Buckley*, in the absence of limits on aggregate political contributions, donors can and likely will find ways to channel millions of dollars to parties and to individual candidates, [producing] 'corruption' or 'appearance of corruption.' The methods for using today's opinion to evade the law's individual contribution limits are complex, but they are well known, or will become well known, to party fundraisers. [Justice Breyer then described three such methods in detail.] The plurality believes that the three scenarios I have just depicted either pose no threat, or cannot or will not take place. Not so. [Justice Breyer then explained in detail why, in his view, the absence of aggregate contribution limits will, in fact, enable substantial circumvention of the base contribution limits.] . . .

"The plurality [substitutes its limited understanding] of how the political process works for the understanding of Congress, [and in so doing it] creates huge loopholes in the law [and] undermines, perhaps devastates, what remains of campaign finance reform."

* * *

Consider the following views:

a. Hellman, Defining Corruption and Constitutionalizing Democracy, 111 Mich. L. Rev. 1385 (2013):

"The main front in the battle over the constitutionality of campaign finance laws has long focused on defining corruption. [But] corruption is a derivative concept, meaning it depends on a theory of the institution or official involved. [What] constitutes corruption in a democracy depends on a theory of democracy. To put the point in a more grounded fashion, what constitutes corruption of legislators depends on a view of the proper basis for decisionmaking by elected officials. [Our] campaign finance case law contains at least three distinct conceptions of legislative corruption. I call these 'corruption as the deformation of judgment,' 'corruption as the distortion of influence,' and 'corruption as the sale of favors.' . . .

"On one view, a legislator ought to exercise his own independent judgment about each decision he faces. [The] legislator, according to this view, should consider only the merits-based reasons that bear on the decision at hand. [Corruption as the "deformation of judgment"] occurs when non-merits-based factors influence the legislator's judgment. . . .

"Corruption as the distortion of influence sees the legislator as properly attentive to the desires and preferences of those he represents. In a well-functioning democracy, the legislator responds to these desires and preferences. [On this view,] corruption occurs when a legislator weighs the preferences of some too heavily, especially when the legislator considers the wishes of wealthy contributors more than others. . . .

"A third view of proper legislative conduct [requires] only that the legislator not actually exchange votes or favors for money. [Corruption], on this view, is narrowly defined as quid pro quo corruption—that is, the sale of some public favor. . . .

"[W]hen the Court defines corruption [in its campaign finance case law], it inescapably puts forward a conception of the proper role of a legislator in a democracy. That is a task that the Court should be cautious to take up. [Because there] are many reasonable ways to instantiate representative democracy, [we] should eschew judicial actions that adopt one view of representative democracy [over another]. Because judicial pronouncements about what constitutes corruption entail commitments to contested conceptions of democracy, there are strong reasons for courts to avoid defining corruption."

b. R. Post, Citizens Divided: Campaign Finance Reform and the Constitution 4, 60-65 (2014):

"[P]roponents of campaign finance reform have failed to advance justifications for regulation that can be inoculated with basic First Amendment principles. They have instead promoted justifications like 'distortion' or 'equality,' which are inconsistent with essential premises of First Amendment doctrine. . . .

"[F]irst Amendment rights presuppose that elections must be structured to select for persons who possess the "communion of interests and sympathy of sentiments" to remain responsive to public opinion. [The concept of "electoral integrity" denominates] elections that have the property of choosing candidates whom the people trust to possess this sympathy and connection. Without electoral integrity, First Amendment rights necessarily fail to achieve their constitutional purpose. If the people do not believe that elected officials listen to public opinion, participation in public discourse, no matter how free, cannot create the experience of self-government. . . .

"The democratic structure and legitimacy of our government depend on electoral integrity. Yet the Court in its campaign finance opinions has not considered the state's interest in promoting the electoral integrity required by the First Amendment. The Court has instead been preoccupied by the attempt to balance First Amendment rights against the need to prevent [quid pro quo] corruption. . . .

"If [we] reformulate our campaign finance jurisprudence upon the principle of electoral integrity, [we] may create a more enduring foundation for the contested area of campaign finance reform. [This] formulation of the issue [requires] us merely to affirm [that] Americans cannot maintain the blessings of self-government unless they believe that elections produce representatives who are responsive to public opinion. [Electoral] integrity is a compelling government interest because without it Americans have no reason to exercise the communicative rights guaranteed by the First Amendment.

"[There] are good reasons to worry that electoral integrity is today under threat. Americans' trust and confidence in their representative institutions has fallen to record lows; we are [experiencing] what most regard as a crisis of representation. In such circumstances it is especially disappointing that the Court seems unwilling to recognize even the existence of the constitutional principle of electoral integrity. . . ."

c. Lessig, What an Originalist Would Understand "Corruption"to Mean, 102 Cal. L. Rev. 1, 3-11 (2014):

"The United States [effectively] has two distinct elections. One election is discrete — call it the "voting election." [All] 'voters' are permitted to participate in that election. [The] other election is continuous — call it the 'money election.' It happens throughout the election cycle. Any citizen [is] permitted to participate in that money election. [To] be allowed to run in the voting election [one] has to do extremely well in the money election. [In] the 2012 election cycle, 84 percent of the House candidates and 67 percent of the Senate candidates with more money than their opponents won. [The] money election produces a subtle, perhaps camouflaged bending [of the process] to keep the funders of the money election happy. [Importantly,] the relevant number of funders is [small]. [In] the 2012 presidential election 0.000032 percent [of Americans] — or 99 Americans — provided 60 percent of the individual Super PAC money spent. . . .

"[The] way we fund elections has created a dependency that conflicts with the dependency intended by the Constitution. That conflict is a corruption. [In] the Framers' language, [the concept of 'corruption'] included a collective sense — the corruption of an institution, or a people, and not just a person. [Congress] was intended to be 'dependent on the people alone.' It has become dependent upon an additional dependence, 'the funders' of campaigns. Because of who 'the funders' are, this additional dependence is a conflicting dependence, and that conflict constitutes 'corruption.'

"This sense of corruption, as constituted by 'improper dependence,' was perfectly familiar to the Framers. It is with this sense of 'corruption' in mind that we can see why our current Congress is 'corrupt.' For the Framers, Congress was [to] have an intended dependence. That dependence was to be, as James Madison wrote in The Federalist No. 52, 'on the people.' [For the Framers,] the anti-corruption challenge was not how to ensure that criminals stayed away from Congress; the challenge was how to secure the influences most likely to align the institution to its proper ends by protecting it from improper dependence. [It] is this fact that makes the current Supreme Court's jurisprudence about 'corruption' so weird. [Only] a non-originalist could embrace [the Court's] position."

d. L. Tribe & J. Matz, Uncertain Justice: The Roberts Court and the Constitution 100-101, 104-105, 108-109, 112-113 (2014):

"*Citizens United* decisively rejected the anti-distortion justification for campaign finance laws. . . . To be sure, money can powerfully advantage a speaker in the marketplace of ideas [and] concentrated wealth, left unregulated, can create a risk that most headlines and TV ads will be controlled by a small group. . . . Still, it would be a mistake to leave judgments about the 'proper' distribution of speech to politicians. Arming them with a roving license to level the playing field by silencing or adjusting the volume of disfavored speakers is an invitation to self-serving behavior and, ultimately, tyranny. The anti-distortion argument can too easily lead down this dangerous path, and [the Court] rightly discarded it. . . .

"[Another argument made against the Court's approach in these cases focuses on a broad conception of 'corruption.'] 'Corruption,' in this view, occurs when politicians become dependent on a wealthy clique and government is no longer responsive to the public interest. [The justices in the majority in these cases] are unreservedly hostile to such arguments. They worry that noble-sounding rationales for campaign finance laws can too easily conceal efforts by incumbents to protect themselves and punish their enemies. [The Court has not adopted] a narrow definition of corruption because it is naïve or apathetic. It has done so because it doubts that the Court [can] create workable First Amendment law that adequately guards against abuse by politicians. Embracing a broader view of the anti-corruption interest risked creating an exception that swallowed the rule. . . .

"In an age of political dysfunction, the extraordinary sums of money that candidates avidly pursue present hard questions about how to reconcile competing national values. [The Court's decisions in these cases will likely affect] policy outcomes by causing an across-the-board realignment of government priorities toward interests backed by big money. Every capable politician has an eye on the next election and a keen sense of who provided support last time, who didn't, who might be persuaded to shift their opinions, and how that might be achieved. [The Court's decisions are] therefore likely to trigger a self-reinforcing cycle. [As] the group of victorious candidates comes to consist mainly of politicians who can successfully navigate these structures and depend on them for reelection, the impetus for change among officeholders will fade. [Perhaps the best solution would be the enactment of new disclosure requirements.] In the post-*Citizens United* era, transparency would provide at least a measure of reassurance. . . ."

See also Tribe, Dividing Citizens United: The Case and The Controversy, 30 Const. Comm. 463 (2015).

dd. Given that the Court has dismissed the equality, corruption, and distortion justifications for campaign finance regulation, might the case for such regulation be strengthened by invoking an "alignment" rationale? That is, is it a problem for democracy if elected officials systematically do not represent the interests of the majority of their constituents? Consider the fact that "individuals who contribute at least $200 to federal candidates are overwhelmingly wealthy, highly educated, male, and white." In 2012, "these donors amounted to just 0.4% of the population, but supplied 64% of the funds received by candidates from individuals." Does it matter that individuals falling within this select group tend to hold views on critical issues of public policy that are very different from those of the majority of the American people, and that legislators tend to act in accord with the views of this tiny minority of very wealthy individuals, even when they conflict with the views of the vast majority of their constituents? Is such "non-alignment" between the views of American citizens and the votes of their elected representatives a sufficiently important concern in a democracy to justify campaign finance regulations of the sort that have thus far been invalidated by the Supreme Court? See Stephanopolous, Aligning Campaign Finance Law, 101 Va. L. Rev. 1425 (2015).

e. In Six Amendments: How and Why We Should Change the Constitution (2014), former Justice John Paul Stevens proposed the following amendment to the Constitution:

Neither the First Amendment nor any other provision of this Constitution shall be construed to prohibit the Congress or any state from imposing reasonable limits on the amount of money that candidates for public office, or their supporters, may spend in election campaigns.

Page 1402.   Before the Note, add the following:

The Supreme Court returned to the problem posed by judicial candidates in Williams-Yulee v. Florida Bar, 135 S. Ct. 1656 (2015), but, on this occasion, it upheld a campaign restriction against first amendment attack.

A Florida rule prohibited judicial candidates from "personally [soliciting] campaign funds." However, it permitted candidates to establish campaign committees that solicited funds, to serve as the treasurers of their own committees, to learn the identity of campaign contributors, and to send thank you notes to donors. Petitioner, a candidate for a seat on a county court, sent a mass mailing to local voters asking for campaign contributions and was disciplined by the Florida Supreme Court. By a 5-to-4 vote, the United States Supreme Court, per Chief Justice Roberts, upheld the ban on personal solicitation. Chief Justice Roberts began his analysis by recognizing that the solicitation restriction constituted "speech about public issues and the qualifications of candidates for elected office" and that it therefore triggered the "highest level of First Amendment protection." Accordingly, the limitation should be strictly structinized to make certain that it was narrowly tailored to serve a compelling interest." Although the state can meet this standard only in "a rare case," the Court concluded that this was such a case. Florida had a compelling interest in preserving "public confidence in the state judiciary. [Simply] put, [the] public may lack confidence in a judge's ability to administer justice without fear or favor if he comes to office by asking for favors." Although the ban might be thought underinclusive because of the exceptions for the activity of campaign committees, it "aims squarely at the conduct most likely to undermine confidence in the integrity of the judiciary: Personal requests for money by judges and judicial candidates." The ban was not overinclusive because it left "judicial candidates free to discuss any issue with any person at any time." In reaching these conclusions, the Court emphasized that

> Judges are not politicians, even when they come to the bench by way of the ballot. And a State's decision to elect its judiciary does not compel it to treat judicial candidates like campaigners for political office. A State may assure its people that judges will apply the law without fear or favor – and without having personally asked anyone for money.

Justice Breyer, and Justice Ginsburg, with whom Justice Breyer joined, filed concurring opinions. Justice Scalia, with whom Justice Thomas joined, Justice Kennedy, and Justice Alito filed dissenting opinions.

Page 1404.   At the end of section 2 of the Note, add the following:

How should we think about the "value" of public employee speech? Consider Kitrosser, The Special Value of Public Employee Speech, 2015 Sup. Ct. Rev. 301:

> *Pickering* and its progeny offer two main justifications for protecting employee speech. The first justification, aptly termed the "parity theory," [is] that government employees should not be robbed "of the First Amendment rights that they would otherwise enjoy as citizens to comment on matters of public interest." [The] second justification, which I call the "special value" rationale, is linked to speech's extrinsic value to the public. From this perspective, public employees deserve free speech protections not because they are just like everybody else, but because they have something *special* to contribute to the marketplace of ideas. . . .
>
> The basic argument is that public employees have a crucial structural role to play in countering government's capacity for deception. [One] aspect of special value consists of the unique insights that public employees gain through their work. But courts disregard to other facets of special value. First, to the extent that employees have special access to internal communication channels, this heightens their free speech value. Second, through the very act of doing their jobs conscientiously and in accordance with the norms of their professions, public employees help to maintain consistency between the functions in which government purports to engage and those that it actually performs. In this sense, public employees are potential barriers against government deception. . . .

2a. *Government motive.* Suppose the government disciplines a public employee for engaging in constitutionally protected speech, but it turns out that the employee wasn't actually engaging in speech at all. Does the discipline in such circumstances violate the First Amendment? In Heffernan v. City of Patterson, 136 S. Ct. 1412 (2016), Heffernan, a police officer, brought a political sign to his bedridden mother as a favor to her. Several police officers saw him with the sign and reported him. He was then demoted for engaging in politicking – something he in fact had a constitutional right to do. The problem, though, was that he wasn't in fact politicking at all. The Court held the disciplinary action unconstitutional because the government's motive was impermissible, even though Heffernan had not in fact been engaged in First Amendment activity. Justice Thomas, joined by Justice Alito, dissented, arguing that there could be no violation of Heffernan's First Amendment rights if he hadn't in fact been exercising them.

Page 1404.   Before section 3 of the Note, add the following:

Lane v. Franks, 134 S. Ct. 2369 (2014) (public employee who testifies under subpoena about a matter related to his public employment is protected by the First Amendment, despite *Garcetti*, where his testimony was not required by "his ordinary job responsibilities").

Page 1417.   Before section 4 of the Note, add the following:

Does it follow from *Wooley* that the government may not engage in viewpoint discrimination when it chooses between specialty license plates designed submitted by motorists? The Court answered this question in the negative in Walker v. Texas Div., Sons of Confederate Veterans, Inc., 135 S. Ct. 2239 (2015), where, in a 5-to-4 decision written by Justice Breyer, it upheld the refusal of the Texas Department of Motor Vehicles to issue a license plate featuring the Confederate battle flag on the ground that the plate consisted of government, rather than private, speech.

> Our determination that Texas's specialty license plate designs are government speech does not mean that the designs do not also implicate the free speech rights of private persons. We have acknowledged that drivers who display a State's selected license plate designs convey the messages communicated through those designs. [*Wooley*]. And we have recognized that the First Amendment stringently limits a State's authority to compel a private party to express a view with which the private party disagrees. But here, compelled private speech is not at issue. And just as Texas cannot require [The Sons of Confederate Veterans] to convey "the State's ideological message," [*Wooley*], [The Sons of Confederate Veterans] cannot force Texas to include a Confederate battle flag on its specialty license plates.

Page 1418.   After section 5 of the Note, add the following:

5a. *Conditions on recipients of public funds.* See Agency for International Development v. Alliance for Open Society International, 133 S. Ct. 2321 (2013), insert in this Supplement for page 1337 of the main volume.

Page 1418.   At the end of section 6 of the Note, add the following:

In Harris v. Quinn, 134 S. Ct. 2618 (2014), the Court considered the constitutionality of an Illinois law that allowed Medicaid recipients who normally would need institutional care to hire a "personal assistant" (PA) to provide homecare services. Under the law, the Medicaid homecare recipients and the state both play a role in the employment relationship with the PAs.

Pursuant to this program, the Service Employees International Union (SEIU) was designated the exclusive union representative for the PAs. SEIU entered into collective-bargaining agreements with the state that included an agency-fee provision, which requires PAs who do not wish to join the union to pay the union a fee for the cost of collective-bargaining expenses, but not for the cost of any political activities of the union unrelated to collective bargaining. A group of PAs who had not joined the union and did not want to pay *any* union fees brought this suit claiming that the law violated their First Amendment right not to be compelled to support the union. Pursuant to *Abood*, the lower courts rejected this challenge and upheld the law.

In a five-to-four decision, the Supreme Court reversed. In an opinion by Justice Alito, the Court cast serious doubt on *Abood,* insofar as it permitted the state to compel non-union members to pay union fees even for the costs of collective-bargaining activities that benefit them. Ultimately, though, the Court invalidated the law without overruling *Abood,* by distinguishing the specific factual situation in the context of PAs from the situations in other public union arrangements. Justice Kagan, joined by Justices Ginsburg, Breyer, and Sotomayor, dissented. Kagan insisted that *Abood* reflected sound First Amendment principles and that the situation in this case was not in any principled way distinguishable from the Court's prior decisions.

For an analysis of the implications of *Harris v. Quinn*, see Estlund, Are Unions a Constitutional Anomaly?, 114 Mich. L. Rev. 169 (2015).

Page 1419.   Before the Note, add the following:

9. *Compelled Abortion Counseling.* Do statutes that require women seeking an abortion to undergo counseling violate the First Amendment? For an argument that they do, see Corbin, Compelled Disclosures, 54 Ala. L. Rev. 1277 (2014). At least one lower court has upheld mandatory counselling against a free speech attack. *See* Tex. Med. Providers Performing Abortion Servs . v. Lakey, 667 F. 3d 570, (5th Cir. 2012). On the other hand, as Corbin points out, some lower courts

have invalidated statutes requiring "crisis pregnancy centers" to disclose the fact that they do not make referrals for abortions or birth control services. Are the two situations distinguishable?

10. *Is there a right not to speak?* Consider Massaro, Tread on Me!, 17 U. Pa. J. Con. L. 365, 368 (2014):

> Contrary to Justice Robert Jackson's rhetorically arresting "no fixed star" celebration of individual freedom from compulsory pledges of allegiance, government often demands private expression, crafts it, or silences it altogether. Constitutionally mandated oaths of office, occupation-specific codes of conduct, audience and context-specific regulation of the content of information disclosures, many employment and civil rights statutes, student conduct codes, conditions on government benefits, anti-fraud laws, and many other forms of government speech regulation demonstrate that there is no across-the-board constitutional mandate against government-compelled expression.

F.   Freedom of the Press

Page 1426.   After section 2 of the Note, add the following:

2a. *Protecting the anonymity of the source.* Instead of focusing on the First Amendment right of the reporter to keep sources confidential, would it make more sense to focus on the First Amendment right of the source to engage in anonymous speech? After all, in a series of decisions, including Talley v. California, McIntyre v. Ohio Elections Commission, NAACP v. Alabama, and Brown v. Socialist Workers, the Court has protected a right to anonymous speech, noting that anonymous speech has "played an important role in the progress of mankind" and that "persecuted groups" throughout history "have been able to criticize oppressive practices either anonymously or not at all." Consider Jones, Re-Thinking Reporter's Privilege, 111 Mich. L. Rev. 1221 (2013):

> A confidential source who does not wish to have her name revealed is analytically indistinguishable from any other author, writer, or speaker who wishes to convey information anonymously. Like the leafleteer in *Talley* . . . and the concerned taxpayer in *McIntyre*, . . . a confidential source offers information that she wishes to make public without attribution . . . for any number of reasons that the Court has acknowledged as valid. [The] source

should be entitled to protection under the anonymous speech doctrine for statements made to a reporter in confidence.

2b. *Investigative journalism or criminal solicitation*? Suppose a reporter persuades a public employee unlawfully to leak classified information. Can the reporter constitutionally be convicted of the crime of criminal solicitation? Recall *O'Brien*. Suppose a journalist conducts an illegal wiretap in order to prove that a congressman took a bribe. Would her conduct be protected by the First Amendment? If not, is criminal solicitation any different? See G. Stone, Top Secret: When Government Keeps Us in the Dark 29-38 (2007) (arguing that because prosecution of journalists for the crime of solicitation would interject "government into the very heart of the journalist-source relationship" and thus "have a serious chilling effect" on legitimate and important journalist-source exchanges, the government should not be able to punish journalists for encouraging public employees to disclose classified information unless the journalist (a) expressly incites the leak and (b) knows that publication of the information would likely cause imminent and grave harm to the national security). Can that position be reconciled with the wiretap example or with *Branzburg*?

Page 1427.   After the citation to R. Tushnet in the second-to-last paragraph of section 8 of the Note, add the following:

Rothman, Commercial Speech, Commercial Use, and the Intellectual Property Quagmire, 101 Va. L. Rev. 1929 (2015).

Page 1451.   At the end of section 4 of the Note, add the following:

Section 230(c)(1) of the Communications Decency Act of 1996 provides immunity from liability for providers and users of an "interactive computer service" who publish information provided by others. Facebook, for example, unlike the *New York Times*, is not liable for otherwise actionable threats, libels, or invasions of privacy posted on its site by users. Does this make sense? Consider Tushnet, Internet Exceptionalism: An Overview from General Constitutional Law, 56 Wm. & M. L. Rev. 1637, 1665 (2015): "Suppose [that] § 230 were replaced by a regime requiring that intermediaries do something to limit the distribution of harmful material — that they adopt a different business model. The question is whether such business-model regulation would be constitutionally permissible, even though the regime might be described as one in which the regulation was adopted for the purpose of restricting the dissemination of harmful information."

VIII
THE CONSTITUTION AND RELIGION

A. Introduction: Historical and Analytical Overview

Page 1466.   At the section 7 of the Note, add the following:

For a recent discussion of how pluralism should affect constitutional doctrine, see John Inazu, Confident Pluralism (2016).

Page 1467.   At the end of section 9 of the Note, add the following:

For recent discussions of this question, see Leiter, Why Tolerate Religion? (2012), offering a perspective from moral and political theory, and Koppelman, Defending American Religious Neutrality (2013), offering a perspective from political theory and law. For a review of these works, see Abner Greene, Religion and Theistic Faith: On Koppelman, Leiter, Secular Purpose, and Accommodations, 49 Tulsa L. Rev. 441 (2013). See also Schwartzman, What If Religion Is Not Special?, 79 U. Chi. L. Rev. 1351 (2012):

> [Many] of the most widely held normative justifications for favoring (or disfavoring) religion are prone to predictable forms of internal incoherence [and] accounts [that] manage to avoid such incoherence succeed only at the cost of committing other serious errors, especially in allowing various types of unfairness toward religious believers, nonbelievers, or both. The upshot of all this is that principles of disestablishment and free exercise ought to

be conceived in terms that go beyond the category of religion. Instead of disabling or protecting only religious beliefs and practices, the law ought to provide similar treatment for comparable secular ethical, moral, and philosophical views.

B.   The Establishment Clause

Page 1494.   At the end of section 6 of the Note, add the following:

6a. Marsh *revisited or extended?* Town of Greece v. Galloway, 134 S. Ct. 1811 (2014), involved the prayer practices of the town board of Greece, a suburb of Rochester, New York. Starting in 1999, the board opened its meetings with, among other matters, a prayer given by guest chaplains chosen from a list of congregations in the town directory, nearly all of which are Christian. Some of the ministers "spoke in a distinctly Christian idiom," including invoking "the saving sacrifice of Jesus Christ on the cross."

Justice Kennedy wrote an opinion that was in part for the Court, and in part only for himself and Chief Justice Roberts and Justice Alito. The Court upheld the town's practices. It relied heavily on *Marsh*, which "[must] not be understood as permitting a practice that would amount to a constitutional violation if not for its historical foundation. The case teaches instead that the Establishment Clause must be interpreted 'by reference to historical practices and understandings.' [The] Court's inquiry [must] be to determine whether the prayer practice in the town of Greece fits within the tradition long followed in Congress and the state legislatures." But "[an] insistence on nonsectarian or ecumenical prayer as a single, fixed, standard is not consistent with the tradition of legislative [prayer]. [To] hold that invocations must be nonsectarian would force the legislatures [and] the courts [to] act as supervisors and censors of religious speech, [which] would involve government in religious matters to a far greater degree [than] is the case under the town's current practice." Justice Kennedy also wrote, "If the course and practice over time shows that the invocations denigrate nonbelievers or religious minorities, threaten damnation, or preach conversion, many present may consider the prayer to fall short of the desire to elevate the purpose of the occasion and to unite lawmakers in their common effort. That circumstance would present a different [case]." Noting that "two remarks" by guest chaplains "strayed from the rationale set out in *Marsh*," he wrote that "they do not despoil a practice that on the whole reflects and embraces our tradition. Absent a pattern of prayers that over time denigrate, proselytize, or betray an impermissible government purpose, a challenge based solely on the content of a prayer will not likely establish a constitutional violation." The town's efforts to locate guest chaplains were "reasonable," and did "not reflect an aversion or bias on the part of town leaders against minority faiths. So long as the town maintains a policy of nondiscrimination, the Constitution does not require it to search beyond its borders for non-Christian prayer givers in an effort to achieve religious balancing."

In the part of the opinion joined only by the Chief Justice and Justice Alito, Justice Kennedy addressed and rejected the argument that the prayer practice coerced participation. As to coercion, "The inquiry remains a fact-sensitive one that considers both the setting in which the prayer arises and the audience to whom it is directed," again "valuated against the backdrop of historical practice." "It is presumed that the reasonable observer is acquainted with this tradition and understands that its purposes are to lend gravity to public proceedings and to acknowledge the place religion holds in the lives of many private citizens, not to afford government an opportunity to proselytize or force truant constituents into the pews. That many appreciate these acknowledgments of the divine in our public institutions does not suggest that those who disagree are compelled to join the expression or approve its content." But "[t]he analysis would be different if town board members directed the public to participate in the prayers, singled out dissidents for opprobrium, or indicated that their decisions might be influenced by a person's acquiescence in the prayer opportunity." Addressing the respondents' claim that "the prayers gave them offense and made them feel excluded and disrespected," Justice Kennedy wrote, "Offense [does] not equate to coercion."

Justice Thomas, joined in part by Justice Scalia, wrote separately. Justice Thomas repeated his argument that the Establishment Clause was not made applicable to the states by the Fourteenth Amendment. In addition, he argued that "the municipal prayers [bear] no resemblance to the coercive state establishments that existed at the founding." The coercion relevant to Establishment Clause analysis "is actual legal coercion, [not] the 'subtle coercive pressures' allegedly felt by [respondents]."

Justice Kagan, joined by Justices Ginsburg, Breyer, and Sotomayor, dissented. Justice Breyer also dissented in a separate opinion. For Justice Kagan, "[t]he practice [here] differs from the one sustained in [Marsh] because Greece's town meetings involve participation by ordinary citizens, and the invocations given — directly to those citizens — were predominantly sectarian. [Greece's] Board did nothing to recognize religious diversity. [The] Town never sought (except briefly when this suit was filed) to involve, accommodate, or in any way reach out to adherents of non-Christian religions." She agreed that "Greece's Board [has] legislative functions," but its "meetings are also occasions for ordinary citizens to engage with and petition their government, often on highly individualized matters. That feature calls for Board members to exercise special care to ensure that the prayers offered [respect] each and every member of the community as an equal citizen." The sessions in *Marsh* at which prayers were offered were "floor sessions [for] elected lawyers. Members of the public take no part. [Greece's] town meetings [revolve] around ordinary members of the community," who "urge [changes] in the Board's policies [and] then, in which are essentially adjudicatory hearings, they request the Board to grant [applications] for various permits."

> Let's say that a Muslim citizen of Greece goes before the Board to [request] some permit. [Just] before she gets to speak her piece, a minister deputized by the Town asks her to pray "in the name of God's only son Jesus Christ." She must think [that] Christian worship has become entwined with local governance. And now she faces a choice—to pray alongside the majority [or] somehow to register her deeply felt difference. [That] is no easy call—especially given that the room is small and her every action [will] be noticed. She does not wish to be rude to her neighbors, nor does she wish to aggravate the Board members whom she will soon be trying to persuade. And yet she does not want to acknowledge Christ's divinity. [So] assume she declines to participate with the others in the first act of the meeting—or even [stands] up and leaves the room. [She] becomes a different kind of citizen. [And] she thus stands at a remove, based solely on religion, from her fellow citizens and her elected representatives. Everything about that situation [infringes] the First Amendment.

Justice Kagan would allow some prayer activities. "What the circumstances here demand is the recognition that we are a pluralistic people. [If] the Town Board had let its chaplains know that they should speak in nonsectarian terms, [then] no one would have valid grounds for complaint. [Or] it might have invited clergy of many faiths to serve as chaplains. [But] Greece could not do what it did: infuse a participatory government body with one (and only one) faith." For her, "[when] a citizen stands before her government, [her] religious beliefs do not enter into the picture. The government she faces favors no particular religion, either by word or by deed. And that government [imposes] no religious tests on its citizens, sorts none of them by faith, and permits no exclusion based on belief. When a person goes to court, a polling place, or an immigration proceeding, [government] officials do not engage in sectarian worship, nor do they ask her to do likewise. They all participate in the business of government not as Christians, Jews, Muslims (and more), but only as Americans—none of them different from any other for that civic purpose."

Justice Alito, joined by Justice Scalia, responded to Justice Kagan in a concurring opinion, calling "the narrow aspect" of her dissent's objections to the holding "really quite niggling." He argued that "there [is] no historical support for the proposition that only generic prayer is allowed," and observed that "as our country has become more diverse, composing a prayer that is acceptable to all members of the community who hold religious beliefs has become [harder.]" Further, "if a town attempts to go beyond simply recommending that a guest chaplain deliver a prayer that is broadly acceptable, [the] town will [encounter] sensitive problems," including possible prescreening or reviewing prayers. The alternative of compiling a list of clergy from numerous traditions to serve as guest chaplains meant that Justice Kagan's objection was only the "[the] town's clerical employees did a bad job in compiling the list" they used.

Page 1499.   At the end of section 2 of the Note, add the following:

Consider these observations, from Koppelman, The New American Civil Religion: Lessons for Italy, Geo. Wash. 41 Int'l L. Rev. 961, 866 (2010):

Douglas Laycock thinks that a lesson [is] that "separationist groups should sue immediately when they encounter any religious practice newly sponsored by the government." That is precisely the right lesson. [New] sponsorship of religious practices is far more likely to represent a contemporaneous effort to intervene in a live religious controversy than the perpetuation of old forms.

D.   Permissible Accommodation

Page 1549.   At the end of section 5 of the Note, add the following:

The Religious Freedom Restoration Act was held unconstitutional with respect to state legislation, but remains applicable to federal legislation. See Gonzales v. O Centro Espirita Beneficente Uniao do Vegetal, 546 U.S. 418 (2006). For a controversial application of the Act, see Burwell v. Hobby Lobby Stores, Inc., 134 S. Ct. 2751 (2014) (rejecting the argument that, with respect to those entitled to raise RFRA claims, the statute "did no more than codify this Court's pre-*Smith* precedents" and holding that a closely held, for-profit corporation with religious objections to certain forms of birth control was entitled to a statutory exemption from a requirement that any insurance policy it provided to its workers cover contraception).

E. Free Exercise, Free Speech, and the Right of Expressive Association

Page 1550.   At the end of section 1 of the Note, add the following:

Observing that "[to] say that the Establishment Clause requires the [ministerial] exemption is to say that regulation of a religious institution violates the Establishment Clause [, which] is very odd," and that "[interference] with religious practice naturally raises Free Exercise concerns, but it is unclear how such regulation *establishes* a religion," Ashutosh Bhagwat, Religious Associations: *Hosanna-Tabor*and the Instrumental Value of Religious Groups, 92 Wash. U.L. Rev. 73, 84 (2014), argues that the decision, while correct, should have rested on a more vigorous application of the right of expressive association.

IX
STATE ACTION, BASELINES, AND THE PROBLEM OF PRIVATE POWER

A.   State Action, Federalism, and Individual Autonomy

Page 1561.   At the end of the Note, add the following:

Is there an "individual action" doctrine that complements the state action requirement? Recall that in National Federation of Independent Business v. Sebelius, 132 S. Ct. 2566 (2012), the Supreme Court held that the "individual mandate" of the Affordable Care Act, which required certain individuals to acquire insurance in private markets, exceeded Congress's power under the commerce clause. (Sebelius is discussed at page 218 of the main volume.) Consider Note, NFIB v. Sebelius and the Individualization of the State Action Doctrine, 127 Harv. L. Rev. 1174, 1174-1175 (2014):

> [Sebelius's] distinction between activity and inactivity [mirrors] [the] state action doctrine. . . .
>
> Both the state action and the individual action doctrines share an analogous analytic framework, and they serve analogous functions. The doctrines police a boundary between the citizen and the state by limiting federal power to contexts either in which the state has acted or in which individuals have acted. In doing so the doctrines construct a realm of individual autonomy free from certain types of governmental intrusions. [Sebelius] transposes and grafts onto the Commerce Clause many of the same commitments that drive the Court's state action jurisprudence, including limitations on the manner in which Congress can regulate nominally private decisionmaking.

C.   Constitutionally Impermissible Departures from Neutrality

Page 1591.   Following the discussion of Lebron, add the following:

The Court reaffirmed the public status of Amtrak in Department of Transportation v. Association of American Railroads, 135 S. Ct. 1225 (2015), but this time in a context that expanded, rather than reduced Amtrak's power. Federal law granted Amtrak and the Federal Railroad Administration joint authority to issue "metrics and standards" that address the performance and scheduling of passenger railroad services. Respondents challenged this authority as an unconstitutional delegation of lawmaking authority to a private entity. (For a discussion of the anti-delegation doctrine, see pp 424-429 of the Main Volume). In an opinion written by Justice Kennedy, that largely tracked the reasoning of *Lebron,* the Court rejected the challenge on the ground that Amtrak was a government actor.

E.   Unconstitutional Conditions and the Benefit/ Burden Distinction

Page 1613.   At the bottom of the page, add the following:

The Court elaborated on its *Nollan* holding in Koontz v. St. Johns River Water Management District, 570 U.S. 133 S. Ct. 2586 (2013), where it held that the same principle was applicable when, instead of accepting the condition, as the landowner had in *Nollan,* the landholder rejected the condition leading to the denial of a permit. Writing for five justices, Justice Alito stated:

> Our decisions [reflect] two realities of the permitting process. The first is that land-use permit applicants are especially vulnerable to the type of coercion that the unconstitutional conditions doctrine prohibits because the government often has broad discretion to deny a permit that is worth far more than property it would like to take. By conditioning a building permit on the owner's deeding over a public right-of-way, for example, the government can pressure an owner into voluntarily giving up property for which the Fifth Amendment would otherwise require just compensation. So long as the building permit is more valuable than any just compensation the owner could hope to receive for the right-of-way, the owner is likely to accede

to the government's demand no matter how unreasonable. Extortionate demands of this sort frustrate the Fifth Amendment right to just compensation, and the unconstitutional conditions doctrine prohibits them.

The second reality of the permitting process is that many proposed land uses threaten to impose costs on the public that dedications of property can offset. [Insisting] that landowners internalize the negative externalities of their conduct is a hallmark of responsible land-use policy, and we have long sustained such regulations against constitutional attack.

Nollan [accommodates] both realities by allowing the government to condition approval of a permit on the dedication of property to the public so long as there is a "nexus" and "rough proportionality" between the property the government demands and the social costs of the applicant's proposal. Our precedents thus enable permitting authorities to insist that applicants bear the full costs of their proposals while still forbidding the government from engaging in "out-and-out . . . extortion" that would thwart the Fifth Amendment right to just compensation.

Page 1620.   At the end of the Note, add the following:

(f) For an interesting unconstitutional conditions decision, see Agency for International Development v. Alliance for Open Society International, 133 S. Ct. 2321 (2013). By statute, Congress authorized the appropriation of billions of dollars to fund efforts by nongovernmental organizations to combat HIV/AIDS worldwide. Congress also imposed two conditions on the receipt of funds: (1) no funds "may be used to promote or advocate the legalization or practice of prostitution"; and (2) no funds may be used by an organization "that does not have a policy explicitly opposing prostitution."

The Court struck down the second condition. It emphasized a distinction between two kinds of conditions: (1) those that define the limits of the Government spending program (specifying the activities Congress wants to subsidize) and (2) those that seek to leverage funding to regulate speech outside the contours of the federal program itself. While Congress may limit its own spending, so that cases that fall within category (1) are permissible, Congress faces constitutional limits when it restricts speech in category (2).

The Court held that the restriction at issue fell in the second category: "By demanding that funding recipients adopt—as their own—the Government's view on an issue of public concern, the condition by its very nature affects 'protected conduct outside the scope of the federally funded program.' By requiring recipients to profess a specific belief, the [requirement] goes beyond defining the limits of the federally funded program to defining the recipient." In the Court's view, the requirement "goes beyond preventing recipients from using private funds in a way that would undermine the federal program. It requires them to pledge allegiance to the Government's policy of eradicating prostitution."

Justice Scalia, joined by Justice Thomas, dissented. He contended that the requirement at issue "is nothing more than a means of selecting suitable agents to implement the Government's chosen strategy to eradicate HIV/AIDS. That is perfectly permissible under the Constitution." In his view, "the government may enlist the assistance of those who believe in its ideas to carry them to fruition; and it need not enlist for that purpose those who oppose or do not support the ideas. That seems to me a matter of the most common common sense. For example: One of the purposes of America's foreign-aid programs is the fostering of goodwill towards this country. If the organization Hamas — reputed to have an efficient system for delivering welfare — were excluded from a program for the distribution of U.S. food assistance, no one could reasonably object. And that would remain true if Hamas were an organization of United States citizens entitled to the protection of the Constitution. [And] the same is true when the rejected organization is not affirmatively opposed to, but merely unsupportive of, the object of the federal program, which appears to be the case here. (Respondents do not promote prostitution, but neither do they wish to oppose it.) A federal program to encourage healthy eating habits need not be administered by the American Gourmet Society, which has nothing against healthy food but does not insist upon it."